# FRESH START

Why Bankruptcy is Faster, Easier and Better Than You Think

# FRESH START

Why Bankruptcy is Faster, Easier and Better Than You Think

**Andrew Balbus**

For Debbie

# Table of Contents

A Roadmap To Using This Book
The Fine Print

**Chapter 1**
**An Initial Consultation Regarding Bankruptcy**
Meet the Epitomes
Their Story
Bankruptcy Is Taboo
Secured Debts
Unsecured Debts
Assets
Income
The Epitomes Did The Right Thing
Debt Became Unmanageable
Consequences Of Unmanageable Debt
The Chapter 7 Solution
The Horrible Things That Happen When You File Bankruptcy
Will You Ever Have Credit Again?
The Process
Ready To Move Ahead

## Chapter 2

Introduction

What Happens When You Do Not Pay Your Debts?

    Liens

    Garnishments

    Bank Account Seizures

Are You "Judgment Proof"?

Your Debt Problem Cannot Be Solved By Better Budgeting

    Tricks Of The Trade

    25% Debt To Income Ratio

Your Debt Problem Cannot Be Solved With More Credit Card Debt

    Debt Consolidation Loan

Your "Bad" Debt Problem Cannot Be Solved With "Good" Debt

    Refinancing

    HELOC

    Reverse Mortgage

    Retirement Accounts

Credit Counseling/Debt Consolidation Services Do Not Work

Debt Negotiation Does Not Work

    Paying Taxes On Forgiven Debt Eliminates Some Of The Benefit

Living Off The Grid Is Unappealing

## Chapter 3

Introduction

Correcting Erroneous Beliefs

    Bankruptcy Is Not Immoral

    Bankruptcy Will Not Ruin Your Credit Score Forever

**Chapter 7**

Exemptions

What Kinds Of Exemptions Are There?

Exemptions May Be Limited Or Unlimited In Amount

Wildcard Exemptions

Can You Keep Your House?

What Is Your House Worth?

Who Owns The House?

**Chapter 9**

    Don't Withdraw Money From A Retirement Account

    Don't Transfer Property Out Of Your Name Or Sell Property For Less Than It Is Worth

Don't Pay Unsecured Creditors

Don't Repay Loans From Friends Or Family

Don't Use Credit Cards After You Decide To File

Try Not To Have Much Money On Deposit When You File

## Chapter 10

It's Faster, Easier And Simpler Than You Think

Hiring An Attorney

Legal Fees

How Do You Pay For Bankruptcy?

Stop Paying Credit Cards

Tax Refunds

Friends And Family

Retirement Accounts

Sell Nonexempt Assets

Pro Bono Appointments

Initial Consultation

Engagement Agreement

Scope Of Representation

Client's Responsibilities

Fees And Expenses

Term Of Engagement

Reaffirmations

Attorney Client Confidentiality

The First Course – Credit Counseling

Filing The Bankruptcy Petition

Notice Of Filing (The "341 Notice")

Court Control Over Your Financial Affairs

The Trustee

The U.S. Trustee

The Second Course – Personal Financial Management

The Meeting Of Creditors (The "341 Meeting" Or "341 Hearing")

Discharge Order

# Preface

In your haste to delve into the more enlightening sections of this book, you may have skipped the Dedication page. If you did, go back and look. The artwork is really cute. But, probably, if you skipped the Dedication page, you skipped this Preface as well. Who reads a Preface? You have no idea what you are missing.

A few pages back, I dedicated this book to my wife Debbie. Of course, I did. This is my first book and we have been married for 38 years. Dedicating this book to Debbie is literally the least I could do in return for her putting up with me all these years. Who else could I have dedicated my first book to?

One candidate might be Rosemary Donahue, my 11th grade English teacher. Mrs. Donahue, who referred to me as "Mr. Balbus," an oddly formal appellation for a 17-year old attending public high school in 1973, made two assessments of me that I have not forgotten (or gotten over).

The first was, "Mr. Balbus, you are a reticent New Englander."

When I was in high school, I did not live in New England. I do now. Mrs. Donahue had not made a prediction. It was an observation. I participated in class discussion rarely and then only reluctantly. The only other "reticent New Englander" I had heard of prior to that was President Calvin Coolidge, who reportedly responded to a bet that he could be made to say more than two words by saying, "You lose." Silent Cal was excellent company to be in. As lengthy as this book is, if I were any less reticent, it could have been a lot longer.

Her second assessment of me was, "Mr. Balbus, you could not write your way out of a paper bag."

Mrs. Donahue's second assessment was less prophetic than her first but more consequential. It was my motivation for writing this book. To prove her wrong. To prove that I could write my way out of a paper bag. And that really is the message of this book.

You have been told that bankruptcy is wrong. That bankruptcy is immoral. That the process is long and uncertain. That your life will be ruined if you file bankruptcy. Do not let what others say hold you back. If you need to, use it as motivation to prove them wrong.

So, thanks, Mrs. Donahue. I secretly dedicate this book to you. When they are finished with it, my readers will crumple it up and dispose of it properly.

# Introduction

Over the past decade, my legal practice has been devoted to representing individuals and small businesses in bankruptcy. I have had the opportunity to help people from a variety of socioeconomic backgrounds, who were struggling with unmanageable debt, find a solution in bankruptcy. Despite their differences, their predicaments tended to be alike.

Typically, their financial problems arose due to circumstances beyond their control, such as job loss, divorce, or illness. They found themselves unable to make minimum monthly payments on their credit cards or regular mortgage payments when the payments were due. They were paying interest on their credit cards at rates so high that no matter how much they paid, the balances never seemed to go down. They were being harassed relentlessly by collectors. The stress of dealing with unmanageable debt was enormous, physically debilitating and taking a terrible emotional toll on themselves and on their families.

I learned something basic and simple: Everyone wants to pay their debts, not everyone can. Debts that were once manageable had become unmanageable.

Despite the obvious benefits of debt relief through bankruptcy, most of the people who came to see me had avoided seriously considering bankruptcy as a solution to their unmanageable debt problem. They believed that filing bankruptcy was wrong, that they would lose their house, that the process was long, complicated and uncertain, and that filing bankruptcy would result in terrible consequences for them, maybe even worse than not paying their debts.

You too have reservations about bankruptcy. The decision to file bankruptcy is not easy an easy decision to make. *"Fresh Start"* is a self-help book for people considering bankruptcy.

*"Fresh Start"* contains all the information you need to determine whether bankruptcy is right for you, how to overcome your fear of filing, and exactly what bankruptcy is all about. If your goals are to return to financial health, to get your life back, and to get a fresh start, this book provides everything you need to know and all the steps you need to take to succeed.

In *"Fresh Start"* you will discover:

- How bankruptcy can eliminate all or most of your unsecured debts, like credit card and medical bills.
- How to determine if you need to file and whether an alternative to bankruptcy might be better for you.
- The mistaken beliefs that keep you from considering bankruptcy, like fear of losing your house or car.
- The harmful mindsets that keep you from pursuing bankruptcy, such as *"Getting out of debt through bankruptcy is immoral," "Bankruptcy is for losers,"* and *"Filing bankruptcy will makes things even worse,"* and how to overcome them.
- An easy-to-follow guide showing you how to determine if you qualify for bankruptcy.
- How to find an experienced bankruptcy lawyer and what it is like to meet with one.

- What steps are involved in the bankruptcy process and how long it will take.
- When you will have access to credit again. It is much sooner than you think!
- The 6 things you must never do before filing bankruptcy.
- Other specialized knowledge known only to experienced bankruptcy professionals.
- Most importantly, that bankruptcy is faster, easier and better than you think.

##  A ROADMAP TO USING THIS BOOK

"*Fresh Start*" is divided into three parts. The first part is a description of an actual initial consultation I had with a prospective client. It explains the circumstances, challenges, and needs of someone considering bankruptcy. It introduces bankruptcy and provides an overview of how bankruptcy can solve the problem of unmanageable debt.

The second part is designed to help allay your concerns about filing. It begins with an explanation of what typically happens when someone does not pay their debts. Possible alternatives to bankruptcy are then presented and analyzed. You will be able to determine whether you need to file bankruptcy. Despite the absence of a good alternative, many people still are reluctant to pursue bankruptcy. I discuss the internal dilemmas prospective clients often face that hold them back: (1) erroneous beliefs; (2) negative emotions; and (3) self-defeating behaviors. I provide suggestions to help overcome those obstacles and move forward.

The third and, by far, the largest part is an explanation of bankruptcy, the different types of bankruptcy, how to determine which type is best for you, whether you qualify for bankruptcy, what you get to keep, what happens to your debts, the things you must not do before filing, and the entire bankruptcy process from start to finish.

"*Fresh Start*" is designed for you to read all three parts or just the parts or sections that seem to apply to you. Feel free to skip or skim anything that does not seem relevant. Because people might not read the entire book or read it out of order, some of the material in the book may seem slightly repetitive. You can be assured there will be a lot to learn. Bankruptcy has its own rules and vocabulary which can turn out to mean the opposite of what you might have expected.

"*Fresh Start*" broadly covers every aspect that someone considering bankruptcy might be concerned with, in sufficient depth to answer most, if not all, of their questions. I have been practicing consumer bankruptcy law exclusively for the last ten years, so I have a fairly good idea of what prospective clients are concerned with, what misinformation they already have, and what they need to know to make an informed decision about bankruptcy. Although a large amount of material is covered, the presentation is designed to be easily understood by a typical prospective client. Abstract concepts are explained using concrete examples. "*Fresh Start*" is not a book for lawyers. There are no code sections, case citations or footnotes that a legal textbook written for lawyers would contain. Sorry, lawyers.

# THE FINE PRINT

"*Fresh Start*" does not purport to provide legal advice, is not intended to constitute legal advice, and should not be construed as a substitute for legal advice from a qualified lawyer. Although I am an attorney, I am not your attorney. You are not my client. Not yet anyway.

Despite my best efforts to ensure the accuracy of the information contained in this book, bankruptcy and related laws change often and, therefore, the content in this book may not reflect recent developments. Dollar amounts for eligibility and exemption purposes, for example, were current when this book was written, but are periodically adjusted for inflation and other reasons.

I am licensed to practice law in Connecticut and New York. Although I have tried to explain bankruptcy law and its application generally, the explanations may not be complete, and may not be accurate in, or applicable to, your jurisdiction. Because the content in this book is general in nature and may not pertain to your specific circumstances, you should not act, or refrain from acting, based on any content without first obtaining advice from a knowledgeable attorney licensed to practice in your jurisdiction. As they say on automobile advertisements on television, "Your mileage may vary."

"*Fresh Start*" is written for individuals contemplating bankruptcy. Certain information may not be applicable to business entities. Similarly, because this book provides a general description of bankruptcy law and its application, there will be exceptions to every single statement contained in the book. I would not be surprised to learn, for example, that the state of Alaska provides special protection to owners of dog sleds. Please do not notify me of my "mistake" of failing to mention the Alaskan dog sled exception.

Congress considers my legal practice to constitute a "debt relief agency" that helps people and small businesses in Connecticut and New York file for bankruptcy relief under the Bankruptcy Code. Congress likes it when I say precisely that. Hopefully, the preceding sentence will suffice to keep me out of jail. Bankruptcy lawyers are the most regulated and scrutinized of all lawyers, "for your protection."

Similarly, overseers of lawyers in Connecticut and New York like it when I say that I have not been certified as a specialist in bankruptcy law by any professional or government authority. The fact that I have a general law degree from Harvard Law School, an LL.M. Master of Laws in Bankruptcy degree from St. John's University School of Law, where I have been an Adjunct Professor, that I have been practicing consumer bankruptcy law exclusively for over a decade, and that articles I have written for professional bankruptcy publications have been cited by bankruptcy and appellate court judges around the country, is not intended to indicate any professional or governmental certification as a specialist in bankruptcy. As my children liked to say, "You're not so smart. You don't know everything." As usual, they are correct.

As a licensed attorney, I am subject to the rules of professional conduct applying to lawyers, one of which is the duty of confidentiality. I cannot go blabbing my clients' secrets to others. Even if they are really good secrets and I am dying to tell my wife. Although 99% of what I learn from a client during a bankruptcy representation is publicly disclosed, the duty of confidentiality bars me from divulging what I learn to you. As they said on the television show "*Dragnet*," "Ladies and gentlemen: the story you are about to hear is true. Only the names have been changed to protect the innocent." All the examples from my practice contained in this book are based on a true story. Client identifiers have been changed to protect client confidentiality.

# CHAPTER 1

## An Initial Consultation Regarding Bankruptcy

## MEET THE EPITOMES

The Epitomes did not want to be in my conference room. Not that day. Not any day. They sat across the table from me uncomfortably, shifting nervously in their seats, arms folded across their bodies defensively. Their facial expressions were glum. We avoided prolonged eye contact, but I could see Julia Epitome was on the verge of tears.

"We never expected to be here. We never planned on this," Julia Epitome began, not knowing quite what to say.

"I get that a lot," I replied. "No one ever wants to be in my office. No ever one wants to be with me. I don't take it personally," I quipped, hoping my small joke would distract Julia from crying the way a magician snaps the fingers on one hand while yelling "Presto" to divert the audience from seeing him conceal a card with the other hand.

Almost everyone who comes to my office for an initial consultation says the same thing – "I never planned on being here." No one ever plans on bankruptcy. No one ever plans on not being able to pay their bills. No one ever plans on the unrelenting harassment and stress that comes when bills are not paid. No one ever plans on being stuck on a Ferris wheel when the power goes out and it starts raining either. But it happens. Bad things happen to good people.

If people planned, they would come in sooner. People postpone the things they fear. Like colonoscopies. Postponing treatment is rarely beneficial.

Fortunately, bankruptcy lawyers are like magicians – we make debt disappear.

# 🦋 THEIR STORY

"Why don't you let me know what's going on. What brings you in today?" I asked, already knowing the answer. I knew what was going on, what had gone wrong. The particular facts and figures may change, but I hear pretty much the same story several times a day, every day. I have for the past decade.

Julia and John Epitome were in my office for an initial consultation regarding personal bankruptcy. Something in their lives had gone terribly wrong and, because of it, they were no longer able to pay their bills. Something had led them to believe that bankruptcy might solve their problem.

Julia Epitome started telling their story. "Well, my husband John lost his job in March. His company shut down due to the pandemic. At first, he thought it would be temporary and he'd get his job back. But, it wasn't. It was permanent. He lost his job. It took a few months before he was able to start collecting unemployment. Without his salary, we had to rely just on my salary. We fell a little behind on mortgage payments. We tried to stay current as best we could. We used our credit cards to make up for some of income we didn't have. John thought he would be able to find a new job right away. But that's not happening as fast as he hoped. He hasn't found anything."

I listened carefully to what Julia was saying. Equally important, I listened to how she said it. Julia Epitome spoke slowly, hesitantly, not carefully, but defeatedly, as if all the life had been drained out of her. I observed her body language. Her subtle actions were consistent with what she was saying. As she spoke, Julia tugged nervously on the bottom of her sweater sleeves, pulling them out beyond the shirt underneath, pulling them until the sweater sleeves almost completely covered her fingers. Her body language was not evasive. Julia was not hiding the truth. Julia was hiding her shame. She was wearing her emotions on her sleeves. I nodded to encourage Julia to continue.

"The credit cards call us asking for payment. I tell them John lost his job. Some seem to understand. Others, just want to be paid. Now, the minimum monthly payments are more than we can afford. I just can't pay them. John doesn't have a job. I don't know what to do. I'm the only one working. We don't have the money. This was not what I expected at this point in our lives. It's all falling apart."

I like to give prospective clients a chance to tell their stories without interruption. It takes some two minutes, others ten. The stories almost always are similar. They were managing their financial affairs, maybe with a little difficulty here and there, but nothing serious, until something unexpectedly went wrong. Usually, a job loss, divorce, or illness. Regular income fell sharply, suddenly. Due to the loss of income, debts that had been manageable quickly became unmanageable. Their lives began a downward spiral. Their hopes for the best were continually disappointed. Things never improved.

Listening to what Julia was saying was less important than giving Julia the opportunity to say it. I hold initial consultations across a large table in my conference room instead of across a smaller desk in my personal office to create more distance, more space, to make prospective clients more comfortable disclosing the most uncomfortable details of their lives. Sitting in a soft, padded chair, in a quiet room with dark furnishings, with an expansive view of trees through the large windows, lets prospective clients feel safe revealing their secrets. Telling her story briefly, uninterruptedly, in my conference room may have been the first time Julia openly discussed her financial problems with anyone, perhaps even her husband.

We do not talk about money. We talk about our jobs with our friends, but we do not discuss our salaries. Husbands and wives often do not discuss their incomes with each other. We especially do not talk about money troubles. We would rather talk about sexual disfunction or marital infidelity than financial problems.

For people who have never experienced dire financial circumstances firsthand, it may be difficult to understand how painful this situation was for Julia.

Imagine the dread of going to the mailbox each day to find another bill marked "Past Due" in red that you cannot afford to pay.

Imagine the indignity of not being able to answer the telephone, because the call could be from a debt collector. Some collectors feign understanding as a strategy to extract any payment now, however small, to instill a behavior pattern that can be manipulated into extracting larger payments later. Other collectors engage in verbal humiliation to extort a larger payment now in exchange for bringing the browbeating to an end. Still other collectors use the scare tactic. I have had clients who were threatened with jail if they did not pay their bills.

Imagine the embarrassment of hearing from your boss that your creditors have been calling the office looking for you or hearing from your bank that your bank account had been seized by a creditor.

Imagine the anxiety of worrying about losing your home.

Imagine not being able to sleep because of the stress.

Imagine the toll the stress takes on your physical and mental health, your relationships, and your career.

Imagine suddenly finding yourself underwater, unable to breathe and unable to reach the surface.

Imagine experiencing that every single day for six months or longer.

That is what Julia was feeling when she sat across the conference room table from me. As she told her story, I recognized the familiar look in her eyes of self-doubt, failure, and shame. I could see the frustration and the incomprehension that this could be happening to her and her family.

Julia continued to relate her story for a few more minutes. When she was finished, Julia's expression had changed. Her face lifted as if a terrible burden had been lifted off her shoulders. Just by telling her story, Julia felt much better. It always does.

 BANKRUPTCY IS TABOO

John Epitome's mood was unchanged. He remained glum. His facial expression reflected the same frustration and anxiety as his wife's, but it was darker. John was angry. For reasons that had nothing to do his performance, John had lost his job. And John was irritated. Although his sleeves were rolled up, as if he were ready to go to work, the opposite was true. John was ready to leave. John was irritated to be discussing his personal financial problems with a bankruptcy lawyer.

When a couple comes in for an initial consultation, usually the wife will lead the conversation. Women tend to oversee the family's finances even when both spouses work. Women tend to be better than men in stretching resources and managing the household budget. When the wife finishes her description of what has gone wrong, I will turn my attention to the husband to see if he has anything to add. Usually, he does not. When he does, the message tends to be similar to what John Epitome delivered to me.

"Mr. Balbus, in my culture, we believe in paying our bills. We consider it immoral and unethical to try to get out of paying them."

"Mr. Epitome," I replied, "People in every culture believe it is immoral and unethical to not pay their bills. Everyone wants to pay their bills, not everyone can."

The sentiment that John Epitome expressed is what virtually everyone believes: bankruptcy is wrong. People pay their bills because paying one's bills is the right thing to do. The idea of not paying one's bills raises emotions of shame and embarrassment. Not being able to pay one's bills is the definition of personal failure. Not being able to provide for one's family leaves one feeling overwhelming guilt. Using bankruptcy to avoid paying one's bills may be the most shameful thing ever considered. Well, perhaps I exaggerate. Clubbing baby seals to death would be considered more shameful. Barely.

John Epitome did not visit me for confirmation that what everyone believes about bankruptcy is true. Everyone also believes that stress causes stomach ulcers and Vikings wore horned helmets. John Epitome came in to be told that what everyone believes about bankruptcy is false. He came to the right place. No one knows anything about bankruptcy and what little "everyone" knows usually is incorrect. That is why I wrote this book. Also, bacteria cause most stomach ulcers and a costume designer for a Wagner opera created the Viking horned helmet.

The Epitomes, like almost half of the people who come in to see me, found me through my law firm's website on the Internet. The other half are referred by local attorneys, accountants and, occasionally, local real estate brokers and bank officers. People who come in for an initial consultation but end up not filing bankruptcy are a larger source of referrals than actual clients who successfully discharged their debts in bankruptcy. Sound surprising? Not really. People are more likely to talk about having had cancer than having been in bankruptcy. Someday, we will wear green ribbons and have parades for bankruptcy "survivors." In the meantime, like cancer in the 1950's, bankruptcy represents something shameful most people would rather not talk about.

When we schedule the initial consultation, we tell prospective clients it is an introductory meeting to learn about their situation, to see if bankruptcy makes sense and, if so, to determine which type of bankruptcy would work best, what the bankruptcy process involves and what it will cost. We let them know that there is no charge for the initial consultation and to expect the meeting to last about sixty minutes. We ask prospective clients to bring with them the answers to eight questions regarding their residency, their income, their assets, and their debts. That is all the information I need to determine whether bankruptcy offers a solution.

Now that the Epitomes have told their story and one of them has been put somewhat at ease, I will begin to ask those questions. There is a structure and a method to asking prospective clients questions. Very few prospective clients have had much experience with lawyers. At most, they may have hired a lawyer to close the purchase of a house or to draft a will. To avoid having prospective clients feel like they are being cross-examined by a criminal lawyer on "*Law & Order*" and making them reluctant or defensive about answering questions, I start off asking easy-to-answer questions: whether they have filed bankruptcy before, how long they have lived in Connecticut or New York, and then some questions about their house and who lives in it, and their cars.

 SECURED DEBTS

"How much is your house worth and how much is the outstanding principal balance of any mortgage on the house?" I asked the Epitomes.

"John and I paid $300,000 for the house around 2015," Julia answered. "We live in the house with our three daughters. According to Zillow, the house is worth $320,000. That sounds a little high. Our house needs a lot of work. We have a first mortgage with Union Savings Bank. We still owe $275,000. We also have a Home Equity Line of Credit with Starbridge Mortgage Company of $35,000."

"Are you current on both mortgages – the first mortgage and the HELOC?" I asked, quickly correcting myself. I think it is important to speak into a prospective client's "listening," that is, the prospective client's understanding of what and how things are, which may be different from the legal perspective. Most people do not think of a home equity line of credit as a second mortgage, but it is. It is recorded on the land records. If it is not paid on time, the HELOC lender can foreclosure, just like a first mortgage.

"The HELOC payment is pretty small, only $175/month. We have been able to remain current on that one," Julia replied. "The mortgage payment is more of a problem. It is $2,800/month. When John lost his job, we fell behind a couple of months. The bank was pretty understanding. We finally caught up on the missed payments. Lately, we have been making each monthly payment, but not on time. Usually, we are a bit late. The payment is due on the first of the month. We don't always have all the money until the end of the month. We are doing the best we can. We never expected to be in this position. We are really worried about losing the house. My eldest is in her senior year at high school. Will we be able to keep the house if we do bankruptcy?" Julia asked. As she finished her question, Julia looked up at me with pleading eyes.

To most people, keeping their house is the most important thing. A man's home is his castle. A women's home is where she raises her children. One of Julia's daughters was in her final year of high school. Moving that child would be traumatic. The other two daughters were in a different school. Being forced to relocate at this time would be another terrible burden to inflict upon the Epitomes.

"Don't worry. You can keep your house in bankruptcy. You will not lose your house," I assured them. Julia looked relieved.

The specific reasons why a house usually can be kept in bankruptcy will be described in detail later in this book. Basically, if the equity in the house (that is, the fair market value of the house minus the outstanding balance of any mortgage or other lien on the house) is below the homestead exemption set by state law, and in some states, the higher of state or federal exemptions, the house can be kept. Here, the fair market value determined by Zillow (which tends to run high) was $320,000. The total of the outstanding balances on their 1st mortgage ($275,000) and their HELOC ($35,000) was $310,000. The Epitomes had $10,000 of equity in their house ($320,000 fair market value minus $310,000 mortgage balances). Since $10,000 in house equity was well below the available state and federal homestead exemptions, the Epitomes could keep their house.

Julia mentioned that their house "needed a lot of work." That is not surprising. People in financial distress rarely can afford to update appliances or to make needed capital improvements, like replacing a roof. Consequently, the Epitomes' house may have been worth less than the $320,000 value estimated by Zillow. In the real world, having more equity in a house is a good thing. In the bizarro world of bankruptcy, having less equity is better. The lower the equity, the easier it is to protect with available exemptions. Ironically, not being able to make home improvements worked to the Epitomes' advantage.

"How about car loans? Do you have any cars with loans on them?" I asked.

Julia shook her head 'yes'.

"More than one?" I asked.

"Two," Julia replied.

"What kinds of cars, how much are they worth and how much is owed on each car loan?" I asked.

Apart from homes, the items people are most worried about losing in bankruptcy are cars. You cannot get to work in most places in the U.S. without a car.

"I have a 2016 Nissan Rogue, which Kelly Blue Book values at $9,150. We still owe $17,550 on that loan. John leases a 2017 Acura RLX. We are current on the Rogue loan and the Acura lease, but with John out of work and all, I am not sure how much longer we will be able to make payments. We need the cars to get to work and, for John, to find a new job."

"You can keep both cars in bankruptcy," I reassured them, "but there may be reasons to get rid of one or both cars in bankruptcy. We will talk more about that later. For now, just keep in mind that if you want to keep both cars, you can keep both cars."

Most people can keep their cars in bankruptcy. A whole section of this book explains why. At this point, just notice two things about our conversation regarding the cars. First, I asked about car loans and Julia answered with a car lease. Once again, there is a legal distinction between a car loan and a car lease, as well as different treatment in bankruptcy, but most people think of a car loan and a car lease similarly, particularly if they have no equity in the car subject to the loan. With both the Nissan Rogue loan and the Acura RLX lease, the Epitomes made monthly car payments to someone they considered to be the owner of the car.

Second, you may be wondering how a 2016 Nissan Rogue worth $9,150 could be subject to a loan of $17,550, almost twice the value of the car. Cars depreciate significantly once they leave the dealer's lot, especially new cars, but that is not what happened here. Welcome to the world of people living in financial distress. What happened here, and it is not uncommon, is that the Epitomes previously owned a car that no longer fit their needs. At the time it was traded in for the Nissan Rogue, the old car had a remaining loan balance of about $7,000. The Nissan dealer "rolled" that old $7,000 car loan balance into the new Rogue car loan leaving the Epitomes liable for a new car loan that was about $7,000 higher than the value of their new car.

The 2016 Nissan Rogue was significantly, hugely, unbelievably "underwater." The Epitomes owed $8,400 more on the loan than the car was worth. Outside bankruptcy, if the Epitomes defaulted on the Rogue loan and Nissan Auto Finance repossessed the car, the Epitomes would still be liable for that amount, probably even more. Bankruptcy offers a way to emerge from that underwater mess. If they were to file bankruptcy in Chapter 7, as most bankruptcy cases are, the Epitomes would have the opportunity to "surrender" the Rogue to the lender and to discharge their entire car loan debt.

Chapter 7 also provides John with a unique opportunity to end his 2017 Acura RLX lease. The Epitomes might prefer to have only one car or a different leased car with a cheaper monthly payment. Outside bankruptcy, if John were to return the Acura RLX and cancel the lease before the end of its term, John would be charged a high early termination penalty. If, instead, he files a Chapter 7 bankruptcy, the Acura RLX could be returned to the dealer, the lease "rejected," and the entire amount owed on the lease discharged.

At this stage of the initial consultation, all the Epitomes want to know is that they can keep their cars. They can. Later, I will pull a rabbit out of my hat and discuss with the Epitomes the amazing opportunity bankruptcy provides to give them relief from an underwater car loan and an unfavorable car lease.

Now that she knows she will be able to keep her home and cars, Julia is beginning to look a lot more relaxed. Her eyes have dried up. More color is coming into her face. She's speaking normally. John is not quite there yet. He is still not happy about the whole bankruptcy thing.

 ## UNSECURED DEBTS

"Now, let's talk about your unsecured debts, that is, debts without collateral. Within a million, what is your total credit card debt?" I asked, jokingly.

Admittedly, it was not a very funny joke. It never gets a laugh. So why bother making a feeble attempt at humor at this stage of the initial consultation? The answer is the psychological principle known as "anchoring." Most people are embarrassed by the size of their credit card debt regardless of the amount. They have no idea whether their credit card debt is large or small compared to other people in financial distress. Whatever it is, the total seems unreasonably and embarrassingly high to them. By setting an "anchor" of a million, no matter how high the Epitome's credit card debt turns out to be, it must be vastly less than one million dollars and, consequently, much less shameful in comparison.

"Our total credit card debt is about $40,000," Julia quietly revealed.

"Is it spread out over a number of bank and store credit cards or is it on mainly one card?" I asked.

"It is mostly Capital One, American Express, Home Depot, Discover, Lowe's Kohl's, Target and TJ Maxx in pretty even amounts. Some of the cards are in my name, some are in John's name."

It may come as a surprise, but, for the most part, it does not matter how much credit card debt you have. There is no maximum credit card debt limit in most bankruptcies. You could owe more than a million dollars in credit card debt and still be eligible for bankruptcy in Chapter 7. Most of my clients have between $40,000 and $60,000 in credit card debt. Occasionally, the total will exceed $100,000. The total does not matter unless it seems excessive relative to the client's gross income, say more than two- or three-times gross income. For example, most credit card issuers will not extend $150,000 of credit to someone with a salary of $50,000. As a result, someone having total credit card debt that high compared to their income suggests that criminality may be involved. Bankruptcy is for honest but unfortunate debtors, not criminals.

Knowing which spouse owed the debt was important. If only one spouse owed the debt, then both spouses might not have to file. Since both Julia and John owed credit card debt, absent other reasons, it was likely both would benefit from filing.

"How about other unsecured debts? I asked. "Do you have any medical debt, tax debt, student loans, or loans from friends or family members? Have you co-signed or guaranteed any debts for someone else?"

"We owe $6,000 to Danbury Hospital, mostly related to an operation I had three years ago that was not fully covered by insurance. We spoke with their lawyer. The hospital won't work with us on it. We just pay them what we can each month. Lately, we haven't paid them anything. We can't. We just don't have the money.

"All of our tax returns have been filed on time and we don't owe any taxes. John still has about $5,000 left on his student loans. Thank God, they went into forbearance when he lost his job.

"My Dad has been great about sending us some money when we get really desperate. Things haven't been easy for him either, since my Mom died two years ago. I promised him we would pay him back what we owe as soon as we can.

"We haven't co-signed or guaranteed debts for anyone else." Julia was getting much more comfortable now answering questions and providing me with a complete picture of their financial position.

The Epitomes' financial situation was common for people contemplating bankruptcy. They had significant credit card debt and some medical debt. Owing money to a family member or friend is not unusual and it is not a problem in bankruptcy, but repaying a family member or a friend right before filing can be a major problem. This book will cover how different types of debts are treated in bankruptcy later. For now, just know that the Epitomes' $40,000 of credit card debt and $6,000 of medical debt will disappear in bankruptcy faster than you can say "Bibbidi-Bobbidi-Boo."

 ASSETS

"Now that I have a complete picture of your debts," I said, "let's turn to your assets, everything you own in whole world. Usually, this is the fastest portion of my show."

It is the fastest part of the initial consultation because almost no one who comes to see me owns anything of value. Typically, people sell everything they can long before they consider bankruptcy.

I went through a standard checklist of the types of property people might own. Things like cars without loans, bank accounts, retirement accounts, jewelry, business property, and life insurance. The Epitomes, like most people in bankruptcy, would be able to keep everything they owned. State legislatures and Congress have established lists of "exemptions," that is, necessary items of property that are exempt from creditors, that debtors in bankruptcy may keep for their fresh start. How exemptions work will be described in some detail later in this book. For now, if you were worried about losing everything you own in bankruptcy and being destitute, forced to live in an old van by the river, you can stop worrying. Most people keep everything they own in bankruptcy.

After completing the asset checklist, I said, "So, basically, you're telling me, 'Balbus we have nothing'."

"Balbus, we have nothing."

"I get that a lot," I said. "If you had valuable assets, probably you would not be sitting here. But, I have to go through the list just to be sure."

 INCOME

"Now that the asset portion of my show is over, it is time for income. What do you do and how much do you make? Let's start with John," I said.

Notice how long the initial consultation had gone on before I asked either Epitome about their income. You might have thought that income was the most important piece of information for me to know. There is a reason for waiting to ask about income. People in financial distress are extremely uncomfortable disclosing where they work and how much money they make. Notice that I did not ask the Epitomes where they worked, just what they did.

Julia answered. "Before he lost his job, John was an account executive at Schmendrick Steel. His annual salary was $80,000. Since he lost his job in March, John has been receiving about $600/week unemployment, but it took a couple of months after he lost his job before he started collecting the unemployment payments. I am the office manager at a veterinary practice in Bethel. My annual salary is $57,500."

Although I had asked John to start, notice that it was Julia who responded. John still had on his mean face. Convincing John that bankruptcy was not wrong would not be easy. Also notice that Julia volunteered the name of John's former employer, but not her own. Former employers do not count. There is less shame in a former employer finding out you filed bankruptcy. Current employers are different. I would need to inject most prospective clients with sodium pentothal before they volunteered the names of their employers. Unless they also happen to be creditors, which is extraordinarily rare, employers are not notified when an employee files bankruptcy, but most people believe their employers will be notified.

I then asked the Epitomes about other sources of income they might have, such as Social Security, disability, pension, alimony or child support, rental or other business income, eBay sales, and part-time bartending. They had no other sources of income.

With that done, I was able to let the Epitomes know whether they qualified for bankruptcy and, in particular, whether they qualified for bankruptcy in

Chapter 7. Before you receive that verdict, it is important that you learn more about the Epitomes. It was information that I would not learn until after the Epitomes had become clients, but it was information that the Epitomes shared in common with most of my clients.

 ## THE EPITOMES DID THE RIGHT THING

The Epitomes were not bad people. Their first large debts were incurred to pay for college. When the Epitomes went to college, tuition was much lower, so John's remaining student loan debt of $5,000 was not particularly high. With their college educations, the Epitomes found good jobs and made excellent livings. They married and moved into an apartment. They saved up for a down payment and bought a house with a monthly mortgage payment that was affordable. As their careers progressed, their earnings rose. Through payroll deductions, they began to save for their retirement. When their family grew to two children, they sold one house and moved into another. To get the space they needed in the desired school district, they had to spend more for their second house. The new house required a monthly mortgage payment that was tougher on their budget than the first house but still within their means. With the birth of their third child, the Epitomes remodeled their house, financed with a home equity line of credit. The HELOC was an extra burden on their monthly budget, but the remodeling increased the value of their house. Instead of paying for cars all at once out of savings, the Epitomes either took out car loans or leased cars.

Mortgages and car loans are often considered to be "good" debts, because they enable the borrower to purchase assets that otherwise would be unaffordable and that make the borrower more productive. "Good" debt carries a lower rate of interest, because collateral secures the repayment of the debt. "Good" debt is less risky.

Credit card debt, on the other hand, is often considered to be "bad" debt, because the purchases made with the debt generally are consumed more quickly. Without collateral as security to support the repayment of credit card debt, interest rates are high, particularly when payments are not made on time. The Epitomes prudently used their credit cards, mainly as a substitute for cash. At the end of every month, the Epitomes paid their credit card balances in full. As their children grew up and the Epitomes occasionally needed more money than they had on hand for a vacation trip or for Christmas presents, the Epitomes used their credit cards. Those extra balances were paid off in full within two or three months.

The Epitomes were pursuing the American Dream. Incurring "good" debt enabled the Epitomes to make major investments in their future: college educations, homes, cars, and remodeling their home to accommodate a third child. They budgeted carefully. Incurring "bad" credit card debt on a temporary basis enabled the Epitomes to make larger purchases at times their monthly budget would not allow. The debts were manageable between their two salaries, reflecting their solid careers. Their prudent use of debt enabled the Epitomes to build high credit scores, which provided greater access to credit at favorable terms. They looked forward to a comfortable retirement. The Epitomes could not have lived the lives they lived if they had to save up in advance to make those purchases. No one would consider doing that today. The Epitomes did the right thing.

Something bad happened to the Epitomes. Something they did not expect or plan for. John lost his job. Due to the Covid-19 pandemic, John's company shut down operations and laid John off. The layoff, temporary at first, became permanent. Unemployment hit John hard. In his entire adult life, John had never been unemployed. Despite the offshoring of U.S. steel manufacturing to China, John had always worked. He thought the Covid-19 shutdown and layoff would be temporary. He was wrong. Without his job, John barely knew who he was.

Nationwide, well over 90% of personal bankruptcy cases are filed by people who lost their job, divorced or separated from their partner, or suffered a serious medical problem. Due to the loss of income or increased expenses attributable to the job loss, divorce or medical issue, debts that once were manageable became unmanageable. To quote the eminent philosopher, professional boxer, and cartoon *"Mysteries"* team leader, Mike Tyson, "Everybody has a plan until they get punched in the mouth."

##  DEBT BECAME UNMANAGEABLE

At Julia's insistence, John reluctantly applied for and began receiving unemployment benefits. That income barely replaced half of John's take home pay. Still, it was some assistance. There are no government benefits to help offset the loss of income when a couple gets divorced or ceases to cohabit and must support two households instead of one. There are no government benefits to help pay the medical expenses that insurance does not cover – especially high deductibles and out-of-network expenses. Even with Obamacare, self-employed people often are required to pay more than $20,000 per year for monthly premiums, co-payments and deductibles before "insurance" begins to cover medical expenses.

Julia tried to spend less to compensate for John's loss of income. She shopped more carefully, substituting "store" brands for "name" brands. She cut back on small "luxuries," using the dry cleaner as little as possible. But the hole in their household budget left by John's unemployment could not be filled by cutting expenses. Most of their expenses were fixed. The first mortgage, HELOC, car loan and car lease had to be paid each month. There was no way to reduce those expenses. At best, they could be paid a month or two late, but late payments triggered late fees and penalty interest rates which dug the budget hole even deeper.

Julia filled the hole in the household budget by using credit cards. That made sense. Credit cards had provided short-term budget flexibility in the past. John expected the Covid-19 shutdown to be temporary. If he could not go back to work at Schmendrick Steel, he expected to be able to find employment with another steel company within a short period of time. He had never been out of work before. He was well-educated, well-trained, and had a lot of experience in his field. Unfortunately, John had no idea what the job market was like for someone his age. No one knew how the Covid-19 shutdowns would affect the economy.

John's prospects for finding new employment at his old salary were worse than he had imagined. What few relevant job listings he found were at companies further away from home and at lower salaries. John was not interested in settling for any job. He wanted to hold out for a position he deserved. As the months passed, credit card usage increased, as did the late payments, the penalties, and the vastly higher interest rates. Credit card penalty interest rates ran close to 30%. Each month, the hole in the Epitomes' household budget became deeper and deeper, harder and harder to climb out of. As their credit card debts rose higher, their credit scores fell further. The debts became unmanageable.

In retrospect, perhaps the Epitomes should have maintained a greater cash surplus to protect against an unexpected loss of income. Had they "saved for a rainy day," the Epitomes would have been better able to deal with the adversity of John's unemployment. The Epitomes were certainly not alone in that regard. According to a January 2021 survey by Bankrate, fewer than four out of ten adults in the U.S. could afford to pay a $1,000 car repair, emergency room visit or other unexpected expense from savings. That is a better result than a recent survey of 2,000 Americans carried out by innovation consultancy Highland, which found that 82% of respondents could not afford to pay a surprise expense of $500. Covid-19 has made the situation much worse. Prior to the pandemic, Highland found that only 50% of Americans could not afford the $500 emergency expense. Highland also found that more than a quarter of respondents had accumulated $10,000 or more in debt since the beginning of the pandemic.

##  CONSEQUENCES OF UNMANAGEABLE DEBT

Unmanageable debt is not solely a financial problem. The physical and mental health consequences can make a dire situation even worse. When he lost his job, John lost the part of himself that was good at doing something, that was productive, that contributed to the benefit of others. He felt disrespected and disregarded by his employer. Losing his ability to provide for his family sapped John's self-confidence and self-esteem.

Anxiety over getting a new job kept John up at night and made him reluctant to get out of bed in the morning. As he became more depressed, John's attitude, his energy, and, worst of all, his hope ebbed. John felt like a failure. He began to withdraw from his family and his friends.

There is a known connection between stress and illness. Mental stress may induce medical problems. Unmanageable debt can make you physically sick. Lack of financial resources may exacerbate existing medical conditions. People often forego scheduled medical treatments or put off seeking medical care for new conditions to avoid spending money. Failure to treat problems at the inception can lead to more serious ailments like digestive tract problems, hypertension, and heart attacks.

Financial distress is frequently ruinous to emotional relationships, turning spouse against spouse. Reportedly, the number one reason for divorce is financial trouble. When I first saw them, from what I could tell, John and Julia appeared to be getting along well. John was clearly angry, but his anger was not directed towards Julia. Often an angry or irritable husband will cut his wife off or correct his wife throughout the initial consultation. That can be hard to sit through. I am a bankruptcy lawyer, not a marriage counselor.

Fortunately, Julia still had her job managing the veterinary practice. The job of managing the household budget without John's income and managing John's deteriorating mental condition also fell to her. Julia had to deal with the past due bills and the calls from collectors. She worried about what would happen if the bills were not paid. Many people relieve the stress caused by unmanageable debt through self-medication – leading to alcohol and drug abuse. Sadly, I have had at least one prospective client take his own life to bring the downward spiral of debt and depression to an end.

The Epitomes were not facing a liquidity problem. They did not just lack sufficient cash to tide them over for a short period of time. That problem had been solved successfully in the past by using credit cards. The Epitomes were facing an insolvency crisis. It was no longer possible to pay their debts.

People often mistake insolvency for illiquidity. They delude themselves into believing another round of debt will fix the problem. More debt never fixes an insolvency problem. Only bankruptcy fixes an insolvency problem.

As the Epitomes struggled to pay their bills, they struggled to find an alternative. They heard about bankruptcy being a solution to the problem of unmanageable debt, but they believed that filing bankruptcy was the "wrong" thing to do.

John made that point explicitly when he said, "In my culture, we believe in paying our bills. We consider it immoral and unethical to try to get out of paying them." Like many prospective clients, John believed that not paying his debts was something an ethical person would not do. Bankruptcy is for bad people who run up bills with no intention of paying them, for cheaters who abuse the system and get away with it. Bankruptcy is not for good people like the Epitomes.

John believed a myth. Everyone wants to pay their debts. Not everyone can. The Epitomes had contractual and ethical obligations to pay their debts. Unexpectedly, their circumstances changed. The Epitomes were not illiquid; they were insolvent. The Epitomes were not choosing to not pay their debts. They had no choice. It was not financially possible for the Epitomes to pay their debts.

The Founding Fathers recognized that their new nation would be better off if individuals facing insolvency were able to discharge their debts in bankruptcy rather than being persecuted by creditors for the rest of their lives, thrown in jail or banished to Australia. They provided all Americans with the right to a "fresh start" in bankruptcy in the Constitution.

Despite the necessity and legality of bankruptcy, people often avoid bankruptcy out of embarrassment or being seen as a failure. Bankruptcy is viewed as being part of the problem, not the solution. Bankruptcy is not for them. Ironically, the same people hold others who have gone through bankruptcy to a less "idealistic" standard. The same people attach no stigma to Chrysler or Hostess for having gone through bankruptcy. They will happily drive Jeeps and eat Twinkies. But fear of filing will often delay or derail their own serious consideration of bankruptcy and the relief it could bring.

Eventually, however, either the financial pressure becomes unbearable or a trigger, such as being served with a lawsuit by a creditor or having a bank account seized or wages garnished, forces people to consider bankruptcy. The Epitomes reached that point, ran a search on Google and the results brought them to my office for an initial consultation. For the Epitomes, the meeting would also be an initial consolation. There was good news ahead. Bankruptcy was a solution to their problem. And it would be faster, easier and better than they thought.

 ## THE CHAPTER 7 SOLUTION

"Congratulations," I said smiling brightly, "you qualify for bankruptcy and, in particular, you qualify for Chapter 7, the fastest, easiest, cheapest and bestest of all possible bankruptcies.

"The 'deal' in Chapter 7 is that almost all your unsecured debts, the credit cards and medical bills, are discharged. 'Poof' they disappear, like magic. You will be stuck with $5,000 in student loans, but they will be easier to pay with no other debt. You get to keep all your income. Hopefully, John will have lots of income after filing. You keep it all. 100%. Creditors get nothing.

"The downside of Chapter 7," I continued, "besides having to deal with me, is that you are limited in what you can keep. What you get to keep is determined by exemptions. Since you do not own any property that I am aware of that is not protected by exemptions, you get to keep everything you own – your house, your cars, your clothes, your furniture, your retirement accounts, your kids, and everything else you own. In addition to those specific exemptions, you likely will also get an additional "wildcard" exemption to cover other items you may have, such as cash in the bank on the day you file bankruptcy.

"Bankruptcy in Chapter 7 works perfectly for you. Your unsecured debts are discharged, you keep all your income, and you get to keep all your stuff. Chapter 7 is such a good deal that Congress limits the number of people who can take advantage of it.

"There are three ways to qualify for Chapter 7. The first and easiest way is to be below median income based upon your household size. Essentially, Congress allows about half of the people of every state automatically to go to Chapter 7. Based upon your household size of 5, the median income threshold is just under $140,000. Your income is well below that threshold.

"If you were slightly above median, you also could qualify for Chapter 7 by passing what is known as the Means Test. The idea is that if you have the means, that is, the ability, to pay creditors, you should not be allowed to discharge all your debts in Chapter 7. Instead, you should be required to pay at least some of your debts in Chapter 13. The math does not work out exactly, but the amount you must pay creditors in Chapter 13 is roughly the amount by which you fail the Means Test.

"The third way to get to Chapter 7 is to have more business debt than non-business debt, which does not apply to you.

"To recap, you get rid of all of your credit card and medical debt. You get to keep all your income going forward. As long as you keep paying the mortgages, you get to keep your house. As long as you keep paying the car loan and the car lease, you get to keep your cars. Unless you would prefer to get rid of one or both cars. I appreciate that you need two cars, but the economically better option would be to get rid of the Rogue and its underwater loan, if you could. If you could borrow a car or buy a clunker now, when your credit improved, you would be able to buy a new car with a reasonable loan at a reasonable rate of interest. And you get to keep all your other property, since there does not seem to be much, if any. Sound good so far?"

Julia was elated. She still had some questions and concerns, but a solution to her unmanageable debt problem existed. Bankruptcy was still scary and unknown, but for the first time in an awfully long time, she could see a future for herself and her family. Even John seemed to be perking up.

 THE HORRIBLE THINGS THAT HAPPEN WHEN YOU FILE BANKRUPTCY

"I know what you are thinking," I said, "this bankruptcy thing sounds too good to be true. What about all the horrible things that happen to you when you file?" I like to simulate a drum roll with my fingers tapping on the conference room table to intensify the drama of the moment. The big reveal.

"Nothing. Nothing bad happens to you when you file. Your credit report will contain a footnote indicating that you filed bankruptcy. Big deal. The fact that you filed bankruptcy will be reported as a footnote on your credit report for up to ten years. That is the worst thing that will happen to you when you file bankruptcy. Filing bankruptcy itself is not factored into your credit score. The score is based upon your income, lines of credit and your ability to make timely payments after filing. My clients who work on rebuilding their credit scores are over 700 within 18 months of filing.

"Credit scores are incredibly sensitive to missed mortgage payments and, to a lesser extent, to missed credit card payments. Since you have been late on two mortgage payments and a few credit card payments, your current credit score is likely to be in the low 500's. If you did not file bankruptcy, your credit score might never reach 700. Filing bankruptcy wipes out your credit history and allows you to restore your credit score much faster than if you did not file.

"You have been living in financial hell fearing bankruptcy over a footnote on your credit report."

## WILL YOU EVER HAVE CREDIT AGAIN?

"You also may be worried about never having credit cards again. Fuhgeddaboudit. Virtually all my clients are offered new credit cards almost immediately after filing. How can that be, you ask? Well, after you file bankruptcy, you are the best credit risk on the planet. All your other unsecured debt has been wiped out and you cannot file bankruptcy in Chapter 7 again for another eight years.

"You may not want to go back to using credit cards, but if rebuilding your credit score is especially important to you, accept all the offers, use the cards to purchase gas and groceries, and pay off the balances in full at the end of every month. The more lines of credit you have and the more you use them, the faster your credit score will go up. Again, my clients who work on rebuilding their credit scores are over 700 within 18 months of filing. There is no way you would be above 600 within the next 18 months without filing bankruptcy.

"If you desperately need to use credit cards during the short period of time after filing and before new credit cards are offered, each of you could file bankruptcy separately one after the other, or you could become an authorized user on someone else's card, say a parent or close friend. Because the authorized user is not responsible for paying off the card, when an authorized user files bankruptcy, the card usually is not shut off.

"Although it is not a concern of yours now, in my experience, filing bankruptcy is not a serious impediment to being eligible for a government-backed mortgage. As a practical matter, it will take two or three years to save up enough money for a down payment on a house. When you are ready to make that down payment, your credit score should be over 700. With those two pieces of the puzzle in place, you will only need a mortgage broker who is capable of explaining why you had to file bankruptcy to qualify."

At this point in the initial consultation, Julia was on cloud nine. The credit card and medical debt would be gone along with the horrible calls from collectors. She would keep all her stuff. She would keep all her income. Nothing bad would happen to her. She would get her life back. Even John was coming around. He still had concerns, but the upside of bankruptcy clearly outweighed his bad feelings about going through it. He became more engaged in the discussion and even had the beginnings of a smile on his face.

 ## THE PROCESS

"Feel better?" I asked. Both shook their heads 'yes'.

"Sound pretty good?" I asked. Again, both shook their heads 'yes'.

"Now that you know that nothing bad will happen to you when you file bankruptcy, let's talk about the whole process, from soup to nuts. It is also faster, easier and better than you thought.

The next fifteen minutes were devoted to my explaining what is involved in filing a bankruptcy case from signing an Engagement Agreement to receiving a discharge. I explained what their responsibilities would be, what paperwork would be required, how much it would cost and how long it would take, all of which is described in detail in Chapter 10. It is a process that will take most clients about four months to complete after which they will get their lives back. You may have played games of *Risk* that lasted longer than four months.

## READY TO MOVE AHEAD

"We've gone through how bankruptcy can give you a fresh start by eliminating your unsecured debts; how you qualify for bankruptcy, because your income is below median for your household size; what you can keep in bankruptcy, everything you own and, if you'd like, you even can get rid of your cars; the horrible things that happen to you after you file, largely nothing other than a meaningless footnote on your credit report; and how quickly you'll be able to restore your credit score and have access to credit. We have covered the process, how long it will take, and what it will cost. Do you have any questions?" I asked. I have done this a few times before, so I did not expect many questions. The Epitomes did not surprise me.

I have often joked about saying at the end of the initial consultation, "So, what is it going to take for me to put you into a bankruptcy today?" like a shady used-car salesman in a David Mamet movie. The high-pressure tactic undoubtedly would "close" more than a few "sales". But it does not work well with bankruptcy. It may not be hard to persuade prospective clients to sign up for bankruptcy. It is hard to get the commitment to follow through. Filing bankruptcy requires a lot of disclosure, which means a lot of paperwork. Some clients finish faster, but, on average, it takes two to four weeks for clients to complete their "homework." The workload is slightly higher than applying for a mortgage, but less than studying for the CPA exam.

Because I want clients who are committed to finishing the process, my preference is to end the initial consultation before the hard close to give prospective clients time to think about the benefits of bankruptcy, how they will pay the fees and when they would like to begin. In some cases, it may be preferable to delay starting the process. The prospective client may need to do a little research, such as valuing assets to make sure they can be kept in Chapter 7 or determining precisely which spouse owns which assets. Once the prospective client is ready to move ahead, we set up a time to review bankruptcy again, sign an Engagement Agreement, and give the client their "homework."

Are you ready to move ahead? The next section of this book will let you know whether you have unmanageable debt and whether there is an alternative to filing bankruptcy that might work for you. Probably, there is not. After that, I will describe and confront the erroneous beliefs, negative emotions and counterproductive behaviors that hold people back from considering and pursuing bankruptcy. After an overview of what bankruptcy is and the different types of bankruptcy, I will provide the information you need to determine if bankruptcy is right for you, whether you qualify for Chapter 7, whether you will be able to keep all your assets in Chapter 7 (spoiler alert: you will). After a description of what happens to your debts in bankruptcy, and a short recap of actions not to take before filing, I will explain the entire bankruptcy process from beginning to end. I have no doubt that you will find bankruptcy to be faster, easier and better than you ever imagined.

# CHAPTER 2

## How You Know You Have To File Bankruptcy

 INTRODUCTION

Towards the end of each initial consultation, I explain the prospective client's non-bankruptcy options. I omitted that discussion from the description of the Epitomes' initial consultation, because it was clear that the Epitomes had no choice other than filing bankruptcy. The Epitomes had no way to pay their debts. They were facing the certainty of lawsuits from unpaid creditors. Maybe you do have alternatives. Let's see. In the next section, I describe what will happen to you if you do not pay your debts and potential alternatives to filing bankruptcy. If no alternative offers a solution to your unmanageable debt problem, you will know that you must file bankruptcy.

## WHAT HAPPENS WHEN YOU DO NOT PAY YOUR DEBTS?

For the Epitomes, as well as for most prospective clients, the debts that tend to go unpaid are "unsecured debts," that is, debts without collateral. Secured debts, such as home mortgages and car loans, tend to be paid first, because the punishment for not making timely payments on secured debts is repossession and loss of the collateral. The consequences for not paying unsecured debts, like credit cards, store charges, personal loans, and medical debts, are less severe but nonetheless unpleasant.

Typically, if no payment at all is made on a credit card for six months, the credit card issuer will stop sending statements and will stop assessing new interest or new late penalties. If it has not happened already, the card will be cancelled, and the account turned over for collection. Shortly thereafter, if the amount owed is large enough, the credit card issuer, a collector for the credit card issuer or, increasingly, a purchaser of the credit card debt, will commence a lawsuit for collection.

Some people are under the misunderstanding that if a credit card debt has been "charged off," they are no longer responsible for the debt. That is incorrect. All a "charge off" or a "write off" means is that the debt has been charged off, that is, removed from, the credit card issuer's accounting records, not that the debt has been forgiven or that the debt cannot be collected. The charged off credit card debt likely has been sold to another party that is in the business of purchasing unpaid credit card debt. Despite the "charge off" by the credit card issuer, the purchaser of the credit card debt can bring a lawsuit for collection.

Before the collection lawsuit may be commenced, the party owning or collecting the debt will send you a letter informing you of your lack of payment and their intention of suing you for collection unless some payment is made immediately. They will also provide you with an opportunity to dispute the debt. Unless your identity has been stolen, usually there is no question of whether you owe the money. If the way interest, late fees or penalties were assessed was unclear, the exact amount owed might be disputable. A debt purchaser is entitled to collect the entire amount owed on the credit card, not just the amount the purchaser paid for the debt, which typically is significantly less than the amount owed.

The particular court in which the collection lawsuit will be brought, generally will depend upon the amount owed. In most states, if the amount owed is below a certain threshold, say $5,000, the case will be brought in the small claims court having jurisdiction over the town or city in which you live. If the amount owed is above the threshold, the case will be brought in the local state court in which all general litigation is brought, which I like to refer to as "adult" court. Both small claims and "adult" courts are civil, as opposed to criminal, courts.

Small claims courts often are administered by magistrates, who are not exactly real judges. Magistrates tend to employ more relaxed rules of evidence than real judges. You do not have to worry about a creditor raising a "hearsay" objection to something you may testify to in smalls claims court. Magistrates also tend to be more debtor friendly. My experience in my local small claims court has been that if the debtor shows up for the hearing, cries, and pleads an inability to pay the amount owed, the default judgment imposed by the magistrate will be $35/week. Inability to pay is not a valid defense to a collection lawsuit, but it may result in an extended payment judgment. I had a recent client who successful proved her inability to pay even $35/week and was ordered to pay her creditor only $5/week. If you faithfully make the $35/week payments for a few years, the debt gets paid and nothing further horrible will happen to you. Maybe you can live with that. Maybe you cannot.

In "adult" court, as in small claims court, debtors generally have no defense to not paying their debts, so they lose the lawsuits, and the creditors obtain judgments against them. I do not have the statistics, but my best guess would be that the vast majority of debtors do not respond to lawsuits, do not show up for their hearings, and lose their cases by default. The result is the same as the judge hearing the case and ruling in favor the creditor. Either way, a judgment enters in favor of the creditor in a certain amount. The punishment tends to be worse in "adult" court than small claims court. With a judgment, a creditor generally can do three things: lien a house, garnish wages or seize a bank account (and, potentially, other property, but that is less likely).

In no jurisdiction in the United States that I am aware of, can a debtor be thrown in jail for not paying a debt. Any debt. We do not have debtors' prisons in the United States. At this point, someone reading this book will jump up screaming, "Wrong, smart guy. I once heard of a guy being thrown into jail in Texas for not paying his student loan." What happened in Texas was that the debtor was thrown in jail for contempt of court, not for failing to pay his student loan. In some cases, a court will order an examination of a debtor against whom a judgment has been entered for the purpose of determining whether the debtor has income or assets that could be used to satisfy the judgment. If the debtor fails to comply with the court order requiring an examination, the debtor could find himself in contempt of court. You can go to jail for contempt of court. In "*My Cousin Vinnie*," Vincent Laguardia Gambini (played by Joe Pesci) was thrown in jail by Judge Chamberlain Haller (played by Fred Gwynne) for contempt of court.

## ❤ Liens

In general (the rules in your state may be different), a creditor with a judgment can take that judgment to the government office in which records related to the debtor's house are located and make that judgment a "lien" against the debtor's house. For that to happen, the judgment must be against a person who has an ownership interest in the house. In other words, a judgment against you cannot be "liened" against a house owned by your mother. In community property states, you could have an ownership interest in a house titled solely in your husband's name. In non-community property states, typically, the house would have to be titled in the name of the debtor for the house to be liened with a judgment against the debtor.

The fact that other people also may have an ownership interest in the house generally does not preclude the house from being liened. If you have a 50% ownership interest in a house also owned 50% by your brother, your 50% ownership interest can be liened. There could be an exception for something called ownership by the "entireties." Both owners of a house through a "tenancy by the entireties" may have to be responsible for the debt before their house can be liened by the judgment.

The primary consequence of having a lien on your house is that you will have to pay off the lien when you go to sell the house, either prior to the sale or at closing. No prospective buyer will want to own a house subject to a lien in favor of Capital One. The lien might be accruing interest either at a judgment rate or a statutory rate of interest. Whether a judgment creditor with a lien can foreclose on, that is, force the sale of, the house is a question for a local attorney. Most states have a "homestead" exemption that protects a home from being sold to pay a judgment creditor depending upon the equity in the home. To be eligible for the state homestead exemption, a few states require the filing of a declaration of homestead. A few other states prohibit homes from being sold to pay judgment creditors regardless of the home equity or exemption.

Assuming foreclosure is not a possibility, most people would prefer not to have a lien on their home, but having a lien on a home generally is not the end of the world, especially if you were not planning on moving anytime soon. You will realize a little less on the sale. If you are elderly and die in the home, your estate will pay off the lien and your heirs will get a little less. Not the end of the world. Again, note that interest may be accruing on the lien, so it may be more expensive to pay off the lien in the future than it is to pay the lien off now.

Judgment liens generally remain on a house until sale, death, or payment. It may be possible to "avoid," that is, remove, a judgment lien from the local land records in bankruptcy. Avoiding judgment liens is a complicated subject for a discussion with a bankruptcy attorney.

## ❦ Garnishments

With a judgment, in most states, a creditor can "garnish," that is, take, some portion of the debtor's gross wages. Typically, before the garnishment begins, the debtor will receive or could receive some additional judicial process at which the debtor can object to the garnishment. The likelihood that the debtor will have a valid objection to the garnishment is small. A portion of the debtor's wages will be garnished.

Each state has laws governing the amount that can be garnished from a debtor's wages. In addition, there are federal limits. Garnishment laws typically allow creditors to take 25% of the debtor's wages, but nothing can be taken if the wages are below minimum wage. There is a lot of math involved in computing the garnishment. You can safely assume that if you earn over $35k/year anywhere in the United States, you will be losing a portion of your paycheck every pay period. Your employer will be directed to send the money directly to your creditor (or its lawyer or perhaps the court) until your debt has been paid in full. The garnishment will appear as a regular deduction on your paystub just like health insurance. In many states, only one creditor can garnish wages at a time.

Who in their right mind would willingly pay creditors a portion of their paycheck every week until the debt was paid in full if bankruptcy could make the debt go away forever? Bankruptcy can discharge a debt even if the judgment was ordered by a court before the bankruptcy case was filed. In other words, if you owe Capital One $5,000 and file bankruptcy, the $5,000 debt can be discharged. If Capital One sues you and gets a judgment before you file bankruptcy and your bankruptcy case is filed before the garnishment begins, the debt can be discharged, and no garnishments will be deducted from your paychecks. If Capital One gets a judgment and begins to garnish your salary before you file bankruptcy, the garnishments will stop as soon as you file bankruptcy, and the debt can be discharged. Even though there was a court judgment ordering you to pay and perhaps even ordering your employer to garnish your wages, the garnishment will stop upon the filing of the bankruptcy case and the debt still can be discharged. The court collection judgment does not trump bankruptcy. Bankruptcy trumps just about everything. That is why it is fun to be a bankruptcy lawyer. It even may be possible to recoup some of the wages that had been garnished and sent to the creditor prior to filing bankruptcy. That is another complicated subject for a discussion with a bankruptcy attorney.

## Bank Account Seizures

The third remedy a creditor with a judgment typically has is the ability to levy or seize a bank account.

In theory, a creditor with a judgment can ask a sheriff to seize the debtor's car, household goods, or other personal property, which the creditor would sell to pay the judgment. In practice, "judgment executions" are rare. Most states have personal property exemptions or outright prohibitions against these types of seizures. I have never seen a credit card collector seize property other than a bank account. I have seen angry former business associates, angry ex-spouses and angry relatives seize or try to seize other assets to satisfy their judgments. Credit card collectors typically will only seize bank accounts.

A creditor can attempt to seize a bank account at any time and multiple times. Usually, the creditor will have a fairly good idea where the debtor banks and when the debtor gets paid. (Hint: you probably gave the credit card issuer that information when you filled out the credit application.) The creditor will seize the bank account shortly after the wages have been deposited, often via direct deposit on Fridays.

There are statutory limits on what funds within a bank account a creditor can seize. In general, debtors are provided with some judicial process at which they can contest the seizure. The bank typically will freeze the funds in the debtor's account for a short period of time during which the debtor can offer some reason, generally a federal or state law, why the funds are protected from seizure. Once funds have been seized from a bank account, it is hard to get them back. And expensive if you need a lawyer. Why would anyone risk having a bank account seized when filing bankruptcy is a safe, easy and effective method of preventing bank account seizures?

The Epitomes had no way to avoid being sued and three very unpleasant potential outcomes when judgments were inevitably entered against them. Your situation may be different. There may be reasons why you do not need to file bankruptcy. You may have alternatives. You might not qualify for bankruptcy. Let us go through some possible alternatives to filing bankruptcy now.

# ARE YOU "JUDGMENT PROOF"?

Even though you may be dealing with unmanageable debt, it is possible that you do not need bankruptcy protection. I frequently see prospective clients who are what we call "judgment proof" or "collection proof."

Remember the three bad things that can happen when you lose a collection lawsuit and the creditor obtains a judgment against you: house lien, wage garnishment and bank account seizure? Well, there are some people who, like bullets bouncing off Superman, are impervious to judgment remedies. They have neither income nor assets that can be lost to creditors.

If you do not own a house, then a creditor cannot put a lien on it. If you lease an apartment, the creditor cannot put a lien on your landlord's apartment building. Please note: this does not mean that you can transfer your house to someone else and lease the house back from them. That kind of transfer is known as a "fraudulent transfer." It probably isn't criminal fraud that could land you in jail, but it is the kind of transfer that could be reversed by a court. Do not transfer property out of your name to avoid creditors without first consulting a knowledgeable attorney.

If you do not have a bank account, then a creditor cannot seize it. Or, if you have a bank account with little or nothing in it, then there will be little or nothing lost to a creditor who does seize it. Most of the people reading this book probably do have bank accounts they would like to keep intact. However, many people across America do not have a bank account or have little on deposit in a bank account.

If you do not earn wages, then a creditor cannot garnish them. If you are unemployed, then you have no wages that could be garnished. If you are receiving a pension, then you likely have no wages that could be garnished. If you are an independent contractor or a freelancer, you probably have no regular wages that could be garnished. Exactly what may be garnished by a creditor will depend upon state law, so speak with a qualified local attorney.

By state and federal law, there are some types of income that cannot be garnished or seized. Social Security benefits fall into this category. By federal law, Social Security benefits, including Social Security disability benefits, may not be garnished, or seized if they are in a bank account. Under the laws of some states, unemployment benefits also fall into this category.

So, if you rent an apartment and your only source of income is Social Security benefits, you do not need to file bankruptcy. You might still want to file bankruptcy, but you do not need to file bankruptcy. There is nothing a creditor can do to you. A creditor with a judgment against you cannot lien your house if you do not own a house and the creditor cannot take your Social Security benefits either directly from the government or once they have been deposited into your bank account.

Just because you are "judgment proof" does not mean that the creditor will leave you alone. Even though the creditor has no legal ability to collect a judgment through garnishment or bank account seizure, the collector can still make your life a living hell. In some states, creditors can attempt to collect a judgment for as long as 20 years.

Consequently, even though you may be "judgment proof," there still may be good reasons to file bankruptcy and discharge the debt. One incredibly good reason would be to stop receiving annoying phone calls from collectors for the next 20 years telling you that you are a terrible person for not paying your debt. Bankruptcy may not be necessary, but it does solve the problem of aggressive debt collectors.

Assuming you are not "judgment proof" and have some assets or income that you would like to protect from creditors, are there still ways that filing bankruptcy could be avoided? Are there viable alternatives to filing bankruptcy? Said another way, how do you know your debt problem really is unmanageable?

##  YOUR DEBT PROBLEM CANNOT BE SOLVED BY BETTER BUDGETING

It is unlikely that you would be considering filing bankruptcy if your unmanageable debt problem could be solved by spending less, but in the interest of being complete, the first alternative to filing bankruptcy to consider would be better budgeting.

Giving up Netflix, switching from Wild Planet Albacore Wild Tuna to Chicken of the Sea Chunk Light Tuna or making a concerted effort to reduce your expenses by 10% every month will improve your monthly cashflow, but probably not enough to make a serious dent in your debt.

### Tricks Of The Trade

One "trick" that can provide some small relief, at least temporarily, is to transfer the entire balance owed on one credit card with a high interest rate to another credit card with a lower interest rate. Credit card issuers often offer 0% introductory or "teaser" interest rates to entice you to switch to their credit cards. The low interest rate of 0% typically is only available for a short period of time, usually six months or less. After the introductory period expires, the interest rate resets to a more normal rate of 20+%. If your credit card balance is $2,000, that six months would save you around $200. After the six months expire, you would need to find another credit card with a 0% teaser rate to transfer that balance to. Note that some credit card issuers will charge a transfer fee of 2% to 4% of the balance transferred, so some of the benefit of the interest rate savings will be offset by the transfer fee. Like white chocolate, transferring credit card balances is not as great as you might have imagined, but it is better than nothing. Eventually, continually transferring credit card balances will prove exhausting and you will focus on solving the problem instead of kicking the can down the road.

Another "trick" is to call the credit card issuer, explain your financial distress and beg them to lower the interest rate. Crying would not hurt. You might end up with some temporary relief from oppressive credit card interest rates.

## ❧ 25% Debt To Income Ratio

Although I have never seen this figure mentioned in any financial planning guide, in my experience, if an individual's or a couple's combined credit card debt exceeds 25% of their gross income, they will have almost no chance of ever repaying it. The debt is simply too high to repay based upon the available income.

How can that be? To start with, federal and state taxes typically take approximately 35% of gross income. In granting a mortgage, bankers generally allocate 40% of gross income towards interest and principal payments. Rental payments usually absorb the same or a greater percentage of gross income. Taxes and housing thus account for 75% of most people's budgets. That leaves 25% for everything else -- food, clothing, medical insurance, other medical and veterinary expenses, utilities, automobile loans and operating expenses or mass transit, pets, insurance, retirement, gym membership, cable TV, leisure, etc. Sure, some of those expenses might be considered non-necessities and trimmed, but after all the other expenses have been paid, there will not be much left for debt service on credit card debt.

It is also true that credit card debt does not have to be repaid in full in one year, but credit card debt compounds at an astronomically high interest rate. At interest rates of close to 30% per annum, which is not uncommon for people in financial distress, who are being assessed a penalty rate of interest, the outstanding principal balance of the debt will double in just under 2-1/2 years. Yes, double in just under 2-1/2 years. Compound interest is why it feels like you are constantly paying your credit card bills but never seem to make a dent in the total amount you owe. Compound interest is why you may have repaid the amount you actually borrowed from the credit card issuer twice but still seem to owe that same amount.

Similarly, when I see a prospective client who is only making minimum payments on their credit card debts, with interest compounding at an astronomical rate, I know that no amount of budgeting is going to create enough available funds to significantly service the credit card debt.

When I see a prospective client whose total credit card debt exceeds 25% of their gross income or who is making only the minimum payments on their credit card debts, I know the prospective client is not going to be able to repay the credit card debt through better budgeting. Better budgeting might enable someone to continue to make minimum payments and thereby carry the credit card debt further into the future, but it will not enable someone to solve the credit card debt problem. In these cases, bankruptcy is not just an option; bankruptcy is a necessity.

##  YOUR DEBT PROBLEM CANNOT BE SOLVED WITH MORE CREDIT CARD DEBT

It may not sound logical to try to solve an unmanageable debt problem by incurring more debt, but people dealing with the pressure of unmanageable debt do not always think rationally. Seeking additional credit from new credit cards or from on-line lenders is often the first alternative to filing bankruptcy most people choose. Some credit card issuers offer "convenience" checks to use to pay-off other debts. If a large percentage of your household budget is already dedicated to making payments on existing credit card debt, incurring additional credit may seem like a logical, maybe even a necessary, albeit short-term, solution to paying living expenses and staying afloat.

When credit limits on existing credit cards have been maxed out and new sources of credit are not available, another short-term respite can be achieved by contacting the credit card issuers and requesting a forbearance, that is, asking them to allow you to skip a monthly payment or two or to waive late fees. That might provide a little extra breathing room. It never hurts to ask.

## ❧ Debt Consolidation Loan

Another alternative, similar to the credit card balance transfer described above, is a debt consolidation loan. There are several on-line lenders, including Prosper.com and LendingClub.com, that offer to "consolidate" multiple, existing credit card debts into one new "consolidated" loan. The existing credit card debts are paid off and the new "consolidated" loan carries a lower rate of interest than the old credit card debts. As a result, the lower monthly payments will provide some additional funds that can be spent on other household needs. The debt consolidation loan may also provide some additional credit either right away or in the future. Obviously, a debt consolidation loan will not solve an unmanageable debt problem. At best, a debt consolidation loan will provide some temporary relief and postpone the day of reckoning. At worst, a debt consolidation loan will exacerbate the unmanageable debt problem.

Eligibility for a debt consolidation loan generally requires a high credit score. Credit scores are very sensitive to on-time mortgage payments and, to a lesser extent, credit card payments. A prospective borrower who has missed a mortgage payment or a few credit card payments may have a credit score that is too low to qualify.

If you do take out a debt consolidation loan, make sure that you use the proceeds for debt consolidation. You must repay existing credit card debt. If you end up filing bankruptcy anyway, particularly if there is a relatively short period of time between incurring the debt consolidation loan and filing bankruptcy, the debt consolidation lender may demand proof that the proceeds of its loan were used to repay existing credit card debt. If the proceeds were not used to repay credit card debt, then the debt consolidation lender might challenge the dischargeability of its debt in bankruptcy on the basis that the debt consolidation loan was fraudulently incurred.

## YOUR "BAD" DEBT PROBLEM CANNOT BE SOLVED WITH "GOOD" DEBT

As mentioned above, home mortgages and car loans are often considered to be "good" debts because they finance the acquisition of otherwise unaffordable assets that will make the borrower more productive in the future. Credit card debts, on the other hand, are often considered to be "bad" debts because they finance purchases that are generally consumed quickly without a lasting benefit to the borrower.

Another alternative to bankruptcy that many people consider is to eliminate unmanageable "bad" debt by refinancing it with, and transforming it into, more manageable "good" debt. Essentially, you borrow money from yourself to repay the credit card debt. That may sound like a great idea, because it does eliminate the credit card debt, and the interest rate that you will be paying on the resulting "good" debt will be much lower than the interest rate you were paying on the old "bad" credit card debt. However, borrowing from yourself may turn out to be a terrible idea for the reasons explained below. First, let's examine the alchemy of transforming "bad" debt into "good" debt.

In general, there are two "good" debt piggy banks that lend themselves (no pun intended) to being raided to repay "bad" debts – a house and a retirement account. For a house to be a source of funds, there must be equity in the house, that is, the value a prospective buyer would pay for the house in the current market must exceed the total amount owed on any existing mortgages or other liens. Borrowing against a house, or more accurately stated, borrowing against the equity in a house, can be accomplished in three ways: (1) refinance an existing mortgage; (2) obtain a second mortgage, sometimes known as a home equity line of credit or by the acronym "HELOC;" or (3) obtain a reverse mortgage.

## ❧ Refinancing

Refinancing an existing mortgage may be an option if you have significantly more equity in your house than when you obtained the mortgage, a qualifying credit score, and a gross income that is high enough to support a larger mortgage. The number of readers of this book who are likely to be eligible is on par with the number of supermodels who are also Mensa members. That said, if you did qualify, the interest rate you would be paying on the refinanced mortgage would be much lower than the interest rate you are now paying on the credit card debt. As a result, the monthly payment would be much more affordable. Also, interest on a home mortgage may be tax deductible, whereas interest on credit card debt is not tax deductible.

## ❧ HELOC

Getting a Home Equity Line of Credit is like refinancing an existing mortgage, except that instead of ending up with one mortgage, you end up with two. The other difference is that a HELOC may be structured either as a fixed amount borrowed with a fixed repayment schedule or as a line of credit, something like a credit card, allowing you to borrow up to a predetermined amount and to pay it back with more flexibility. So, a HELOC could provide access to some additional credit after the proceeds were used to repay existing credit card debt. The other benefits of a HELOC are the same as those for a refinancing.

## ❧ Reverse Mortgage

As you may have heard Tom Selleck say on late night TV commercials, "a reverse mortgage allows homeowners age 62 and older to access equity in their houses." Those funds could be used to pay credit card debt.

Unlike a regular mortgage, which requires monthly payments of interest and principal, a reverse mortgage usually does not require any repayment until the homeowner permanently leaves the house, typically at death, or when the house is sold. Qualifying for a reverse mortgage may be easier than qualifying for a refinancing or a HELOC, because the borrower's current income and credit score are not relevant. Since no monthly payments are made on the reverse mortgage, the lender is not concerned about the borrower's financial ability to make them.

The amount that can be borrowed on a reverse mortgage, called the "principal limit," is based largely on the house's equity and the borrower's expected longevity. The older you are, the higher the value of your home after subtracting outstanding mortgage balances, and the lower current interest rates are, the higher the principal limit, and the more money you can borrow.

Like the other mortgage alternatives, the advantages of using a reverse mortgage to repay credit card debt include a lower rate of interest, possible tax deductibility of interest and possible excess funding or additional available credit with sufficient house equity. Reverse mortgages are heavily regulated and are more expensive to obtain than regular mortgages.

Most reverse mortgages are insured by the Federal Housing Administration (FHA) under its Home Equity Conversion Mortgage (HECM) program. A small number of private lenders make reverse mortgages outside of the HECM program. To be eligible for a HECM government insured reverse mortgage, you and your house must satisfy certain requirements. Consult a knowledgeable real estate attorney.

Economically, using a reverse mortgage to repay credit card debt is exactly like one of the three consequences of not paying credit card described above. A reverse mortgage is a lien on your house. Instead of the lien being in favor of the credit card issuer, the lien is in favor of the reverse mortgage lender. Either way, the lien will be paid when the house is sold. In effect, the person who really bears the burden of the credit card debt or the reverse mortgage is the heir who otherwise might have inherited a house without a lien.

Using home equity to repay credit card debt has its advantages. Unless you qualify for bankruptcy. Then it is terrible idea. You will have transformed a debt that bankruptcy can discharge – credit card debt -- into a debt that bankruptcy cannot discharge – a mortgage.

By tapping into the equity in your house to repay credit card debt, you are betting that nothing bad will ever happen to you. You will never experience a loss of income. You will never become seriously ill and miss work or incur significant medical expenses. You will never get divorced. You will never be called upon to care for an aged or disabled family member. If one of those unfortunate events happens, you will have no equity or less equity in your house to call upon. You may even find yourself in greater danger of losing your house.

Also take into consideration that even though mortgage interest rates are relatively low, closing costs, including title services, the preparation of closing documents, obtaining credit reports and appraisals, property surveys, inspections, loan processing, and other similar charges, "points" or loan origination fees, mortgage insurance and legal fees can be expensive and will offset the benefit of repaying the higher interest rate credit card debt.

As bad as using house equity to pay credit card debt may be, using funds in retirement accounts is even worse.

## ❦ Retirement Accounts

Instead of tapping into the equity in a house to repay credit card debt, some view tapping into the funds in a pension or retirement account, like an IRA or 401(k), either through a withdrawal or through a loan, as an alternative to filing bankruptcy.

An early withdrawal from a tax-deferred retirement account can be expensive. Typically, if a tax deduction was taken when the money was contributed to an IRA, the withdrawn money will be taxed as current income and will be subject to a 10% penalty if withdrawn before age 59-1/2.

Borrowing against a retirement plan can be a better option than taking an early withdrawal, because it avoids triggering the recognition of taxable income and the early withdrawal penalty. Often, it may be possible to borrow against a 401(k), Roth IRA or pension account, but not against a regular IRA. Many retirement plans allow owners to borrow up to 50% of the value of the account, which must then be repaid over five years. Interest must be charged on the loan, but the interest rate will be lower than the interest rate on the credit card debt and, best of all, the interest will be paid to the account (i.e., to you), not to the credit card issuer.

This alternative is not likely to be widely available. Nearly 40% of American workers do not have either an IRA or any retirement savings. For those with retirement savings, raiding what little may be available to fund retirement as a "solution" to an unmanageable debt problem is a terrible idea.

First, if you have taken a loan from an employer-sponsored retirement plan and you later lose your job, you may be required to immediately repay the full borrowed amount or to pay income taxes and penalty as if the loan were an early withdrawal from the retirement plan.

Even worse, however, is that retirement savings are heavily protected by law. Congress encourages people to save for their retirement by providing tax advantages to retirement plan contributions and by heavily protecting those savings from creditors. Creditors cannot attach, seize, or garnish funds within retirement accounts whether a debtor is in bankruptcy or not. It makes no sense to use funds that are protected from creditors to pay creditors. Instead, save your retirement funds for your retirement. You will need them then. Never use retirement savings to pay creditors if bankruptcy is an option.

# CREDIT COUNSELING/DEBT CONSOLIDATION SERVICES DO NOT WORK

Not-for-profit credit counseling agencies and for-profit debt consolidation or debt elimination businesses offer assistance with credit card debt. The names are often used interchangeably.

As used here, "credit counseling" refers to counselors who offer budgeting advice. Typically, for a small monthly fee, a credit counselor will work with you to create a monthly budget and a debt management plan that will enable you to repay all your debts. Eventually. Usually, the credit counselor will get you a discount on interest rates and late fees, but you still will be required to pay the full amount of credit card debt that you owe. It may take you years to pay off the full credit card debt, during which time you will be making monthly payments to the credit counselor, and your ability to use credit cards likely will be cut off. Credit counseling is not the worst thing in the world, but it is unlikely to solve an unmanageable debt problem. Also, because the funding for the "non-profit" agency often comes from the credit card issuers, credit counselors strongly advise their clients (you) against filing bankruptcy.

"Debt consolidators," also known as "debt eliminators," promise even more. You may have seen their advertisements on television hawking "the secret that credit companies don't want you to know" and "if you have $5,000 in credit card debt, we can save you thousands." They claim that they will negotiate with your credit card issuers so that you can pay off your credit card debts for less.

The basic "concept" behind debt consolidation and debt elimination is that all of your little credit card debts will be "consolidated" into one giant new debt that will be serviced by the debt consolidator. The debt consolidator promises that it has negotiated "deals" with all your creditors enabling you to pay less than 100% of what you owe. You make one payment each month to the debt consolidator, which then pays all your participating creditors, perhaps at that time, perhaps at a later time in a one-lump settlement payment. After you make, usually, 60 monthly payments to the debt consolidator, whatever remains of your credit card debt will be forgiven by the credit card issuers.

The promised advantage of debt consolidation is that the monthly payment you make to the debt consolidator will be less than the monthly payments you would otherwise make to the separate credit card issuers. If you have enough income to afford the monthly debt consolidation payment, this sounds like a great deal. But, just like "What happens in Vegas stays in Vegas," debt consolidation does not always work out as promised.

There are a few problems with the debt consolidation "concept." First, not all creditors participate in the debt consolidator's reduced interest rate/debt forgiveness plan. You likely will not be told whether your creditors are participants or not. If all of your creditors are not on board with the debt consolidator's plan, interest and late charges will continue to accrue, your non-payment will be reported to credit agencies, and the non-participating creditors may not stop collection activities, including sending bills, calling, or bringing a collection lawsuit.

Second, ordinarily, all your credit cards will be shut down while the debt consolidation plan payments are being made, so you may have no access to credit during the term of the debt consolidation plan.

Next, the savings may be less than you expect. Debt consolidators charge a fee, roughly between 2% and 2-3/4 % of your total credit card balances. By the time you have made enough monthly payments to allow a lump sum settlement, the additional interest, late fees, and debt consolidator fees can eat up much of the savings.

And, to the extent that there is a savings from debt forgiveness, that savings comes at an additional cost. You must pay taxes on the amount of debt forgiven at ordinary income rates of taxation. The amount of credit card debt that is not paid is treated as income that you received and is taxed. The extra taxes can erode a significant portion of the savings. How will the IRS know that you had debt forgiven? The credit card issuer will send you and the IRS a 1099-C in the amount of forgiven debt. That is a requirement for the credit card issuer to take a "bad debt" tax deduction on the amount of debt forgiven. In contrast, there is no income tax on debt discharged in bankruptcy.

But wait, there's more. It gets worse. Usually, you need to make 60 monthly payments for the promise of debt forgiveness to be realized. What happens if during that 60-month period a monthly payment is missed? Typically, if you miss one monthly payment during that 60-month period, the debt consolidation plan terminates. Let's face it, you are in financial distress. It is highly likely that you will experience a cash short fall at least once during the 60-month plan period causing you to miss one monthly plan payment. After months of faithfully making payments, all your credit card debts will come back to life, some perhaps even higher than they were before due to additional interest and penalties. You may have paid large up-front fees and made monthly payments to the debt consolidator for absolutely nothing.

Despite purported special endorsements by the local Better Business Bureau, debt consolidators often are not licensed, not regulated, and have no office in your state. In some states, debt consolidation is illegal. Guess which type of business has a remarkable tendency to go out of business or declare bankruptcy within 60 months? Survey says -- debt consolidator.

There may be legitimate debt consolidators. Big Foot, the Loch Ness Monster and Chupacabras may also be real. I cannot disprove their existence. Most bankruptcy lawyers consider debt consolidation to be a scam. Not a scam like an email from a Nigerian price who needs your bank account number to send you millions of dollars. More like sugary breakfast cereals will lower your cholesterol scam. Few, if any, of the promised benefits are realized by most people who sign up. I see at least one prospective client every year who had enrolled in a debt consolidation plan that failed. The prospective client was out considerable fees and was left with more debt than they had before, a trashed credit score and no alternative except to file bankruptcy.

If you have the ability and the desire to pay some of your credit card debt over three to five years, bankruptcy offers a much better solution than debt consolidation. Chapter 13 is a debt consolidation plan with lower fees than debt consolidators typically charge and, because it is supervised by the bankruptcy court, a Chapter 13 plan is not a scam. You will get the promised debt relief after three to five years with no adverse income tax consequences.

#  DEBT NEGOTIATION DOES NOT WORK

A variation on debt consolidation that actually benefits people with unmanageable debt looking for an alternative to bankruptcy is debt negotiation. Although terms like debt consolidation, debt settlement and debt negotiation are used interchangeably, I am using "debt negotiation" here to refer to direct negotiations between a credit card issuer and a credit card debtor in which the credit card debt is settled for less than what is owed.

Here's how debt negotiation works. You stop making payments on your credit card debts. Instead, you open a savings account and start making regular monthly payments into that savings account. Typically, after a credit card debt has gone unpaid for a few months, the credit card issuer will send a letter offering a settlement deal: "Pay $x amount now and the entire outstanding credit card balance will be considered paid in full." The credit card issuer would prefer to receive some cash now rather than chase a delinquent credit card debtor for payment in full later.

That mailed settlement offer is the credit card issuer's first offer. It is not necessarily the credit card issuer's best offer. It may be possible to settle the outstanding balance for less than the mailed offer. By waiting a little longer to settle the debt, you may be able to achieve a settlement that is more favorable to you. But, in the meantime, interest will be running, and collection calls will be making your life a living hell.

It is a negotiation. You are attempting to convince the credit card issuer that you cannot pay what they are asking. The credit card issuer is attempting to convince you that you would be better off paying what they are asking now rather than dragging out negotiations. Your negotiating position – that you cannot afford to pay the amount they are requesting – is enhanced by demonstrating that you cannot afford to pay. You have lost your job, other expenses have arisen that make paying credit card debt impossible, or some other hardship exists. The best way to demonstrate that you cannot afford to pay a credit card debt is to not pay the credit card debt. While all this is happening, you need to be building up your savings account so that you will have the cash available to settle the debt.

According to most debt negotiation books, the "sweet spot" for negotiating the best settlement is right before the debt is "charged off." Typically, credit card issuers will charge off a debt after six months of non-payment. When a credit card debt is charged off, it means that the credit card issuer has written the debt off its accounting books as a bad debt. It does not mean that the credit card issuer has forgiven the debt or that the credit card issuer cannot still legally attempt to collect the debt.

Generally, once the debt has been written off the credit card issuer's books, the debt is sold to another party who will attempt to collect the debt. According to most debt negotiation books, you can negotiate the most favorable settlement with the credit card issuer right before they sell the debt to another party. The credit card issuer would be happy to settle the debt with you for slightly more than what they would receive from the debt purchaser.

The problem is that you do not know how much of a discount the credit card issuer is taking when it sells the debt to a debt purchaser, so it is hard for you to know how much to offer the credit card issuer. A good rule of thumb is to start your offer at 25% to 33% of the amount owed and be prepared to accept a settlement in the range of 50% of what is owed. It is highly unlikely that the debt purchaser will be paying more than 50% of what is owed. Probably, it will be paying much less. It is also possible for you to negotiate a debt settlement with the debt purchaser after six months. My experience has been that debt purchasers are far more likely to commence collection lawsuits for amounts owed under $5,000 than are credit card issuers.

Most people are uncomfortable negotiating anything, especially a credit card debt they may feel guilty about not paying. Still, negotiating is one of the most important skills you can learn. I recommend buying one or two of the top ranked debt negotiation books on Amazon for a quick education. Start your negotiation with an offer of 20% of what you owe. Be prepared for the debt negotiation to last four or five rounds. The first person you speak with will claim that they are not authorized to accept a settlement or that there is a minimum amount they can accept which is higher than what you are offering. That may or may not be true. Ask to speak with a supervisor. Offer a little bit more each time you speak with a new person. Try to get each new person to improve their offer as well. Crying does not hurt. It is not illegal to lie to a credit card issuer or a collector. They may not be telling you the truth either about how little they will accept. You must negotiate just as hard as they do.

For debt negotiation to work, you need cash. The credit card issuer will not accept a settlement with payment over time. The credit card issuer is already being paid over time by you. To reach a settlement, you need to offer something better than the extended payments the credit card issuer is already receiving. The credit card issuer will accept less than what is owed today because it will be paid immediately. That is why you have been funding a savings account instead of making credit card payments. Do not forget to fund the savings account! Debt negotiation does not work unless you have cash to settle the debt.

Always try to get the credit card issuer to agree to remove any negative items from your credit report in exchange for the debt settlement payment. The credit card issuer may not agree. If it does, try to get that promise in writing before you pay. An alternative might be for the credit card issuer to agree not to challenge you when you dispute the debt being reported on the credit report as having been "delinquent." It never hurts to ask.

Prospective clients often ask if I would negotiate a debt settlement on their behalf. The problem with paying me, or anyone else, to settle a credit card debt is that your principal negotiating position is that you cannot afford to pay the debt. If you hire someone else to conduct the debt negotiation for you, you are weakening that argument. You are demonstrating that you have enough money to pay someone else to negotiate on your behalf. Maybe you have a lot more. The other problem, for me, is that there is no "fair" amount that I could charge. My estimate of how much time it will take to settle the debt invariably will be wrong. Whatever fee I set, based upon that estimate, will be wrong. Either the process will take less time and the client will feel cheated or the process will take more time and I will feel cheated. If all I did was settle credit card debts, I might have a better idea of the average time required, but I don't. Instead, I give prospective clients the same advice I have provided above with the caveat that if that advice does not work, the prospective client may come back and I will negotiate the debt on their behalf. To date, not a single prospective client, including lots of little old ladies, has come back and asked me to settle debt on their behalf.

Debt negotiation can be a particularly good alternative to filing bankruptcy, especially where bankruptcy may not be the best solution, because you do not qualify for Chapter 7, you would pay 100% of your debts in Chapter 13, or the cost of bankruptcy exceeds the benefit. For example, if you only owe $5,000 and the total fees for filing bankruptcy are $3,000, it makes no sense to file bankruptcy. You almost always can negotiate a credit card debt settlement for 50% of the amount owed. Paying 50% of $5,000, that is, $2,500, to the credit card issuer makes more sense than paying $3,000 to file bankruptcy. Usually.

## ❧ Paying Taxes On Forgiven Debt Eliminates Some Of The Benefit

As mentioned above, to the extent you realize a savings from debt forgiveness by a credit card issuer, that savings comes at a cost. You must pay income taxes on the forgiven debt. The credit card issuer will report "discharge of indebtedness income" in the amount of forgiven debt on a form 1099-C which it will send to you and to the IRS in order for the credit card issuer to take a "bad debt" tax deduction on the amount of forgiven debt. The IRS will expect you to pay income tax on the "discharge of indebtedness income" at ordinary income rates of taxation unless you qualify for an exception. If an exception applies, you may be able to avoid paying tax on "discharge of indebtedness income."

One way to avoid paying taxes on "discharge of indebtedness income" is by being insolvent at the time the debt was forgiven. Being insolvent, for this purpose, means that your liabilities (debts) were greater than your assets at the time the debt was forgiven. For example, if you have $10,000 in assets (car, jewelry, cash in the bank), and $40,000 in debt (car loan and credit card debt), then you are insolvent by $30,000, because your $40,000 debts exceed your $10,000 assets by $30,000. As long as the debt forgiven is $30,000 or less, you would not have to include that amount in your taxable income. On the other hand, if the $40,000 in debt was all credit card debt, no car loan, and all the credit card debt was forgiven, then you would have to pay income tax on $10,000 of the forgiven debt. $40,000 in debt was forgiven, but you were insolvent by $30,000, so only the excess $10,000 is taxed.

The way insolvency is calculated includes assets that are often excluded for other purposes. For example, retirement accounts, which are excluded from creditors in bankruptcy and in state court collection lawsuits, are counted as assets for the purpose of determining whether you were insolvent when debt was forgiven. You may also need to adjust the tax basis of other assets you own to have the forgiven debt excluded from taxable income. This area is extremely complicated. If you are seeking to avoid taxation on forgiven debt, work with a knowledgeable CPA or tax professional who can explain the requirements and complete the necessary paperwork to qualify for the exception.

The other main exception to paying taxes on "discharge of indebtedness income" is to file bankruptcy. There is no "discharge of indebtedness income" recognized on any debt discharged in a bankruptcy case. There is no insolvency test or other qualifications or limitations in bankruptcy. As a result, even if you can negotiate a debt settlement in which you end up paying less than what is owed, the adverse tax consequences may make filing bankruptcy a better option.

# LIVING OFF THE GRID IS UNAPPEALING

I keep a small antique suitcase in my conference room. One side is hand painted "Cuba." I am not sure of the origin of the suitcase. I bought it on eBay. It does not appear to ever have been used for travel. I use it a prop when filing bankruptcy in any chapter is not a viable option. At the end of initial consultation, the prospective client will look at me and ask, "Well, if bankruptcy will not work, what can I do?" I point to the suitcase. "The U.S. has no extradition treaty with Cuba," I respond, intending to be facetious not cruel. Then I spend some time explaining debt negotiation.

Just because there are no really good options does not mean there are no really bad options. Some bad options are still worse than other bad options. Unless you are an aficionado of classic cars from the 1950s, fleeing to Cuba is unlikely to work out well. There are debt management books that seriously suggest the best option under these circumstances is to go underground, perhaps assume a new identity, and live off the grid.

It may be true that if you move constantly, you may be able to evade your creditors. Eventually, however, they tend to find you. It is difficult to avoid leaving any digital footprint in the Internet age. Everything you do is tracked and recorded. I often see prospective clients who are being sued on a debt incurred a long, long time ago in a place far, far away. The prospective clients either forgot about the debt or never realized the creditor had obtained a judgment. Ten or fifteen years later, the debt surfaces. The old judgment may be from a court located in a former state and "domesticated" in a court in the state in which they currently live. The prospective client may not have had income or assets ten or fifteen years ago, but they have income and assets now.

If you move, ignore mail and calls from creditors (who also will be contacting every relative and employer of yours they can find in a legal attempt to locate you), avoid owning bank accounts or other assets in your name, and earn income that cannot be garnished, you may be able to achieve some measure of success in evading creditors. Obviously, your credit score will be trashed and you will have limited access to credit. Depending upon how successful you are in creating a new identity, banks may not want to deal with you.

If you fancy yourself an amateur lawyer, you could try disputing your debts. It is extremely difficult to find legitimate defenses for not paying your debts, but it is not inconceivable that you could find mistakes in the paperwork that could constitute a violation of the Fair Debt Collection Practices Act (FDCPA). It is possible that if you make yourself a pain in the neck, the creditor might leave you alone. I have never heard of that actually happening, but that is what the "live off the grid" books suggest. My guess is that the credit card issuer will brutally prosecute and persecute you to make an example of you so that others do not try the same tactic.

It takes an extraordinarily strong stomach and extremely thick skin to even consider pursuing this path. Prospective clients often have qualms about the morality of filing bankruptcy. Living off the grid to evade creditors is presidential assassin-level immorality. If bankruptcy or debt negotiation were viable options, why on earth would anyone ever consider living off the grid?

By this point, it is likely that you have no viable economic alternative to bankruptcy. But, if you are like most prospective clients, you still are not convinced that filing bankruptcy is the "right" thing to do. You have beliefs and emotions about bankruptcy that hold you back. Let's tackle those objections next.

# CHAPTER 3

# What's Holding You Back?

# INTRODUCTION

Despite the economic necessity and the absence of good alternatives, people often refuse to consider bankruptcy as a solution.

Information, attitudes and expectations conveyed by the media, popular culture, religious and social institutions, as well as family and friends, create beliefs that can be unstated and unconscious. They often seem obvious, despite never having been challenged or shaped by rational thought. Beliefs can be easy to cling to and hard to change.

People have lots of conscious and unconscious beliefs about bankruptcy. Most are unfavorable. Most are untrue. Bankruptcy is almost universally considered to be wrong. Morally wrong. Ethically wrong. Even financially wrong.

Beliefs can generate emotions and behaviors that maintain and support the beliefs. Left unchallenged, erroneous beliefs may result in negative emotions and counterproductive behaviors. People in financial distress often feel as though they are under siege. The assault is not just financial, it is emotional as well. Their personal identity and self-respect are under attack. The emotional defense mechanisms that come to the rescue tend to bolster their beliefs.

The inability to pay one's debts or provide for one's family can be devastating to one's self-image and self-worth. It evokes feelings of failure, shame, and guilt. Those feelings, in turn, can lead to depression and debilitating behaviors that can interfere with taking remedial actions.

Negative emotions and behaviors create a dismal feedback loop unconsciously defending the negative beliefs which, in turn, reinforce the negative emotions and behaviors. Bankruptcy, which could be a solution to the problem of unmanageable debt, instead is barred from consideration. *"I'm a failure." "Only losers consider bankruptcy." "Bankruptcy is wrong." "Bankruptcy makes a bad situation even worse."* The emotional side of the brain hijacks and holds the analytical side hostage to neither side's benefit.

This section identifies the erroneous beliefs, the negative emotions and the self-destructive behaviors that hold people back from considering or pursuing bankruptcy. It explains why those beliefs are erroneous, those emotions are misplaced, and those behaviors are counterproductive. It offers suggestions for overcoming the dark side of the unmanageable debt sepulchral force and moving forward towards the light of a fresh start. Filing bankruptcy will not make things worse than they are. Things are terrible enough already.

# CORRECTING ERRONEOUS BELIEFS

## Bankruptcy Is Not Immoral

Almost universally, people believe that filing bankruptcy to obtain debt relief is wrong, morally wrong.

Morality is a difficult concept to define. Not everyone's ethical sensibilities and limitations are the same. Actions that are acceptable to some may be reprehensible to others. Still, some actions do seem to be innately right or wrong. Acting in a fair and ethical manner is important to most people. Few people think of themselves as immoral or bad or wish to have their actions seen as immoral or bad by others.

Bankruptcy will result in debts going unpaid. That is an undeniable fact. Creditors will not be repaid what they are owed. Even if some of what creditors are owed is repaid, most will not be repaid by debtors in bankruptcy. Does it follow then that bankruptcy is innately wrong or morally reprehensible? Does bankruptcy shock everyone's conscience? Or, are there circumstances in which bankruptcy might be considered not only not morally abhorrent but necessary?

There is a belief, widely held across countries and cultures, that paying one's debts is an especially important thing to do and, therefore, that not paying one's debts is a wrong or immoral thing to do. This belief has penetrated deeply into our psyches and is reflected in our popular culture. As the HBO television series "*The Game of Thrones*" made abundantly clear, "A Lannister always pays his debts." That was the motto of House Lannister. Lannisters may have plundered gold mines, betrayed alliances, ruled ruthlessly and regularly engaged in murder, but they always paid their debts. Somehow, the multitude of Lannister sins were absolved because the Lannisters always paid their debts.

Why is paying one's debts so important? After all, repaying a debt is just an obligation. We routinely ignore or violate other obligations. How many dates have you contrived an excuse to get out of? How many white lies have you told to spare someone's feelings? Showing up for a date and telling the truth are obligations. Why is failing to honor the obligation to meet a friend or tell the truth morally acceptable but failing to honor a financial obligation morally unacceptable?

Anthropologist David Graeber addressed this issue in his book, "*Debt: The First 5,000 Years.*" He did not reach a conclusion as to why debt repayment became so relatively important as a moral obligation, but he does note that there is at least some conflict about it: "most everywhere, one finds that the majority of human beings hold simultaneously that 1) paying back money one has borrowed is a simple matter of morality, and 2) anyone in the habit of lending money is evil." So, at the same time we believe that lending money is evil, we believe that paying back the evilly-lent money is not just the right thing to do, but one of our higher moral obligations.

It is possible that debt repayment became regarded as such an important moral obligation simply because creditors were powerful marketers, just as the apple is regarded as the most potent of all fruits because the apple growers trade association has convinced us that "eating one apple a day keeps the doctor away."

More likely, the reason we consider paying our debts to be so important is that we experience moral loss when something we do causes harm to another. When we fail to repay money that was lent to us in good faith, we cause harm to another. Our moral loss reflects the economic loss we cause the creditor.

Perhaps the most basic, fundamental human precept is to "Do unto others as you would have others do unto you." It is commonly referred to as "The Golden Rule." That precept is considered a "Natural Law," sometimes a "Divine Law" that applies to the universe and all its inhabitants. It underlies all of mankind's rules and regulations. When debt goes unpaid, property of the creditor is taken. No one desires to have their own property taken from them. Taking the property of others causes harm to others.

That harm is experienced very differently by different creditors. In my practice, I am keenly aware of the loss experienced by a local day care center that had extended credit to the parents of children in the center's care when the parents filed bankruptcy. In contrast, I literally could care less when my clients discharge tens of thousands of credit card debt every day. The harm suffered by the local day care center by non-payment is far greater than the harm suffered by American Express.

The economic hardship imposed on American Express is negligible. The risk of non-payment is one of many risks American Express expects and mitigates against in its business model, in part, by charging 20+% interest. Mitigating the risk of non-payment is not as easy for the local day care center. The local day care center does not routinely extend create and, therefore, cannot protect itself against the expected loss in advance by charging all parents slightly higher tuition.

Also embedded in the higher sense of immorality of not paying the day care center as opposed to the credit card issuer is the notion of reciprocity. Morality seems to require some reciprocity; a moral obligation should go both ways. The day care center was doing my clients a favor by extending them credit so their children could attend. The day care center appears to have been taken advantage by the absence of repayment. It seems unfair. Our moral sensibilities are not as incensed by the non-payment of credit card debt because credit card issuers are not typically viewed as acting morally towards their clients. Absent the reciprocity, the credit card issuer does not appear to have been cheated by non-payment.

Credit card issuers routinely try to collect debts with the pitch that non-payment is dishonest. They also regularly claim that dishonest people who file bankruptcy impose a cost on honest card carriers in the form of higher interest rates. The loss experienced by the credit card issuer from the dishonest bankruptcy filers, they say, must be recouped by charging the honest card carriers higher rates of interest than they would otherwise be charged. The honest must pay for the sins of the dishonest.

If the claim that credit card interest rates reflect the issuer's bankruptcy loss experience were remotely true, we would expect to see interest rates charged on credit cards increase with increases in bankruptcy filings and decrease with decreases in bankruptcy filings. That has not happened. The number of consumer bankruptcy filings has declined steadily since 2005, dropping over 30% alone between 2019 and 2020. Despite the decline in filings, interest rates charged on credit cards have not decreased at all. If honest card carriers really were subsidizing dishonest bankruptcy filers, credit card interest rates today should be much lower than they were in 2005. Instead, credit card interest rates have consistently topped 20% since 1978. In that year, the Supreme Court decided that state usury laws, which typically capped credit card interest rates between 12% and 18%, did not apply to nationally chartered banks operating in states like South Dakota, where credit card interest rates could be as high 24%. Guess why your credit cards are all issued by banks based in South Dakota?

Note also that the cost of money for credit card issuers, that is, the interest rate credit card issuers pay to borrow money to finance their business, has steadily declined since 2005, and especially since 1978. That means, the "spread," which is the difference between the rate at which the issuer lends money to its customers and the rate at which the issuer borrows money to finance its operations, which is an indication of the issuer's profitability, has never been higher. For any lender. In the history of mankind. Excluding the Mafia. Currently, the "spread" is around 20%.

In addition to charging interest rates so high they would have led to stoning in biblical times, credit card issuers routinely engage in other behaviors that could hardly be considered morally reciprocal. One such behavior is offering credit cards without performing due diligence to determine whether the target can afford the line of credit being offered. Most people do not have MBAs in finance. The easy availability of credit often encourages people to incur more debt than they can afford. Credit card issuers have access to huge stores of financial information. They could easily tailor the credit offer to the target's income. Instead, high lines of credit are indiscriminately offered to anyone with a zip code and a pulse. Credit card issuers know that a large number of target customers will default. It does not matter. Like paying Samuel L. Jackson to appear in its TV commercials, default is simply a cost of doing business for the credit card issuer. The issuer's business model, with 20%+ rates of interest and a gigantic "spread," allows the issuer to absorb a high rate of default. Credit card issuers can offer credit wildly indiscriminately and still be very profitable. Don't cry for me, Chargentina. Default causes much greater harm to the card holder. The consequences of default are hardly symmetrical or reciprocal.

I acknowledge that it may be a teensy bit unfair to blame American Express for what could be considered the profligacy of its clients. Afterall, American Express does not force anyone to take its cards. American Express does not force anyone to use its cards, although it knows that people tend to spend more money, faster, and with less thought, with credit cards than with cash. American Express does not force anyone to incur debt on its cards. And, to its credit, American Express does tell its customers how long it could take to repay their credit card balances if only minimum monthly payments were made. I know. I just checked my statement.

In my current monthly statement, American Express disclosed that it would take me eight years to repay the balance I owed, assuming I incurred no new debt and I made the minimum monthly payments on time. American Express also disclosed that it would take me 480 months to repay the same balance if I missed a due date and the late payment penalty interest rate of 29.24% applied. Does 480 months sound faster than 40 years? They are the same. Moses and the Israelites exited Egypt and reached the Promised Land in the same amount of time.

The non-penalty rate and the penalty rate disclosures contained two different rates of interest. However, the two presentations contained another difference that was not disclosed. The minimum monthly payments also differed. Curiously, in the penalty interest rate calculation, the monthly payment was assumed to be almost 20% higher than the monthly payment disclosed in the non-penalty interest rate presentation. If the same monthly payment were used in the penalty interest rate presentation, I literally would be the oldest human alive when I made my last payment. In fact, I would be the oldest human to have ever walked the earth. I appreciate the effort, Amex, but the disclosure of repayment information in my credit card statement was about as useful as the disclosure of hotel room rates on the inside of hotel room doors. To paraphrase Samuel L. Jackson, "What's in my wallet?"

The moral precept of "Do unto others as you would have others do unto you" works both ways. As Spiderman stated so succinctly, "With great power comes great responsibility." Karma may not be instant, but creditors who take advantage of debtors eventually tend to reap the harvest of the seeds sown.

Another notion embedded in the immorality we assign to not paying one's debts is ability to pay. "A Lannister Always Pays His Debts" is the Lannister House motto because the Lannisters have the means to pay their debts. They have the ability to pay their debts either through income derived by taxing their subjects at Casterly Rock, by selling their assets – gold from their mines, or through sheer ruthlessness. The Lannister House motto does more than just boast about the Lannisters' wealth. The motto "A Lannister Always Leaves a 25% Tip" could have accomplished that mission. The ability to pay one's debts suggests more than wealth. It suggests intention, reliability, and competency as well. Even if the Lannisters are facing financial difficulties, they will find a way to pay their debts.

But what if the Lannisters cannot pay their debts? What if a fire breathing dragon destroys the Lannisters' castle and roasts every living Lannister to death, except, perhaps, small children who have been sent to live as hostages with potential adversaries? What happens to a moral requirement that becomes impossible to fulfill?

There is a difference between choosing to not show up for a date or choosing to tell a white lie to spare someone's feelings and failing to repay a debt due to inability to pay. In all three cases, an obligation has not been honored, a promise has not been fulfilled, but in only two of the three cases can the person be seen as having made a choice.

We sense that to hold someone morally culpable for an action, the person must have possessed the power and capacity to have done something else. To have someone's action be considered immoral, the person must have been able to make a choice. There must have been a morally acceptable alternative to the chosen action before we judge the action to be immoral.

People facing unmanageable debt cannot fulfill their moral obligation to pay their debts, because paying their debts is not economically possible. People facing unmanageable debt file bankruptcy because there is no economic alternative. Filing bankruptcy is not a choice to renege on a moral obligation; it is forced by economic necessity. Bankruptcy is not immoral.

"Do unto others" is a fundamental precept, a Natural Law, because the purpose of law is to create and preserve societal harmony. Societal harmony is required for individual well-being, or "the pursuit of happiness" as Thomas Jefferson put it in the Declaration of Independence. This Natural Law may be immutable, but it is subject to countervailing laws, just as the "law" of gravity is subject to the countervailing "law" of levitation. Allowing debtors who cannot repay their debts to discharge their obligations in bankruptcy countervails the "Do unto others" precept precisely because it preserves societal harmony and individuals' well-being. Bankruptcy is not immoral.

That is not to say that there will not be creditors who will be harmed. Creditors who are unable to anticipate debts being discharged in bankruptcy and who cannot offset that cost in advance by charging all their customers slightly more than they otherwise would have been charged will suffer harm. But the number of such creditors is relatively small.

As for the largely mythological creature who wildly runs up credit card debt buying expensive handbags and shoes and files bankruptcy to escape paying for them, bankruptcy law reflects the distinction between debts honestly incurred that cannot be repaid due to absence of means and debts dishonestly incurred with no intention of being repaid. The latter are deemed fraudulent and are not dischargeable in bankruptcy. Intentionality matters.

By the way, the above discussion should in no way impugn the business practices, business model or motives of American Express. I have nothing against American Express. One of my best friends works for American Express. I have an excellent professional relationship with lawyers for American Express. I have been a "member" since 1981 and I would like to continue to be a cardholder. Amex, please do not cancel my card. I don't leave home without it.

## Bankruptcy Will Not Ruin Your Credit Score Forever

People often have the erroneous belief that filing bankruptcy will ruin their credit score and they will never be able to restore it.

Your credit report is a record of how you have incurred debts and repaid them. It contains a history and description of the status of your debts as reported by creditors to one of the three major national credit bureaus: Experian, Equifax, and TransUnion.

Credit scores are an attempt to summarize in one number your credit history and, therefore, your likelihood of repaying debts, based upon your income, the number of lines of secured and unsecured credit you have, the length of time they have been open, how close you are to the credit limit in each line, and, most importantly, how diligent you have been in making timely payments on those lines of credit. The more lines of credit, the longer they have been open, the further away from their limits, the better you have been at making on time payments, the higher the credit score. Credit scores are extremely sensitive to mortgage payments being made on time and, to a slightly lesser extent, to credit card payments being made on time.

There are several types, or brand names, of credit scores. There is no one scoring system that all credit bureaus and creditors use, but about 90% of the credit scores used by creditors are issued by one company, which is also the best known --- the FICO score, which stands for the Fair Isaac Corporation.

Most of the prospective clients I see have missed at least one mortgage payment and several credit card payments. Their FICO credit scores tend to hover in the mid-to-low 500's. Credit scores do not go much lower. To be eligible for favorable interest rates on car loans and home mortgages, credit scores generally need to exceed 700. Interestingly, credit scores take the biggest hits when a debt is reported as being 30 or 60 days overdue. Credit scores are not that negatively impacted by debts being further overdue, say being 90, 120, or 150 days late.

You do not have to be Nostradamus to be able to predict that someone with a credit score in the mid-to-low 500's, who is struggling with unmanageable debt, will never get their credit score above 700 without filing bankruptcy. It simply is not possible for someone in dire financial straits to make all future debt payments on time.

Surprisingly, bankruptcy actually improves the likelihood of restoring a favorable credit score. The bankruptcy discharge causes your credit history to be wiped out. You start fresh. Your future credit score is based on your income, lines of credit, and your ability to make debt payments on time in the future. Having your existing debts wiped out in bankruptcy makes on-time payment of your future debts infinitely more likely. My clients who accept offers of credit after filing and are diligent in making on-time monthly payments, regularly see their credit scores rise above 700 within 18 months, and sometimes within six months, of filing bankruptcy.

Credit reports contain a footnote indicating bankruptcy filings within the prior ten years (possibly less with a filing in Chapter 13). Big deal. There is a footnote on your credit report. The footnote is not a factor that goes into determining your credit score. You can live with a footnote on your credit report.

## ❦ Bankruptcy Will Not Leave You Without Access To Credit Forever

People often believe that filing bankruptcy will render them ineligible for credit cards or home mortgages in the future. That belief is false. Bankruptcy filers have ample access to credit after filing and, often, very shortly after filing.

Believe it or not, virtually all my clients are offered new credit cards almost immediately after filing. How can that be? They just filed bankruptcy! Who in their right mind would offer credit cards to deadbeat bankruptcy filers? The answer is -- very sophisticated credit card issuers.

After someone files bankruptcy, assuming they will receive a discharge (which is a fairly safe assumption), that person is the best credit risk on the planet. All their other unsecured debt will be wiped out. They cannot file bankruptcy again in Chapter 7, where credit cards debts are eliminated, for another eight years. If you were a credit card issuer, would you rather extend more credit card debt to someone already struggling with credit card debt or to someone who has no other credit card debt and cannot seek debt relief for another eight years?

In the past, my clients were only offered secured credit cards. The available line of credit on the secured credit card reflected the deposit the cardholder made into a savings account established for the benefit of the credit card issuer. The savings account "secured" the credit card. There was almost no risk of loss for the credit card issuer. If the cardholder failed to make a monthly payment, the issuer would deduct the payment from the savings account. Once the issuer became comfortable with the "creditworthiness" of the cardholder, the issuer would release the savings account and extend credit on an unsecured basis. Those days are long gone. Today, all my clients are offered unsecured credit cards with high credit limits.

Just because a client is offered credit cards after filing does not necessarily mean they should accept them. The invitation of more credit can be a temptation to over-spending that might best be avoided. However, where rebuilding a credit score is especially important, the best strategy is to accept all the credit cards offers, use the cards to purchase gas and groceries, and pay the outstanding balance off in full at the end of every month. The more lines of credit you have and the more you use those lines of credit, the faster your credit score will go up.

In my experience, filing bankruptcy also is not an impediment to being eligible for a mortgage in the future. As a practical matter, it will take two- or three-years following bankruptcy to save up enough money for a down payment on a house. Typically, to be eligible for a government-backed home mortgage, your credit score should be over 700. As explained above, certainly within two- or three-years following bankruptcy your credit score should be over 700. With those two pieces of the puzzle solved, you will only need a mortgage broker to originate the mortgage who can explain why you had to file bankruptcy.

## ❦ Bankruptcy Requires Little, If Any, Court Activity

Many people shy away from bankruptcy out of the mistaken belief that they will be required to plead their case in a court presided over by a judge. Very few people have any experience in court and whatever experience those people may have had likely was not pleasant. The prospect of filing any kind of legal case is scary. People are understandably terrified of having to go to court, to appear before a judge, to speak in public, to plead their case, to disclose the most unfortunately details of their lives, and to risk having their case fail.

Fortunately, for virtually everyone who files bankruptcy, none of those things happen. For most people, filing bankruptcy involves as much court activity as filing an income tax return. Most people who file bankruptcy file their cases in Chapter 7. They never go to court. They never see a judge. There are no pleadings before a judge in their cases. Judges do not approve or deny their cases. Judges do issue discharge orders, but discharge orders ordinarily are issued automatically, unless an objection to discharge has been raised.

Are there exceptions? Sure. Just as there are a few people who file income tax returns and end up in court. Generally, for similar reasons -- not telling the truth. If there were an issue regarding whether you qualified for Chapter 7 or whether your prior conduct may have disqualified you from receiving a discharge of your debts, in whole or in part, that issue could be heard and decided by a bankruptcy court judge.

Bankruptcy is for honest people to whom something unfortunate has happened. If you misrepresent your income, if you conceal property you own, if you incur a debt with no intention of ever paying it, or if you otherwise act in a fraudulent manner, your honesty is put into question. A bankruptcy court judge might have to determine whether you acted dishonestly and, if so, whether your actions were bad enough to deny you debt relief. That should apply to exactly no one reading this book.

Bad acts that could cause a bankruptcy court judge to deny a discharge, in whole or in part, are exceedingly rare. When they do arise, they tend to arise more in business cases than in consumer cases. If you have any doubt as to whether your actions might be construed as being dishonest, consult a knowledgeable attorney.

I once saw a prospective client who was seeking relief from a state court judgment. The prospective client had beaten someone up in a fist fight in a bar. The victim sued for damages. The court ordered the prospective client to pay compensation to the victim. Beating someone up is the rare kind of intentional bad act that would cause the resulting debt to be declared non-dischargeable in bankruptcy court in a consumer case. For my own health and welfare, I try to avoid taking on clients with a history of beating people up. For both reasons, I declined representation of the brawler.

The third part of this book is all about qualifying for Chapter 7. After you read it, you will have a good idea whether you qualify for Chapter 7 and whether your debts are dischargeable. Although Chapter 7 does not involve going before a judge, there is Meeting of Creditors that will require your participation. For most people, that meeting involves ten minutes of answering questions. That is it. The entire bankruptcy process is explained in Chapter 10 of this book, so all your fears should be allayed. Hiring a knowledgeable attorney would also help.

In contrast to Chapter 7, cases filed in Chapter 11, Chapter 12 and Chapter 13 do involve going to court to obtain confirmation of a plan detailing how creditors will be paid and to defend against any objections to confirmation by creditors, among other matters. Few of those matters, however, require oral testimony or other significant participation by an individual debtor in a non-business case.

## ❦ You Will Not Lose Your Home Or Car In Bankruptcy

Many people who would be helped by bankruptcy avoid it due to the unfounded belief that they will lose their home or car in bankruptcy. Unexpectedly losing a home or car in bankruptcy is rarer than unexpectedly being eaten by a shark. It does not happen. If it did, cable television would run "Bankruptcy Week" right after "Shark Week."

Property potentially can be lost in Chapter 7. The "deal" in Chapter 7 is that your unsecured debts get discharged and you get to keep all your future income, but the "catch" is that you lose property that is not "exempt" from creditors. That "nonexempt" property will be sold by the Chapter 7 Trustee and the proceeds will be used to pay your creditors. Although the potential for property to be lost is there, no one who knew what they were doing would file a case in Chapter 7 without knowing whether they could keep everything they owned. Certainly, no one who had read this book or retained an attorney would be at any risk of losing a home or a car.

A "fresh start" does not mean starting from scratch. As explained in Chapter 7 "What Can You Keep In Bankruptcy?" under state or federal bankruptcy law, houses and cars usually are "exempt" from creditors. Most people can keep their house and car. Where exemption laws do not provide sufficient protection for items of property, such as a house or a car, Chapter 13 can be selected instead of Chapter 7. In Chapter 13, creditors are repaid some or all of what they are owed, but there is no risk of losing property. Retention of nonexempt property is one of the main reasons people choose Chapter 13 over Chapter 7.

## ❧ You Will Not Be Discriminated Against Due To Bankruptcy

Another erroneous belief keeping people away from bankruptcy is the fear of being discriminated against in employment, housing, or student loans as a result of having filed bankruptcy.

As mentioned above, a bankruptcy filing likely will appear as a footnote on a credit report for as long as ten years after filing. There are employers and landlords who request access to credit reports from applicants before making their hiring or rental decisions. The fear that those employers or landlords might deny employment or an apartment lease based upon the footnote disclosure of bankruptcy in the credit report is understandable.

Consider this: to request and obtain access to a credit report requires a fair amount of sophistication (and lawyering). To deny employment based on a credit report, the employer must provide an explanation to the applicant. Would a sophisticated employer or landlord, who presumably also is a sophisticated user of the information contained in a credit report, prefer to select someone who has filed bankruptcy and has no debt or someone who has not filed bankruptcy and is still dealing with unmanageable debt? Which candidate is more likely to steal? Which candidate is more likely to be able to afford to pay rent and fulfill other financial obligations in the future?

There may be another reason for requesting a credit report from a job applicant. Some businesses use credit scores as a proxy to measure cooperativeness. The idea is that a higher credit score indicates a higher degree of compliance with financial obligations, which implies a higher degree of compliance with employment obligations. On balance, employers prefer to hire candidates who can be relied upon to do as they are told. Whether the idea of equating a high credit score with a high degree of workplace compliance makes any sense, or why anyone would want to work in such a place, aside, as explained above, filing bankruptcy will enable someone to improve a poor credit score much faster than the credit score would improve without filing bankruptcy.

By law, a governmental unit may not "deny employment to, terminate the employment of, or discriminate with respect to employment against," a person who has filed bankruptcy. In other words, no part of the government at any level can refuse to hire you, or fire you, or treat you differently than any other person, just because you filed bankruptcy. There can be no discrimination against you in the future, for example, if you were to apply for a student loan for yourself or a child, just because you filed bankruptcy. The decision to offer a student loan by a governmental agency must be made without reference to the applicant's or the applicant's parent having filed bankruptcy.

Laws prohibiting discrimination against bankruptcy filers are a little weaker for private employers. By law, a private employer may not "terminate the employment of, or discriminate with respect to employment against," a person who has filed bankruptcy. Courts in most of the U.S. have held that a private employer can refuse to hire a person based solely upon the fact that the applicant filed bankruptcy. So, it is legally possible for an employer to use a bankruptcy filing as a reason to deny a job applicant employment. But, once again, why would a sophisticated employer prefer to hire a prospective employee who is still dealing with unmanageable debt over a prospective employee who has filed bankruptcy and has no debt? Which prospective employee is more likely to steal?

Filing bankruptcy will not preclude a terrible employee from being fired. The terrible employee just cannot be fired solely based on having filed bankruptcy. But what if an employee was fired whose performance was not objectively terrible? Could an employee who was fired and who had filed bankruptcy sue the employer for bankruptcy discrimination? It sounds fanciful. As far as I know, no such case has ever been filed (which is one indication that no one gets fired for filing bankruptcy). Terminated employees sue former employers based on racial and gender discrimination all the time. The terminated employees frequently receive large settlements to avoid having the matter decided in court. If I had any clients who were ever fired, I would seriously consider bringing a "bankruptcy discrimination" case.

## Your Neighbors Will Not Know About Your Bankruptcy

Even in the Internet age, everyone wants their financial affairs to be kept as private as possible. People often are reluctant to file out of the belief that their neighbors will learn about their financial difficulties and their bankruptcy filing. They worry that the bankruptcy filing will be reported in the local newspaper or that a big white sign will be erected on their front lawn. Those concerns are misplaced.

Although bankruptcy case filings are judicial filings that the public may have access to, the reality is that the public never learns about, or the details of, consumer bankruptcy filings.

As a rule, local newspapers do not report on individual, non-business Chapter 7 or Chapter 13 bankruptcy filings. Local newspaper editors understand the embarrassment local people, who may be their subscribers and advertisers, would feel if their filings made the news. There is no need to warn the community about a consumer bankruptcy filing, as there might be with an arrest. To the extent bankruptcy filings receive coverage in the local media, the stories usually are about Chapter 11 filings by businesses with local employees, suppliers or customers. Those bankruptcies could have an economic impact on the local area. There is no requirement to post a "legal notice" of a bankruptcy filing in the paid advertising section of a local newspaper, the way some legal actions must be noticed. Big white signs are erected on front lawns to give notice of judicial sales of houses in foreclosure cases, not bankruptcy cases.

Bankruptcy filings contain significant financial disclosures. As judicial filings, they are public records. In theory, anyone can go to the bankruptcy courthouse in which the case was filed and examine the bankruptcy filings. As a practical matter, however, it is quite difficult to enter a federal courthouse these days. Your neighbors are not going to know that your financial disclosures are available to be examined at the federal courthouse or know how to get access to see the documents.

Bankruptcy filings are not available to the public on-line. Your bankruptcy case docket cannot be Googled. All judicial records can be accessed on Pacer, but that system is not designed for browsing by non-registered parties. As with any public disclosure, it is not impossible for someone to learn of a bankruptcy filing, but it is highly unlikely. The small risk is greatly outweighed by the enormous benefit.

One tip I have discovered to make the filing of a bankruptcy case even less accessible to nosy busybodies is to use the filer's full name, including full middle name or names. Official bankruptcy forms require the filer's full name, but many people just disclose a middle initial or fail to disclose a middle name at all. Using the full name makes a difference. It makes it less likely that the bankruptcy case will show up in an Internet search. Here's why: You can be certain that no one who invited Lee and Marina over for cocktails or a BBQ in Dallas knew Lee Oswald's middle name. They called him "Lee" or "Bud." Assuming Lee filed bankruptcy and his nosy neighbors wanted to learn more, they would Google "Lee Oswald" or "Bud Oswald." If Lee had filed bankruptcy using his full name, including his middle name, an on-line search for "Lee Oswald" or "Bud Oswald" likely would not produce any results for a bankruptcy case filed by "Lee Harvey Oswald."

Prospective clients occasionally raise the concern that their employers will be notified about their bankruptcy. No one wants their employer to learn about their bankruptcy filing. Unless the client owes the employer money, the employer will not receive notice of the bankruptcy filing. Same for landlords and everyone else. No debt, no notice. Generally, only creditors and co-debtors receive notice of bankruptcy filings.

## ❦ Both Spouses Do Not Have To File

Married couples often believe that both spouses must file bankruptcy even though only one spouse needs to file. That is incorrect. You do not have to drag an unwilling spouse into bankruptcy. Both spouses are not required to file. Either or both spouses may file. It may be a very good idea for both spouses to file, but it is not required. In deciding whether one or both spouses should file, the following should be considered:

## *Who Owes The Debt?*

If both spouses have incurred credit card or other unsecured debt, especially if both owe money to the same creditors, probably both spouses will need to file. The exception would be if the couple absolutely, positively needed access to credit immediately after filing and there was no way to get access to credit through being an authorized user on someone else's credit card. In that case, you might have one spouse file, get a discharge, get credit, and then have the other spouse file. Having only one spouse file bankruptcy at a time leaves the other spouse with access to credit.

## *Who Owns Which Assets?*

If one spouse owns assets that cannot be kept in Chapter 7, for example, an Andy Warhol painting or a house with too much equity to protect with the homestead exemption, only the other spouse, who owns assets that can be kept in Chapter 7, should file.

The benefit of both spouses filing together is the cost. Most lawyers will charge the same fee for one or both spouses. If you file two separate cases, you will incur two separate legal and filing fees.

Regardless of whether one or both spouses file, their eligibility for Chapter 7 will be determined based on their combined incomes.

There is a lot of misinformation about bankruptcy. About 90% of what people believe when they come to see me for an initial consultation is wrong. They might as well believe that Julius Caesar invented the Caesar salad.

In a way, that is not surprising. The beliefs seem true because they are repeated so often without being corrected. There is no bankruptcy trade association that fact checks, disputes, or debunks the misinformation. Apart from a local bankruptcy attorney here and there, no one promotes bankruptcy. There are no advertisers trying to convince you that filing bankruptcy will make you stronger, younger, more popular, more confident, prettier, or smarter. Almost all the national advertising that mentions bankruptcy comes from debt consolidators instructing listeners not to file bankruptcy. Debt consolidators denouncing bankruptcy is like Weight Watchers warning about the dangers of broccoli.

To solve your unmanageable debt problem and achieve your goal of a fresh start, you must first change your negative beliefs about bankruptcy. If you still are not convinced that the beliefs I have just discussed are incorrect, I encourage you to research them further. Changing beliefs is not easy. Confirmation bias leads us to find and interpret new information in a way that tends to support our pre-existing opinions. Like wheel alignments, mental adjustments are often necessary. Once your negative beliefs about bankruptcy have been addressed, there may be negative emotions holding you back.

# NEGATIVE EMOTIONS

People often harbor erroneous beliefs regarding bankruptcy because erroneous beliefs camouflage negative emotions that are too painful to admit or address. Those negative emotions include fear of failure, guilt, shame, humiliation and embarrassment. No one wants to confront those emotional explosives. We would rather duck and cover. To quote the eminent modern psychologist Eric Clapton, "You've been running and hiding much too long. You know it's just your foolish pride, Layla."

As we saw with the Epitomes, unmanageable debt happens to good people, people who never expected to be in financial distress, people who did the right things, people who worked hard to build a solid financial future for themselves and their family. The Epitomes were playing the "Game of Life" and winning. They were moving their car token around the gameboard from "Start" to "Retirement", choosing their careers, family, vacation, and other milestones. They had the satisfaction that comes with professional advancement, a loving family, excellent health, and caring friends. In short, the Epitomes were successful.

Like most people, the Epitomes did not consider making money an explicit goal. Money was not considered the root of all evil either. Rather, money was an implicit goal, a means to an end. To the Epitomes, success meant having the things that money could buy, not merely possessions, but also good health, security and the ability to overcome problems. The Epitomes were not spending money carelessly. They were not earning money, as comedian George Carlin quipped, "to buy things they did not need to impress people they did not like."

Maybe the Epitomes wanted "to keep up with the Joneses" next door. It would not be unusual for people like the Epitomes to see who was ahead in the real game of life by comparing their wealth, status, and appearance to others around them. Money is more tangible and easier to measure than happiness, wellbeing, and love. It would not be surprising if the Epitomes were a little envious of neighbors who bought fancier cars or who took more exotic vacations. Similarly, it would not be surprising if the Epitomes worried about being seen as losing the game of life by their neighbors.

The Epitomes were expecting a future in which things would be even better. But something unexpected happened to the Epitomes. The Covid-19 pandemic arrived. John lost his job. With less income available, debts that were once manageable were manageable no longer.

## Failure

No one wants to admit to being a failure at the game of life. Not to themselves. Not to others. Considering bankruptcy can be viewed as an admission of failure in the game of life, so it is avoided. People would rather continue to star in their own personal horror movie, "Night of The Living Debt," than consider a solution that appears to be a concession of failure. Bankruptcy is more terrifying to their self-esteem than the nightmare of unmanageable debt.

Fear of failure takes a very nasty vector around the consideration of bankruptcy, because three notions of failure get triggered simultaneously. First, there is performance failure. I cannot pay my debts. I failed at providing for my family. I failed at managing my family's finances. I failed at the game of life. Next comes identity failure. Because of my performance failure, I will not be respected and loved by my family and friends. I am not worthy of the approval of others. I am a failure as a human being. Under other circumstances, the "bad hand" that has been dealt might be accepted, played, and made the best of. Here, the possible solution, bankruptcy, triggers a third failure – moral failure. Not paying my debts is immoral. Considering bankruptcy as a solution to my unmanageable debt problem is morally wrong. How could I ever forgive myself if I resorted to bankruptcy? Instead of solving them, bankruptcy compounds performance failure and personal failure. Part of performance failure and personal failure is the inability to control events and circumstances. As an unknown, bewildering process that is reputed to make things worse, the immoral solution of bankruptcy is seen as turning performance failure and personal failure into an even greater catastrophic failure.

Bankruptcy lawyers do not receive professional training in psychology. But, as a parapsychologist, I have sensed that fear of failure and fear of being seen as a failure are more pronounced in men than women. Men tend to attach much more of their self-worth to their occupation. When men suffer a job loss, they are more likely than women to view themselves as being defective. Financial failure is not just something that happened to men, it is something men are. Something is wrong with them. Identity failure is more closely related to performance failure in men than women. In my experience, women have an easier time separating the bad event that has happened to them from who they are. Women are less likely to equate financial failure with personal failure. Considering bankruptcy seems to be less of an assault on a woman's ego than a man's ego.

## 🦋 Guilt And Shame

Related to the fear of failure are the emotions of guilt and shame. The notion of guilt is that something we *did* is wrong. We feel guilty when we cannot pay our debts. We feel guilty when we consider using bankruptcy to escape paying our debts. Guilt comes from performance failure. The notion of shame is that something we *are* is wrong. We are bad people because we cannot pay our debts. We are bad people because we are considering bankruptcy as a way out. We feel ashamed that we did not manage our finances better. We feel ashamed that we did not live up to the image we believe our family and friends have of us. We are unworthy of the respect or love of others. Shame comes from identity failure. Shame is a doubly insidious emotion because we are ashamed that we are ashamed. It does not help to tell ourselves that we should not feel ashamed, because that just triggers guilt about feeling ashamed. These emotions are self-defeating. Internalizing guilt and shame can lead to serious feelings of helplessness and despair.

Shame is more often associated with bankruptcy than humiliation because shame is something we tend to believe is deserved. Humiliation is something we believe is not deserved. If we consider bankruptcy as a solution to our failure to pay our debts, that would be shameful. We brought shame upon ourselves. If an involuntary bankruptcy were filed against us by our creditors, that would be humiliating. Embarrassment is a less painful emotion than shame or humiliation that generally carries with it the notion that what has happened to us regularly happens to other people and they get over it. People often feel deeper emotions than embarrassment when contemplating bankruptcy. Embarrassment is not the impediment to moving forward that are failure, guilt and shame.

## ❧ Overcoming Negative Emotions

How do you get beyond these negative emotions? For starters, notice that the negative emotions exist. Acknowledge them. These negative emotions do not exist independently in nature. Shame is not on the menu at Chick-fil-A. Our brains cause these emotions to exist. We create them. We inflict suffering on ourselves by conjuring these evil spirits into existence. By noticing and acknowledging the negative emotions, we can begin to deal with them.

Next, understand that while guilt and shame may serve a valuable purpose as deterrents against committing the bad act that generated the emotions again in the future, guilt and shame are not terribly helpful with respect to something you had little control over. The unmanageable debt exists. Feeling guilt and shame about being unable to pay the unmanageable debt will not make it go away. The job loss, divorce or medical condition that likely caused the unmanageable debt might possibly happen again, but that possibility is largely out of your control. Feeling guilt or shame about things out of your control is an unnecessary punishment and a waste of time.

It sounds cliché, but it bears repeating: Life is not fair. Bad things happen to good people. You are not a bad person. You are a good person to whom something bad has happened. You did not incur debt without any intention of repaying it. You regularly and responsibly repaid your debt until something happened to make repayment impossible. The debt became unmanageable. You are not a failure. Failure is something that happened. Failure is not who you are. Failure does not define you.

You may lament your current situation and feel guilt or shame that things are not as they "should" be. Considering bankruptcy as a solution may also seem "wrong" because bankruptcy is not the way things "should" be either. But things are only how they are, not as they "should" be. How things are now is unmanageable and unacceptable for a healthy life. The word "should" derives from the Anglo-Saxon word "sceolde." You need to stop scolding yourself. Do not allow yourself to think that the cure – bankruptcy -- is worse than the disease – unmanageable debt. Bankruptcy will not make things worse. That is the shame talking.

Ask yourself, "How will it help me to have these negative emotions and how will it hurt me?" List the advantages and disadvantages on a piece of paper, if necessary. When you see that the disadvantages far outweigh the advantages, you can begin to change your feelings. You can stop feeling guilt and shame for the things you did that you "should" not have done or the things you did not do that you "should" have done. Then you can focus on solving the unmanageable debt problem instead of using up all your energy blaming yourself and feeling guilty.

You cannot change your life unless you change the way you think and feel about yourself and the way you talk to yourself. The more positive your thoughts, the more productive, capable, lovable, and happy you will feel. What you tell yourself helps determine how you feel and what you are capable of. Tell yourself, "There is a way to solve this unmanageable debt problem." This book gives you the tools to know whether bankruptcy is the answer.

It may be disappointing and difficult for your friends and family to learn that you filed bankruptcy, but bankruptcy is something you do. Bankruptcy does not define you. Bankruptcy transforms you. Bankruptcy is not the end of your path. Bankruptcy is a fresh start on your path. What you make of your fresh start following bankruptcy will define you.

One of the best movies about financial failure and redemption is "*It's a Wonderful Life.*" Feeling the shame of his Building & Loan's unexpected failure to manage its financial obligations (after Uncle Billy misplaced the deposits), George Bailey contemplates suicide. George changes his mind after his Guardian Angel provides a vision of what the lives of George's family and friends would have been like had George never been born. Those same people rally to George's support, solve his financial problem and toast George as "the richest man in town." Your choices make a difference to you and those around you. Your choices define you.

Guilt and shame can be tough emotions to get over even after bankruptcy. The bankruptcy process itself does nothing to help people overcome feelings of guilt and shame. Debtors rarely go to court. As a result, there is no public "forum" in which debtors can confess what they may consider to be their sins. They never get to apologize to creditors whose debts will not be paid. They cannot publicly resolve to never file bankruptcy again. There is no "price" to be paid for debt relief (apart from legal fees) for almost all debtors in Chapter 7. There is no punishment. No judge provides absolution. There is no forgiveness in bankruptcy.

I have had a few clients who remained haunted by feelings of guilt and shame after their Chapter 7 cases had ended. They felt underwhelmed by the absence of contrition and the lack of a cathartic experience during the bankruptcy process. They expected some punishment, to pay some penance. They felt betrayed by the ease with which their debts were discharged. It would be easy to write them off as crazy, like the clients who fail to appreciate my sense of humor, but the unease was real. To help assuage their guilt, I offered to send them an especially large bill. No one ever took me up on that offer.

To help address these feelings, many bankruptcy lawyers employ a ritual. The lawyer takes the client's credit cards and cuts the cards in half in front of the client. The split cards fall into a giant glass urn containing the cut credit cards of other clients. The ceremony usually is performed when the bankruptcy case is filed. The credit cards likely would have been cut off at filing anyway and the client should not have been using credit cards prior to filing, but the card cutting does inflict some symbolic punishment on the client. The ritual has the added value of connecting that client's single experience with the experiences of many other past and future bankruptcy filers just like that client. That connection gives the ritual extra meaning. The client is not alone. The credit card cutting ceremony can make the filing experience more tangible.

While I am a big proponent of some rituals, knocking on wood for good luck and sacrificing virgins to end droughts come to mind, I do not employ the credit card cutting ceremony. My practice, instead, is to ask clients to write anonymous testimonials for my website. I do this for a few reasons. First, testimonials are a terrific source of information for people who are considering bankruptcy. Testimonials provide first-hand insight into what the clients were thinking and feeling during the bankruptcy process. Testimonials explain how bankruptcy turned out to be easier, faster and better than they had expected.

Testimonials can help the clients writing the testimonials even more than they help prospective clients. Studies have shown the value of expressive writing as a way of healing victims of trauma. Shame thrives on secrets. When people share their stories and experiences, they reveal their secrets. Sharing the good news of bankruptcy with people standing in the same shoes as the testimonial writer, who are grappling with the same erroneous beliefs and negative emotions, is a way of "paying it forward." The good deed of writing the testimonial may not reverse the harm caused by discharging debt, but it can help the testimonial writer move forward into a positive future. Writing a testimonial in a caring, sympathetic way can be the cathartic experience some clients need to forgive themselves and let go of any remaining guilt and shame. Testimonials can provide closure.

##  COUNTERPRODUCTIVE BEHAVIORS

When dealing with unmanageable debt, the negative emotions of failure, guilt and shame can lead to depression and helplessness, which can then cycle back to create more feelings of failure, guilt, and shame. The negative emotions may influence or cause negative behaviors. There are several negative behaviors that hold people back and prevent them from moving forward to consider or pursue bankruptcy. I do not encounter most of them in my practice because most prospective clients have already decided to at least consider filing bankruptcy when they meet with me, but they are real problems for many people struggling with unmanageable debt.

### Denial

Isn't it better just to pretend that everything is awesome? Yes, there may be an unmanageable debt monster living under the bed, but maybe it will go away like the other monsters living under the bed. Is this really something that must be dealt with right now? Could this really be happening to someone who did all the right things, like you?

Refusing to admit unmanageable debt exists may allow you the luxury of avoiding the problem, at least until the calls from debt collectors start making your life a living hell. Denial enables you to maintain the façade that if only you had not done a series of things, like take a job, get married, buy a house, buy a car, or have children, you would not be staring down the barrel of the unmanageable debt revolver today. Your life magically would be happier. Who knows? Maybe. Maybe not. A whole lot of living would have to unwound to put you back in your happy place. Dwelling in the fan fiction of what might have been is not terribly helpful. It delays moving towards a solution. Your current situation may be beyond your most terrifying expectations, but it is the reality you face.

Denial does not come completely without a cost. Denial comes with what economists call an "opportunity cost." We must make choices. In a way, denial is a choice. A choice not to do something. Choices involve sacrifices -- things that we give away, now or later, to do something. There are opportunities that we sacrifice when we make a choice, even if the choice is do nothing. When we refuse to consider bankruptcy as a solution to unmanageable debt, we sacrifice our health and well-being. What is worse, if we continue to make token payments on debts that can never be fully repaid, we sacrifice funds that could be better spent providing for our family.

## ❧ Self-Pity

Unmanageable debt is not a problem that can be ducked out on. It will not fix itself. It does not go away. Acknowledging the problem can be overwhelming for many people. It triggers the negative emotions described above. Feelings of failure and shame lead to feelings of hopelessness and despair. The self-pity and resulting paralysis can become so overpowering that seeking a solution becomes nearly impossible.

Feeling sorry for yourself may be comforting, but it is self-destructive and does nothing to improve your situation. Do not resign yourself to sadness, depression, and self-pity. Do not sell yourself short.

## ❧ Can't vs Won't

For many people who recognize that life is not fair and that dwelling in self-pity is not beneficial, the next limiting behavior they encounter is one that says they "can't" move ahead when what they really mean is that they "won't" move ahead.

People say they can't file bankruptcy because they won't file bankruptcy. To consider bankruptcy is to admit that life has not worked out exactly as planned.

Sometimes the "can't" is rephrased so that the power is taken out of their hands. They can't file because a spouse or a parent won't allow it. What they really are saying is that they won't file because they won't risk the disapproval of the spouse or the parent.

Well, guess what? No one wants to file bankruptcy. Filing bankruptcy is not an item on a single person's bucket list of things to do before they die. Not one. No prospective client comes into my office without saying, "I never wanted to be here. I never thought this would happen to me."

Saying that you can't file bankruptcy allows you to feel like a victim with no responsibility over your life. That may be a genuine emotion, but it obviously is neither helpful nor true. "Can't" is not the same as "Won't." You must take responsibility for your own life.

You must put your own needs and the needs of your family first, and not feel bad about doing something your spouse, your parent, society, or anyone else disapproves of. You cannot live your life to please other people, particularly when dealing with unmanageable debt can hardly be called "living."

## ❧ Resistance To Change

Change is hard. Change is even harder when it invokes the disapproval of one's own internal voice, society at large, and friends and family. Stepping outside one's comfort zone to pursue something completely unknown is terrifying. Not a lot of us try skydiving. But, just because change is hard does not mean change can be shied away from. Just because a task is difficult does not mean the task should not be taken on.

Resistance to change often comes from aversion to loss. Economists note that we tend to overvalue what we have, and we are reluctant to give up what we have for something else. Because of loss aversion, potential losses weigh more heavily on us than potential gains. Loss aversion is a particular problem with bankruptcy, because very few people have any idea of what is involved or what the future will be like. The mistaken belief that bankruptcy will make things worse weighs heavily against considering it. A miserable present may outweigh an uncertain future.

One way for you to overcome resistance to change and to consider bankruptcy is to imagine your future free from unmanageable debt. What would you gain from being debt-free? Financially and emotionally. Think about how your family life will improve. Your health. Think about where you will be in five years after a fresh start. Contrast that to where you will be in five years if you continue to struggle with unmanageable debt. Although the task ahead is hard, the pay off is high enough to convince you to change, to pursue bankruptcy.

## ❦ Procrastination

Even after the decision to change has been made, many people still have trouble getting into action. The choice is not whether to begin, it is when to begin. Many people are ready to bear the present discomfort for the future benefit, but they would prefer to postpone that discomfort a little longer. They procrastinate. Procrastination is particularly prevalent in bankruptcy because so few people know anything about bankruptcy, what the process will be like and how things will turn out. Children show more enthusiasm for vaccinations than most prospective clients show for bankruptcy.

The future is an uncertain place. We do not know exactly what will happen. The best we can do is draw on our knowledge and other experiences to anticipate what the future will be like. Fortunately for you, you have this book to guide you. This book details exactly what bankruptcy is, how it works, what the process is and what is involved. Procrastination is no longer an option for you.

I have never had a client regret filing bankruptcy. Almost universally, their only regret was not having filed bankruptcy sooner.

 ## GETTING INTO ACTION

It has been said that there are two kinds of people in the world: those who divide the world into two kinds of people and those who do not. I am in the first group -- the dividers. To me, there are two kinds of people in the world: those who acknowledge their situation and make results happen and those who make lots of excuses for not making results happen.

You may not have had control over the events in your life that led to your unmanageable debt predicament, but you do have control over getting out of it.

Think about another time in your life when you faced adversity and the odds seemed overwhelming. What happened? You got creative. You visualized a solution. You told yourself, "I will." You set goals. You developed a plan. You committed yourself to following the plan and achieving the goals. You got resourceful. You got into action and you got the job done. The same applies now.

Fear can be a valuable emotional tool to help us evade or avoid danger. But fear of filing in the face of unmanageable debt inhibits eliminating the danger, which diminishes our quality of life. Neutralizing fear requires courage. To activate courage requires desire. You really have to want it. You have to want to overcome the self-inflicted negative feedback loop of failure/guilt/shame. You have to want to get your life back. You have to want the joy of being debt-free. Existential joy, by the way, is the greatest wealth you can acquire. It is priceless. (For everything else, there's Mastercard).

If your desire is great enough and you choose to pursue bankruptcy, you will be in good and familiar company. Here is a partial list of famous people who are reported to have filed personal or business bankruptcy: Kim Basinger, Toni Braxton, Francis Ford Coppola, Walt Disney, Zsa Gabor, MC Hammer, Don Johnson, Larry King, Burt Reynolds, Cyndi Lauper, Dave Ramsey, P.T. Barnum, George Foreman, Wayne Newton, Meatloaf, Mickey Rooney, Anita Bryant, Marvin Gaye, David Bowie, Mick Fleetwood, Isaac Hayes, Ulysses S. Grant, Tammy Wynette, David Crosby, Jackie Mason, Cindy Lauper, George McGovern, Red Foxx, Latoya Jackson, Bowie Kuhn, Francis Ford Coppola, Henry Ford, J.C. Penney, Nicholas Cage, Mike Tyson, 50 Cent, and, of course, Donald Trump (not personally, only for his casinos).

Bankruptcy did not stop these people. After using bankruptcy for relief from unmanageable debt, each went on to greater professional triumph.

The old proverb is that a journey of a thousand miles begins with a single step. The rest of this book provides all steps you will need to take. Get started. Don't wait until conditions are perfect. Conditions will never be perfect. As they say on late night televisions commercials, "Act now!" Once you start, your feelings about bankruptcy will change. You will see that bankruptcy is faster, easier and better than you thought.

# CHAPTER 4

## Overview Of Bankruptcy

The odd word "bankruptcy" is thought to have derived from the Italian phrase "banca ratta," which means "broken bench or table," not "bankers are rats," as some may have assumed. In medieval Italy, when a merchant failed to pay his debts, his creditors literally would break the bench or table from which the merchant conducted his business. Presumably, the prospect of having his place of business busted up provided the merchant with a strong incentive to pay his debts. At some point, however, creditors finally realized that breaking the merchant's bench or table was an inherently futile, self-defeating gesture that significantly diminished the likelihood of their ever being repaid. Who says creditors are slow learners?

The non-obvious idea that allowing debtors to escape unmanageable debt benefitted societal harmony and productivity more than allowing creditors to endlessly inflict violence and punishment on debtors and their families preceded the rise of banking in Italian city-states by a very long time. The Old Testament states: "At the end of every seven years you shall grant a release and this is the manner of the release: every creditor shall release what he has lent to his neighbor" (Deuteronomy 15:1-2). The ancient Israelites knew that the likelihood of a creditor being repaid by a debtor with little income or few assets was lower than the likelihood of either getting blood from a stone or turning a rod into a snake (Exodus 7:19). At some point, allowing a creditor to inflict violence on a debtor in default on his debt was more of a detriment to society than a benefit. When Moses came down from Mount Sinai bearing the big stone tablets inscribed with the ten commandments, murder, adultery, theft and bearing false witness made the naughty list, but "Thou Shalt Not Default on Debts" did not (Balbus 17:7).

The idea of providing debt forgiveness through bankruptcy made its way from the Old World to the New World. The Founding Fathers gave Congress, the legislative branch of government, the power to enact "uniform laws on the subject of bankruptcies" in Article 1, Section 8 of the United States Constitution. The Founders were less explicit about the nature of such bankruptcy laws – what debts should be forgiven, under what circumstances and who should make the determination. From the first U.S. bankruptcy law, passed in 1800, to the most recent version - the Bankruptcy Code enacted in 1978, which was significantly amended in 2005 by the Bankruptcy Abuse Prevention and Consumer Protection Act, a tension has existed between debtors, who view debt forgiveness as a fundamental (or biblical) right, and creditors, who view debt forgiveness as a privilege that should be limited and, ideally, granted with their permission.

This tension between the competing interests of debtors and creditors was one reason why the Founders provided in the Constitution that bankruptcy laws were to be "uniform" throughout the states. The Founders were concerned that some states might enact bankruptcy laws that were too punitive towards debtors while other states might enact very liberal debt forgiveness laws to become debtor havens.

Despite the uniformity requirement in the Constitution, the application of bankruptcy laws, which are federal laws enacted by Congress, is a little different in each state. For example, one of the three ways to qualify for Chapter 7 is to be below median income based upon household size. However, the median income is not a federal median income uniform throughout the states. The median income threshold for Chapter 7 qualification varies from state to state. A spouse in a household of four in Connecticut may qualify for Chapter 7 with a household gross income currently just under $131,000, while a spouse in a household of four in Mississippi would only be eligible for Chapter 7 with a household gross income currently just under $72,000. Same federal bankruptcy law, different application in different states.

The notion behind using median income as a tool for determining eligibility for Chapter 7 was that about half of the residents of every state would automatically qualify. But, median incomes vary widely from state to state. Had the bankruptcy law adopted a uniform federal median income for Chapter 7 eligibility, say $100,000 for a household of four, more than half of the households in Connecticut would qualify for Chapter 7 but far less than half of the households in Mississippi would qualify.

Another non-uniform application of "uniform" bankruptcy law can be seen in the assets debtors are allowed to keep in bankruptcy. Which assets a debtor in Chapter 7 may keep is determined under state exemption laws in all states. Additionally, in 19 states and the District of Columbia the debtor has a choice of using state exemptions or the federal bankruptcy exemptions. Depending upon the property the debtor is trying to protect in those 19 states, one set of exemptions might provide better protection than the other. Exemption laws can vary significantly among states. Florida and Texas, for example, have very generous "homestead" exemptions that currently protect an almost unlimited amount of equity in a home. In contrast, the homestead exemption in Alabama, which currently does not allow the option of selecting the federal bankruptcy exemptions, currently protects only about $15,000 of equity in a home or $30,000 with two spouses on title. The non-uniform application of "uniform" bankruptcy laws among different states makes it easier to file bankruptcy in Chapter 7 in some states than others.

The fundamental ideas reflected in U.S. bankruptcy laws are: (1) an honest but unfortunate person seeking relief, known as a "debtor," should be entitled to the release of personal liability, known as a "discharge," of debt and a fresh start, with the extent of the debt relief somewhat related to the debtor's ability to pay; (2) filing bankruptcy should put an immediate end to creditors separately pursuing collection of their individual debts, known as the "automatic stay" and; (3) any money or other property of the debtor that is to be paid to creditors, known as a "bankruptcy estate," will be administered by a trustee supervised by a bankruptcy court judge and will be divided among creditors depending upon the priority of collection status assigned to the creditors' claims under bankruptcy law.

Bankruptcy cases are filed in federal bankruptcy courts. There are no state bankruptcy courts. Each bankruptcy court is administered by a federal bankruptcy court judge. The U.S. currently is divided into 94 bankruptcy districts. Each state has at least one district. One district has at least one bankruptcy court. The state of Connecticut, for example, is one federal bankruptcy district with three bankruptcy courts located in Bridgeport, New Haven and Hartford, each presided over by a separate bankruptcy court judge.

Bankruptcy cases generally begin with the debtor filing a document, known as a "petition," in bankruptcy court. The petition happens to be similar for most debtors even though they could be individuals, couples, unincorporated businesses, major corporations, foreign corporations with U.S. operations and non-profit associations.

There are six basic types of bankruptcy cases, which are called "chapters" based upon the chapter of the Bankruptcy Code that describes them. Chapter 7, sometimes called "liquidation," is used primarily for individuals with lower incomes and few assets who are seeking a complete discharge of their debts. Chapter 13 is used primarily by individuals whose incomes are too high to qualify for Chapter 7 or who own assets they could not retain in Chapter 7, who will repay a portion of their debts to creditors pursuant to a court approved "plan" over three to five years. Chapter 11 is used primarily by corporations to reorganize their operations and capital structures to operate profitably in the future, pursuant to a "plan of reorganization" approved by the bankruptcy court and accepted by the requisite number of creditors. Chapter 12 was designed specifically for family farmers and fishermen, who had excellent lobbyists in Congress, to provide them with a better result than the farmers and fishermen would have obtained under the relatively similar Chapter 13. Chapter 9 is for municipalities, such as cities, but not for states. Chapter 15 is used primarily by foreign corporations with subsidiaries operating in the U.S.

There is nothing absolute, immutable, or sacrosanct, either in moral or economic terms, about bankruptcy laws. They are inherently arbitrary policy choices based upon compromises derived from the relative political power of classes of debtors and creditors at the time the laws were enacted. Bankruptcy laws are constantly subject to change as the fortunes and political power of those classes ebb and flow.

As an example, in 2019, Congress added a new subchapter to Chapter 11 to expedite reorganizations for small businesses, particularly small businesses with one or a small number of secured creditors who support the small business reorganizing and continuing to operate. The new provisions largely favor secured creditors over unsecured creditors, but both groups of creditors do better having the small business reorganize in Chapter 11 rather than liquidate in Chapter 7.

When the current Bankruptcy Code was enacted in 1978, some degree of relief existed for debtors with student loans. Today, absent unusual circumstances, most student loans are not dischargeable, in whole or in part, in bankruptcy. With the total amount of student loan debt now exceeding the total amount of credit card debt, the dischargeability of student loan debt in bankruptcy is likely to change in the not-too-distant future. As a matter of politics alone, the number of people with unmanageable student loan debt is so large that Congress will be called upon to provide some measure of student loan debt relief. Because student loan debt is largely guaranteed by the federal government, creditors holding student loan debt may have little economic incentive to oppose student loan debt relief. Federally guaranteed student loans will be paid regardless of whether the loans are discharged in bankruptcy.

Bankruptcy laws change not only over time, but also in their interpretation by different courts. The same bankruptcy laws are often subject to different interpretations by different bankruptcy judges around the country. Different interpretations of the same law can lead to different application and different results in different parts of the country, despite the supposed "uniformity" of bankruptcy laws.

For example, a divorced husband who was awarded 50% shared custody of his two biological children in his divorce and who has been living with his girlfriend for the last two years might be considered a "household" of four in some bankruptcy districts, a "household" of three in others, and a "household" of two in still other bankruptcy districts. Because qualification for Chapter 7 purposes depends, in part, upon a debtor's household income and household size, the difference in how courts interpret the meaning of the word "household" can result in some debtors qualifying for Chapter 7 and others not qualifying, even though the debtors' living situations are the same.

With that rudimentary overview of bankruptcy law under our belt, let's take a quick look at the main bankruptcy chapters for individuals and how to determine which chapter is best for you.

# CHAPTER 5

## Which Type Of Bankruptcy Is Best For You?

 INTRODUCTION

There are four types, or chapters, of bankruptcy that are available to individuals: — Chapter 7, Chapter 11, Chapter 12, and Chapter 13. (Please do not ask why three of four chapters were assigned numbers associated with gambling). By "individual," I mean a human being, not a business entity. For this purpose, an "individual" includes someone who operates a business as a sole proprietor, such as an individual who provides tutoring services.

If you operate a business inside a business entity that you own, such as an LLC, "S" corporation, or partnership, you can file bankruptcy as an individual. Just because you file as an individual does not mean that the entity must or should file bankruptcy. If it were to file, the entity would be required to file bankruptcy separately from the individual owner of the entity. Entity filings are another book.

The type of bankruptcy that is best for you will depend upon which chapter you qualify for and which chapter provides you with the greatest benefits. In some cases, there may not be a choice; only one chapter may be available. When a choice among chapters is available, that choice must be made based upon the specifics of your situation.

 CHAPTER 12 (FAMILY FARMERS AND FISHERMEN)

If you are engaged in farming or fishing, you could be eligible for Chapter 12. Chapter 12 was designed by lobbyists working primarily for family farmers and, to a lesser extent, by lobbyists working for fishermen, whose East Coast votes were needed to get the Midwest farmers their special bankruptcy. As far as I know, very few fishermen take advantage of Chapter 12.

Chapter 12 is like Chapter 13 in that the debtor must propose and confirm a plan, overseen by a trustee, pursuant to which some, but usually not all, of the debtor's outstanding unsecured debts are repaid, usually over five years. Chapter 12 has some important advantages over Chapter 13.

First, the debt limits are significantly higher in Chapter 12 than in Chapter 13. Currently, debtors in Chapter 13 may only have unsecured debts of approximately $420,000 and secured debts of approximately $1,250,000. In contrast, debtors in Chapter 12 can have total debt of approximately $10,000,000, but at least half of the debt must be related to the farm. If your total debt exceeds the debt limits, you are not eligible to file in the chapter. With higher debt limits, it is easier to qualify for Chapter 12 than Chapter 13.

Second, debtors can modify a mortgage on their principal residence in Chapter 12 but not in Chapter 13. In Chapter 12, a farmer with a farmhouse worth $500,000, subject to a $750,000 mortgage will be able to restructure the mortgage such that only $500,000 will be treated as secured and paid over up to 30 years at an interest rate that is likely to be much lower than the original rate of interest in the mortgage. The $250,000 unsecured portion of the $750,000 mortgage will be paid like credit card debt out of available income, usually over five years, but most of the unsecured debt will not be paid at all. The unpaid portion will be discharged at the end of the plan.

Third, farmers in Chapter 12 can structure payments around the cash flow of their farm. Farmers may have more available cash in some months, such as after a harvest, than in other months.

Fourth, there are significant tax benefits that are available to farmers who sell their farms during the term of their Chapter 12 plans that are not available in Chapter 13.

To be eligible for Chapter 12, you must be engaged in farming. If you are a full-time bankruptcy lawyer, you are not eligible for Chapter 12. But, if you derive at least a majority of your income from farming, you would be eligible to file in Chapter 12 even if you were also engaged in some other business as a sideline.

For example, if you were a full-time bankruptcy lawyer, but also had a little farm in the country that raised sorghum that you sold every Sunday at the local farmer's market, the percentage of your total income from farming likely would be below the majority threshold for Chapter 12 eligibility. On the other hand, if raising sorghum for sale at farmers' markets was where you derived the majority of your income and you merely dabbled in practicing bankruptcy law as a sideline, then you could be eligible for Chapter 12.

Ordinarily, if you were eligible for Chapter 12, that chapter would provide you with the greatest benefits. But not always. Perhaps you were tired of the hard work of farming and wanted to switch careers into something easier, like trading securities on Wall Street. In that case, you might prefer to eliminate your farming debts entirely and quickly, rather than paying some or all your debts back over time. Since you would be moving to Wall Street, you might not care about losing your farmland or farm assets.

Giving up the farmland and farm assets in exchange for being completely relieved of all your debt might be a great trade. The first great trade of your new career! In that case, based upon the specifics of that situation, Chapter 7 might be the better chapter to file in.

Chapter 12 is more streamlined than Chapter 11 and, accordingly, faster and cheaper. But, if your debts exceed the $10 million debt limit for Chapter 12 or if you face one unusually recalcitrant creditor, you might prefer to try to confirm a plan of reorganization over that creditor's objection in Chapter 11.

There could be situations in which the farm aspect of the reorganization was relatively unimportant. Chapter 13 might then be a faster and cheaper option than Chapter 12. If you are a farmer or fisherman, find a knowledgeable lawyer. I have never represented a farmer or fisherman. The law is so specialized that further discussion of Chapter 12 would be of little benefit to anyone who is not a farmer or fisherman. Sorry, farmers and fishermen. Shouldn't that be fisher-people?

 ## CHAPTER 11 (REORGANIZATIONS)

Chapter 11 is for transforming an unprofitable business into a profitable business. This is accomplished by allowing the business, under court supervision, to close unwanted business operations, to sell unwanted assets, and to terminate or restructure unfavorable leases and contracts. Secured debts generally can be restructured or renegotiated. Unsecured debts generally can be paid at a small percentage of what is owed, providing significant debt relief. Typically, the previous equity ownership is eliminated and either new equity owners provide new capital or previous debt holders are given new equity in exchange for their debt. By focusing on the profitable operations and by reducing the cash flow that previously went to servicing debts and paying creditors, the reorganized business can emerge from Chapter 11 poised for success.

Chapter 11 bankruptcies usually are managed by the debtors themselves. Debtors in Chapter 11 need to propose a bankruptcy "plan of reorganization" that identifies all of the operational and capital structure reorganizational steps the business proposes to make, and to have that proposed plan approved by the bankruptcy court and by the vote of the requisite number of creditors at a formal court hearing known as "confirmation."

Chapter 11 is primarily used by businesses, but it can also be used by individuals with high incomes and high debts. The need to obtain creditor approval and confirmation of a plan of reorganization by a bankruptcy judge generally makes Chapter 11 cases longer, more complicated and, consequently, more expensive, than the other types of bankruptcy cases.

For individuals with high incomes whose debt levels exceed the eligibility threshold for Chapter 13, currently a little under $420,000 for unsecured debts and a little over $1,250,000 for secured debts, Chapter 11 may be the only available option for obtaining debt relief while maintaining the business.

In my practice, I once filed a Chapter 11 case for a veterinarian whose practice had suffered a serious decline in revenue following a flood. The practice had been purchased a few years earlier entirely with borrowed funds. The assets of the practice, including cages, tables, lights, cabinets, and tools, "secured," that is, were collateral for, the loan used to purchase the practice. Following the flood, the value of the veterinary assets was significantly less than their value when the practice was purchased. The amount of debt the veterinarian was left with was impossible to pay with the base of customers remaining after the flood. Filing in Chapter 13 was not an option because the amount of debt the veterinarian owed exceeded the debt limits for Chapter 13.

For the veterinarian, filing in Chapter 11 had several benefits. The creditor that had loaned the veterinarian money to buy the practice was prevented from foreclosing, that is, taking away, the practice from the veterinarian due to non-payment of the debt. Under his Chapter 11 plan, the veterinarian was able to renegotiate the amount he owed that creditor down to an amount that more closely reflected the value of the assets after the flood and the ability of the veterinarian to pay given the lower number of customers. The veterinarian also received significant debt relief from unsecured creditors who were paid only a portion of what they were owed. The veterinarian was left paying some, but not all, his debts, which allowed him to continue practicing. Over time, all the creditors received more in Chapter 11 than they would have received had the veterinary practice been liquidated in Chapter 7.

For some individuals, filing bankruptcy in Chapter 11 may provide significant benefits even if no plan of reorganization is ultimately approved or, if approved, completed. One of my Chapter 11 filings was for a hotel developer who owned several hotel projects that were in various stages of development. One of the finished hotels had run into financial trouble and was unable to make mortgage payments. The bank that held the mortgage started a foreclosure action. In essence, the bank said, "You're not paying your debt, we're taking your hotel which is our collateral." Despite his financial difficulties, the developer believed that the finished hotel had the greatest potential for appreciation of all his hotel projects. What could the hotel developer do to save the "trophy" hotel property from being foreclosed?

Filing Chapter 11 stopped the hotel foreclosure and provided the developer with the opportunity to sell the hotel projects he was less interested in keeping, so that he could use the proceeds from their sale to pay the mortgage on the hotel he wanted to keep. Although that was the reason for filing the case and the focus of his plan of reorganization, the developer did not necessarily need to have a plan of reorganization confirmed by the bankruptcy court and approved by creditors to accomplish his goal. Stopping the foreclosure case and being able to continue operations in Chapter 11 provided the hotel developer with enough time to sell the unwanted hotel projects and become current on the delinquent hotel mortgage. Once that goal was accomplished, the Chapter 11 case could be dismissed.

The facts and circumstances surrounding the veterinarian and the hotel developer described above are unusual. Chapter 11 filings for individuals with small businesses are the exceptions, not the norm. The bankruptcy "deck" is stacked against individuals in Chapter 11. Interpretations of the law in many jurisdictions make it difficult and, therefore, unpredictable and costly, to confirm reorganizations plans for individuals.

It is also difficult and costly to operate a small business as a "debtor-in-possession" in Chapter 11. The business must open new "debtor-in-possession" bank accounts with new "DIP" checks. Monthly operating reports must be field with the bankruptcy court detailing the income, expenses, and operating results of the business. Those reports are available to the public. Preparing them requires accountants with bankruptcy reporting expertise, which small business accountants typically do not possess. Preparing the monthly operating report also requires a great deal of the small business owner's time that could otherwise be devoted to turning the business around.

There is great deal of legal work for a bankruptcy lawyer in Chapter 11 even after the case is filed. Depending upon the animosity of creditors and their willingness to oppose the reorganization, the bankruptcy lawyer may need to spend a considerable amount of time in court obtaining the bankruptcy court's permission to engage in what otherwise might have been routine business operations, such as using cash in the business's bank account. After the initial permissions have been obtained, the bankruptcy lawyer's focus turns to drafting a plan of reorganization, getting the creditors to vote in favor of the plan and the bankruptcy court to confirm the plan. All of that also requires a lot of time from the small business's owner.

The plan of reorganization establishes different classes of creditors depending upon the nature of their claims. It describes how each class of creditors will be treated and what each class will receive. To be confirmed by the court, the plan must be approved by a certain number of creditors and classes of creditors who vote on the plan. Deciding how to classify creditors and what to pay them based upon how they are expected to vote requires some strategy. The entire Chapter 11 process can be overwhelming for the accountants, lawyers, turnaround specialists and business managers of a Fortune 500 company. It is almost impossible for an individual owner of a small business. Many of the Chapter 11 bankruptcies that are filed for individuals with small business end up being converted to Chapter 7 bankruptcies.

If you find yourself in situations like the veterinarian or hotel developer described above, where filing Chapter 11 might offer some benefits, consult a bankruptcy attorney who is familiar with and willing to file cases for individuals in Chapter 11. There are not many.

## ❧ New Subchapter V

In 2019, Congress enacted The Small Business Reorganization Act (SBRA), which created a new subchapter within Chapter 11 to enable small businesses to reorganize in a faster, more cost-effective manner than "regular" Chapter 11.

To qualify, the debtor must have been engaged in business or commercial activities. Courts are divided as to whether the debtor must be operating when the case is filed. The original debt limit was $2.7 million, but that has been raised currently to $7.5 million. More than half of the debt must be from business or commercial activities. Debt owed by affiliated parties is included in the total debt. Debtors must elect Subchapter V treatment.

If elected, unlike "regular" Chapter 11, there is no creditors committee, there are no fees paid to the U.S. Trustee, it is easier for the business owner to retain ownership because there is no "absolute priority rule," reorganization plans move towards confirmation on an expedited basis, and it is easier to confirm a plan over the objection of an "unreasonable" unsecured creditor. The biggest benefit may be the ability to modify a mortgage on a home to the extent that proceeds of the mortgage were used in the debtor's business.

In Subchapter V, although the debtor is left in possession of assets and in control of the business, a trustee is appointed to oversee the case and monitor the debtor. The trustee is supposed to act as a "consultant" to the debtor, providing input as to the feasibility of the proposed reorganization plan and acting as a mediator to obtain the consent of creditors to the plan. In some cases, the trustee may make disbursements to creditors. The trustee's fees are paid by the debtor.

Subchapter V is new. The jury is still out as to whether small business debtors will prefer it to "regular" Chapter 11. My own guess is that Subchapter V will be useful in cases in which one or very few secured creditors have a keen interest in keeping the debtor in operation, instead of being liquidated in Chapter 7.

 CHAPTER 13

The way to think about Chapter 13 is that it is essentially a debt consolidation plan in which unsecured debts, such as credit card debts and medical debts, are paid back, usually not in full, generally over five years, but perhaps in as few as three years. Secured debts, such as car loans and home mortgages, generally are paid in full as they were prior to filing bankruptcy, although there are exceptions. Chapter 13 can offer some debt relief, particularly if the portion of the debtor's income that will go towards repaying creditors, known as "disposable income," is low.

As with non-bankruptcy debt consolidation, in Chapter 13 the debtor makes payments to creditors pursuant to an agreement, known as a "plan." Negotiations over how much will be paid to unsecured creditors in the plan are conducted primarily with a Chapter 13 Trustee and are based upon the debtor's projected "disposable income," an amount largely, but not entirely, determined under the Bankruptcy Code. The amount that unsecured creditors will receive in Chapter 13 is much more dependent upon the debtor's expected earnings than the amount of debt the debtor owes. The payment plan proposed by the debtor and negotiated with the Chapter 13 Trustee must be approved by a bankruptcy court judge in a judicial process known as "confirmation." Following confirmation, the judge will remain available to adjudicate any disputes that might arise during the term of the plan.

Monthly payments are made by the debtor to the Chapter 13 Trustee. In turn, the Chapter 13 Trustee makes monthly payments to the debtor's creditors. The Chapter 13 Trustee ensures that payments made by a debtor in Chapter 13 end up being received by creditors and that any debt remaining at the end of the payment plan that is not required to be paid under the plan is legally discharged. In contrast, debt consolidators cannot always be counted on to fulfill their end of a non-bankruptcy debt consolidation plan.

Another significant difference between Chapter 13 and a non-bankruptcy debt consolidation is that during the Chapter 13 case, creditors are prohibited from engaging in any collection activity. Creditors cannot call, send letters, or bring a lawsuit to collect a debt while the Chapter 13 case is in progress. That is quite different from a non-bankruptcy debt consolidation, during which creditors are not restrained from calling, sending letters, or bringing a lawsuit against a debtor.

So, if you are willing to pay creditors and have sufficient income or other funds to be able to pay creditors over time, Chapter 13, with its administration by a Chapter 13 Trustee subject to supervision by a bankruptcy court judge, is vastly superior to a non-bankruptcy debt consolidation plan.

## ❧ Eligibility

Not everyone can take advantage of Chapter 13. There are eligibility requirements. The first are debt limits. These are limits on the amount of debt you can have in two different categories of debts. If your total debts in either category exceed the debt limit for that category, you are ineligible to file in Chapter 13. Congress made a policy decision that debtors with high debts should be forced to file in Chapter 11 where creditors get to vote on the debtor's plan of reorganization and, accordingly, have more involvement in whether a debtor will receive debt relief. Unfortunately, Congress did not set the Chapter 13 debt limits in either category especially high.

The debt limit for the total amount of unsecured debts, including credit card debts, personal loans, medical debts, student loans, and income tax debts, currently is just under $420,000. The debt limit for the total amount of secured debts, including home mortgages and car loans, currently is limited to just over $1,250,000. If either your total unsecured debts or your total secured debts exceed their respective limits, you are not eligible to file in Chapter 13.

Admittedly, there may not be a lot of people with mortgages and car loans that total over $1,250,000. I do see prospective clients who own large homes in fancier towns in Connecticut with large mortgages who fail to qualify. Similarly, I also see prospective clients with $100,000 of credit card debts, which alone would be under the unsecured debt limit, but who also owe $150,000 in student loans, $50,000 in income taxes and $125,000 in alimony. They are over the unsecured debt limit and thus ineligible to file in Chapter 13. The debt limits described above are current debt limits. The limits adjust every three years with inflation.

The other important eligibility requirement is that to be a debtor in Chapter 13 you must have "regular income." If you have an unmanageable debt problem because you lost your job, filing Chapter 13 probably is not an option, at least not until you find a new job. Congress made a policy decision that people without regular income would not be able to fund a repayment plan.

## ❦ Advantages of Chapter 13 Over Chapter 7

Assuming the eligibility requirements for both chapters were met, under what circumstances would someone prefer Chapter 13 to Chapter 7? There are not many.

### Stop Foreclosure

The principal reason people file Chapter 13 is to stop foreclosure and save their house. When a home mortgage goes unpaid for six months or more, the mortgage lender, typically a bank, will begin a legal action in state court, known as a "foreclosure," to obtain legal ownership of the home. In some states, mediators are automatically appointed to work with the homeowner and the lender to modify the mortgage. By extending the term of the mortgage, that is, the number of years over which the mortgage is paid, the monthly mortgage payment can be reduced to an amount the homeowner can afford. If mediation fails and the mortgage otherwise cannot be modified, the lender typically will end up owning the home.

Since lenders are in the business of making loans and not owning homes, the lender will sell the home to recoup the money it is owed on the mortgage.

If the house is sold for more than what is owed, the homeowner will receive the excess. That almost never happens. Ordinarily, the house is sold for less than what is owed. In many states, the amount still owed on the mortgage becomes a "deficiency judgment" the homeowner will remain liable for. In many other states, mortgages are "non-recourse" and no deficiency judgment will arise. Many states do not have judicial foreclosures, so the simplified description above may not apply. Suffice to say, if a mortgage goes unpaid long enough, the lender will seek to obtain ownership of the house. Chapter 13 can be used to thwart that process.

Filing a bankruptcy case triggers the application of an "automatic stay" which "stays," that is, stops, all collection activity, including foreclosure. It does not matter when during a foreclosure case the bankruptcy case is filed. The bankruptcy case could be filed as soon as a notice of foreclosure is received. The bankruptcy case could be filed at any time during the foreclosure case. The bankruptcy case could even be filed after the foreclosure case had ended and the home was about to be auctioned off to the highest bidder on the courthouse steps (different states handle this process differently). Even at that extremely late stage, the filing of the bankruptcy case would stop the sale of the home, because every single event I have described is an action to collect a debt. The automatic stay stops all collection actions in their tracks.

It is important to notice that the filing of a bankruptcy case by itself stops the foreclosure. Nothing other than filing bankruptcy is required to stop the foreclosure. You do not need a bankruptcy lawyer to file a case. In the courts in which I practice, over half of the Chapter 13 cases are filed "pro se," that is, without a lawyer. The homeowner files a bankruptcy case in Chapter 13 to stop the foreclosure. But, stopping the foreclosure does not give the homeowner a free house. Once the bankruptcy case is filed and the foreclosure stopped, then what?

To keep a house facing foreclosure in Chapter 13, the homeowner must propose a plan that details how the homeowner intends to make current mortgage payments shortly after the case has been filed as well pay the arrearage, that is, the amount the homeowner owes for unpaid principal, interest, late fees, escrow, and legal fees incurred up to the time the bankruptcy case was filed. In other words, a homeowner can keep a home in Chapter 13 if the homeowner can make the current monthly mortgage payments shortly after the case is filed and can repay the old amount owed on the mortgage over time, usually over five years.

In some bankruptcy courts, the debtor may have the opportunity to modify the mortgage in Chapter 13, but that generally requires the cooperation of the mortgage lender. Bankruptcy judges can be very persuasive, but if the mortgage lender refuses to extend the term of the mortgage to reduce the monthly mortgage payment or is convinced the homeowner still lacks the income to make the proposed reduced monthly payment amount, it may not be possible to modify the mortgage.

Chapter 13 is a better bankruptcy option than Chapter 7 for stopping a foreclosure and saving a house, because only Chapter 13 provides the mechanism for the homeowner to catch up on the mortgage arrearage over time. Filing a case in Chapter 7 would trigger the application of the automatic stay, which would immediately stop the foreclosure, just as it would in Chapter 13. However, because there is no plan pursuant to which the mortgage lender would be paid the arrearage it is owed in Chapter 7, the mortgage lender could ask the bankruptcy court to terminate the automatic stay. Generally, debtors have no "cause" for opposing the termination of the automatic stay. The debtor owes the arrearage and cannot repay it. Once the bankruptcy court "lifts," that is, terminates, the automatic stay, the mortgage lender can return to state court and restart the foreclosure case. Often, a mortgage lender will choose not to ask the bankruptcy court to "lift" the automatic stay. Most Chapter 7 cases are completed within four months of filing. Once the Chapter 7 case ends, the automatic stay also ends. The mortgage lender then can return to state court to restart the foreclosure case. Instead of asking the bankruptcy court to lift the automatic stay, the lender can wait for the automatic stay to terminate on its own when the bankruptcy case ends in four months. So, filing Chapter 7 can stop a foreclosure case, but generally not for very long.

If your goal is to stop foreclosure, you can achieve a longer stop in Chapter 13. This does not mean that every homeowner is successful in Chapter 13. Very few of the "pro se" debtors mentioned above ultimately are successful in proposing, confirming, and completing a plan that repays the mortgage lender the arrearage it is owed. But, the process during which all of this takes place can last six months or twelve months or longer. During that time, the foreclosure is stopped. As a result, Chapter 13 can be an effective tool for postponing foreclosure even if it is an unsuccessful tool for repaying the arrearage and keeping the home.

*Is "Saving" A Home A Good Idea?*

A question rarely asked is whether using Chapter 13 as a tool to postpone foreclosure is a good idea. Is postponing foreclosure really in the best interest of the homeowner? Both states in which I practice, Connecticut and New York, offer mandatory mediation to every homeowner against whom a foreclosure case is brought. Typically, the mediator will try to tack the entire arrearage onto the outstanding principal balance of the mortgage and re-amortized the new balance over as long a period as possible, usually 30 years. If that reduced monthly payment of interest and principal still exceeds what the homeowner can pay, usually about 40% of gross income, then the homeowner cannot afford the home.

In states without mandatory mediation where Chapter 13 is used as the mortgage modification forum, filing Chapter 13 still may not be necessary to modify a mortgage. The last thing a mortgage lender wants is a non-performing mortgage loan on its books and another house in its inventory of foreclosed homes. Every additional home a mortgage lender takes into inventory is another home that will hit the market at a depressed price further reducing the value of every other repossessed home the mortgage lender is trying to dispose of.

Some homeowners may read that last paragraph with incredulity. They honestly believe that Wells Fargo is doing everything it possibly can to take their house away from them. I beg to differ. Wells Fargo may be greedy. Wells Fargo may be evil. But Snidely Whiplash no longer runs the mortgage workout department at Wells Fargo. A computer program makes the decisions now. The computer program does not want to take away your house. Wells Fargo would prefer to have a valuable asset, a performing loan, on its books than a liability, a non-performing loan and a house that will cost Wells Fargo even more money to maintain and dispose of. If Wells Fargo can be convinced that the homeowner has a high enough gross income such that 40% of it can go towards debt service, Wells Fargo will refinance the mortgage without having to resort to Chapter 13.

Obviously, Wells Fargo was merely being used as an example of a mortgage lender in the previous paragraph. I have nothing against Wells Fargo. My office is located next to a Wells Fargo branch and I occasionally use notaries who work for Wells Fargo. Wells Fargo, please don't cut them off.

"Saving" a house is not always in the economic best interest of the homeowner. A homeowner with significant equity in a house who falls behind on the mortgage can sell the house, pay off the entire amount owed and keep the remaining equity. No one needs Chapter 13 to accomplish the sale of a house with equity. The houses being "saved" in Chapter 13 are the houses that are "underwater," that is, the amount owed on the mortgage or mortgages exceeds the value of the house. Homeowners cannot sell those houses. If the homeowner could sell the house via a "short sale," there would be no proceeds left for the homeowner. In most cases, after the short sale, the former homeowner would end up paying more money to rent the same amount of space. Thus, the need to "save" the house.

Here's an illustration: Homeowner owns a house worth $100,000. The total amount owed on the mortgage, including unpaid principal, interest, late fees, escrow for real estate taxes, and legal fees for collection, is $120,000. Of the $120,000 total amount owed, $20,000 has not been paid in the last twelve months and is "in arrears." The $120,000 owed on the house exceeds the $100,000 value of the house by $20,0000. The homeowner cannot sell that house and retain any of the proceeds. All the $100,000 proceeds would go to the mortgage lender, assuming the lender agreed to a "short sale." It is called a "short sale," because the proceeds of the sale are "short" of what is owed the mortgage lender.

If the current mortgage payment is $2,000/month and the cost of renting similar space is $2,250/month, you can see why the homeowner would want to save the house. He "saves" $250/month by "saving" his house. So, to save his house, the homeowner files a Chapter 13 bankruptcy case. Foreclosure immediately stops. In his Chapter 13 plan, the homeowner proposes to start making the $2,000 monthly mortgage payments shortly after filing and he proposes to pay the $20,000 arrearage in 60 equal monthly installments over five years. Great deal, right? Save the house, save monthly expenses? Well, not so much. Let's do the math.

The homeowner ends up making a monthly payment of $2,333, comprised of the $2,000 current monthly mortgage payment plus $333, the monthly portion of the $20,000 arrearage over 60 months ($20,000/60 = $333). The homeowner is paying $2,333/month to the mortgage lender in Chapter 13 instead of $2,250 in rent for a new house. The monthly mortgage payment exceeds the monthly rent payment by $83/month.

Paying $83/month extra is not a good thing, but at the end of 5 years he will own the house. That's a good thing, right? Not so much. He will own a $100,000 house, but he will own a $100,000 house for which he has paid $120,000. Here is what I ask every prospective client facing the same situation, "Would you pay $120,000 today for your $100,000 house?" Not a single prospective client has answered 'yes' to that question. So, why would I put you into Chapter 13 plan where you will pay $120,000 to "save" your $100,000 house? It makes no economic sense to pay $120,000 for a house worth $100,000. It makes no economic sense to pay more for a house than the house is worth.

In my opinion, and it is by far a minority opinion among bankruptcy attorneys, keeping a homeowner in a home he or she cannot afford is not doing the homeowner a favor. If the homeowner could not afford the monthly mortgage payment prior to filing Chapter 13, how exactly is the homeowner going to be able to afford the monthly mortgage payment plus the monthly arrearage payment in Chapter 13? Even if the mortgage is modified in Chapter 13 and the monthly mortgage payment is reduced, if the new monthly mortgage payment plus the monthly arrearage payment is a stretch for the homeowner to afford, how exactly will the homeowner be able to afford the considerable regular maintenance and capital expenditures a home requires? How will the homeowner by able to pay to replace the roof and the boiler when those repairs are required? "Saving" a home may not be a great reason for preferring Chapter 13 over Chapter 7 after all.

### Keep Nonexempt Property

The other major reason Chapter 13 is often preferred over Chapter 7, assuming the debtor qualifies for both, is that Chapter 13 imposes no limits on what property a debtor may keep. As described in more detail later, debtors in Chapter 7 receive complete relief from most unsecured debts, but they are limited in what property they can keep. Chapter 13 can be a better "deal" if the amount of property that cannot be kept in Chapter 7 is unacceptably high.

The items of property that can be kept are listed as "exemptions," that is, exempt from the clutches of evil creditors. Every state has a list of property that is exempt from creditors. The same list of exemptions that protects property against seizure by a creditor with a judgment from a state collection lawsuit applies to protect property of a debtor in bankruptcy from a Chapter 7 Trustee appointed to represent and distribute property among creditors. In addition, currently 19 states and the District of Columbia also offer debtors in bankruptcy the option to choose between the better of their state exemptions and the federal bankruptcy exemptions.

Most states allow their residents to keep enough assets to get a fresh start. Some states, like Texas and Florida, have very generous exemptions to protect houses, known as "homestead" exemptions. Other states, like Alabama and New Jersey, are less generous with their homestead exemptions. If you own a house in Alabama or New Jersey with $75,000 of equity you will not be able to keep it in Chapter 7. The Chapter 7 Trustee will sell the house, pay you the amount of the homestead exemption you are entitled to and, after paying himself some fees, distribute the remainder to your creditors.

If you don't like that "deal" in Chapter 7 and you want to keep the house in New Jersey with $75,000 in equity, you must file bankruptcy in Chapter 13 (or, perhaps, Chapter 11). But, filing in Chapter 13 can be costly. The amount you must pay creditors in Chapter 13 generally is the greater of two amounts. The first amount is your "disposable income." The second amount is the value of nonexempt property you are seeking to keep. The idea is that you can keep 100% of your assets, but if your creditors would have received proceeds from the sale of those assets in Chapter 7, then you must pay creditors at least that much in Chapter 13. You get to keep the assets, but you must pay creditors for them, unless your "disposable income" is higher. If your "disposable income" is higher than the value of your nonexempt assets, then you have to pay creditors your "disposable income." That's win-win for the creditors.

Continuing with the illustration above, assume that the available homestead exemption in New Jersey is $25,000. That means you can keep a house with $25,000 of equity. If the house equity exceeds $25,000, then you get to keep $25,000 of the proceeds from the sale of the house by the Chapter 7 Trustee. You can only keep $25,000 of house equity. In Chapter 7, the Chapter 7 Trustee would sell the house with $75,000 of equity, pay you your $25,000 homestead exemption and pay your creditors $50,000 (ignoring fees). If your house has $75,000 of equity, you likely would prefer to keep the house by filing Chapter 13 instead of Chapter 7.

To keep your New Jersey house with $75,000 of equity, of which $50,000 was not exempt, you would have to pay creditors in Chapter 13 the greater of $50,000 or your "disposable income." If your "disposable income" was $5,000/year for a total of $25,000 over the five-year term of your Chapter 13 plan, then the $50,000 of nonexempt house equity would exceed the $25,000 of "disposable income." Your Chapter 13 plan would call for you to pay creditors $10,000/year for five years. On the other hand, if your "disposable income" was $15,000/year for a total of $75,000 over the five-year term of your Chapter 13 plan, then the $75,000 of "disposable income" would exceed the $50,000 of nonexempt house equity. Your Chapter 13 plan would call for you to pay creditors $15,000/year for five years.

Assuming your "disposable income" was the lower $5,000/year for a total of $25,000 and you had to pay creditors the greater amount, the $50,000 of nonexempt equity, you would need to pay creditors $50,000 over five years to keep your house in New Jersey in Chapter 13. Chapter 13 might be better than Chapter 7, but the next question is whether filing bankruptcy makes sense at all. To answer that question, you would need to compare the cost $50,000 (plus fees) to the benefit – how much debt relief are you getting in Chapter 13?

For example, if your total credit card debt was $150,000, filing bankruptcy in Chapter 13 would make sense. In effect, you would be paying creditors $50,000 over five years to "settle" $150,000 of debt. Settling $150,000 of credit card debt for $50,000 is a rather good deal and it is a deal that you are assured will come to fruition, provided you keep your end of the bargain by making payments for 60 months, because the Chapter 13 plan is supervised by the bankruptcy court. At the end of 60 months, the $100,000 unpaid credit card debt would be discharged. And you keep your house.

On the other hand, if your total credit card debt was only $75,000, filing bankruptcy in Chapter 13 might not make sense, because you generally can negotiate a credit card debt settlement for 50% of what is owed outside of bankruptcy. It makes no sense to pay $50,000 to creditors in Chapter 13 if you could negotiate a debt settlement for $37,500 outside of bankruptcy.

The other issue with Chapter 13 in this example is funding the plan. Assuming your "disposable income" was $5,000/year but the plan called for $10,000/year in payments to creditors, you would have to find a way to fund the incremental $5,000/year.

*Can You Keep "Luxury" Assets?*

Chapter 13 allows debtors to keep nonexempt assets, but it may not allow debtors to keep all nonexempt assets. Most Chapter 13 Trustees and most bankruptcy judges do not look favorably upon Chapter 13 plans that propose to pay creditors less than 100% of what they are owed while allowing the debtor to keep "luxury" assets. For example, no state that I am aware of has an exemption that would protect a valuable speed boat, certainly not above a small "wildcard exemption." A valuable speed boat would be a nonexempt asset. Although debtors are normally allowed to keep nonexempt assets if creditors are paid at least the value of those nonexempt assets in Chapter 13, most Chapter 13 Trustees and judges would consider it "abusive" for the debtor to retain ownership of a speed boat while not paying their unsecured debts in full and, as a result, would refuse to allow confirmation of the debtor's Chapter 13 plan. If you want to keep a luxury asset, that is, an asset not generally recognized as being needed for a "fresh start," your Chapter 13 plan will have to propose paying creditors either 100% of what they are owed or, in addition to whatever "disposable income" may be required, the full nonexempt value of the luxury asset. Fair is fair.

Notice that when I say a debtor will be required to pay 100% of his debts, the debtor will not just be paying 100% of his debts in Chapter 13. He will also be paying the Chapter 13 Trustee a statutory fee for her services, which can be as high as 10% of the payments the Trustee makes to creditors, but more often comes in around 6% to 7%. The Chapter 13 debtor will also be paying a fee to a bankruptcy lawyer. So, being in Chapter 13 and paying 100% to creditors costs a lot more than the total of 100% of the debts. If you had the ability to pay 100% of your debts, why would you ever choose to pay more than 100% of your debts in Chapter 13?

Indeed economically, the breakpoint is much lower than 100% of your debts. Most credit card debt can be settled for 50 cents on the dollar. If you negotiate hard, you might be able to get a credit card issuer to accept as little as 33 cents on the dollar. The advice given in most debt negotiation books on this subject is to "Offer one-third, settle for one-half." When you add on Chapter 13 Trustee and bankruptcy lawyer fees, Chapter 13 looks like a bad economic deal unless your Chapter 13 plan discharges at least 2/3 of your unpaid debts. Yes, you would need cash to settle those debts for 50% or less outside of bankruptcy, but, if you can manage the debt negotiation process, you likely will achieve a better economic result than you would in Chapter 13.

Connecticut has among the highest median household incomes of any state. The current median income for a household of four is over $130,000. What tends to happen in my practice is that prospective clients who earn more than the median income do not earn just a little over median income. They tend to earn a lot over median income. In other words, these prospective clients are not making $135,000/year. They are making $200,000/year and are still unable to pay their debts. As a result of being significantly over median income, the "disposable income" they would be required to pay creditors in Chapter 13 would be enough to repay 100% of what they owe. Most of the prospective clients I see who fail to qualify for Chapter 7 by being over median would end up paying more to creditors in Chapter 13 than they would to settle the debts outside of bankruptcy. When I explain the economics to these prospective clients, very few are still interested in filing in Chapter 13. I end up talking myself out of a lot of bankruptcy clients.

Nonetheless, there are a few situations in which someone who qualified for Chapter 7 and who could settle his or her unsecured debts for around 50% of what was owed outside of bankruptcy might still find some advantage in Chapter 13. Those situations do not apply to many people. I will cover them briefly.

### Mortgage "Strip Offs"

In Chapter 13, but not in Chapter 7 or Chapter 11, it is possible to eliminate, technically, "strip off," a wholly unsecured second mortgage from a house. Let's unpack that. Second mortgages, generally home equity lines of credit ("HELOCs"), are "secured," that is, the house is given by the homeowner as collateral for the loan. But, over time, the value of the house may have declined to the point where the value of the house is only sufficient to cover just the balance of the first mortgage, leaving the second mortgage without any collateral supporting it, that is, "unsecured."

Here's an example: The Smiths bought a house in 2005 for $300,000 with a standard 30-year, self-amortizing mortgage (the first mortgage). In 2010, the house had appreciated in value to $375,000. To pay to remodel the house in 2010, the Smiths borrowed an additional $50,000 with a HELOC (the second mortgage). In 2018, the main employer in town moved its operations to China. Local home values collapsed. Mr. Smith lost his job. Currently, the house is worth $250,00 and has two mortgage liens: the first mortgage lien with $275,000 still outstanding and the second mortgage (HELOC) lien with $45,000 still outstanding. Although the house has two mortgage liens securing two mortgages, because the $275,000 owed on the first mortgage exceeds the $250,000 value of the house, there is no collateral value to support the HELOC. In foreclosure, the house would be sold for $250,000. All the proceeds would go to the first mortgage (ignoring transaction costs). The HELOC would get nothing. The HELOC is thus wholly unsecured and totally "out of the money."

In Chapter 13, a wholly unsecured second mortgage lien can be "stripped off" the property records. The gigantic windfall the Smiths would receive is that after the completion of their Chapter 13 plan, the Smiths would own a home with only one mortgage. The unpaid portion of the HELOC would be discharged. The HELOC lien would be removed from the property records. The Smiths could thereafter sell the house and keep all the proceeds of the sale after repaying the then-outstanding balance of the first mortgage. The house might be worth $500,000 in 2030. The Smiths would pay off the say $175,000 owed at that time on the first mortgage and keep the remaining $325,000 (ignoring transaction costs). The HELOC would get nothing.

Again, this bankruptcy magic only works if the HELOC is wholly unsecured. If the house were worth $1 more than the outstanding balance on the first mortgage, then the HELOC would be secured by that $1 of collateral value. With even $1 of collateral value securing it, the HELOC would not be "wholly unsecured" and could not be "stripped off."

Sounds amazing, doesn't it? The Smiths get to keep their house free of a second mortgage. Like many things that sound too good to be true, this panacea does not always pan out. The HELOC does not just disappear. The amount owed on the HELOC gets added to the unsecured debt the Smiths owe. So, their unsecured debt just increased by $45,000. If the Smiths have little "disposable income," the extra unsecured debt may not matter. In Chapter 13, the amount that is paid to unsecured creditors is the greater of nonexempt assets or "disposable income." As long as the Smiths' other unsecured debts already exceed that amount, the addition of $45,000 in unsecured HELOC debt makes no difference to the Smiths. The amount the Smiths will have to pay unsecured creditors will not increase as a result of adding the $45,000 HELOC debt to their unsecured debts. On the other hand, if the Smiths have few other unsecured debts and their "disposable income" exceeds $45,000, then the $45,000 HELOC debt will be paid as an unsecured debt over the five-year term of the Chapter 13 plan. So, stripping off a wholly unsecured second mortgage only makes economic sense if you have extremely low "disposable income" and few nonexempt assets. Otherwise, you could be worse off in Chapter 13. Outside of Chapter 13, you would have more than five years to pay off the HELOC.

And there is one other catch. To strip off the wholly unsecured HELOC in Chapter 13, the Smiths must complete their Chapter 13 plan. The Smiths must make all payments to creditors that are required under the plan. If the Smiths fail to make mortgage payments on the first mortgage and plan payments to all the unsecured creditors, then the Smiths will not complete their Chapter 13 plan, they will not receive a discharge and the HELOC lien will not be stripped off. Remember, the Smiths have a house with a wholly unsecured mortgage because Mr. Smith lost his job when his employer closed shop and moved operations to China. What is the likelihood that the Smiths will have sufficient income to make all their required plan payments over five years? Statistically, not very high. Nationwide, the estimate is that over 80% of Chapter 13 plans fail. Not just Chapter 13 plans with lien strip offs. All Chapter 13 plans. 80% fail. That is a rate of failure almost unknown in any other form of human endeavor. Indeed, the failure rate is so gigantically high that one could (and should) ponder why Congress does not eliminate Chapter 13 entirely.

### Car Loan "Cram Downs"

Like the magic of "stripping off" a wholly unsecured second mortgage lien, Chapter 13 can be used to "cram down," that is, to reduce, the amount of a car loan under certain circumstances. The notion behind this procedure is that if the value of the car has declined below the amount owed on the car loan, then the amount of the loan should be reduced to match the value of the car. Cram downs are allowed for all vehicles purchased more than 310 days (2-1/2 years) prior to the Chapter 13 bankruptcy filing. For vehicles purchased less than 310 days prior to the Chapter 13 bankruptcy filing, cram downs are allowed unless the loan is secured by a "purchase money security interest" in a motor vehicle acquired for the debtor's personal use. So, you can always cram down a refinancing, such as an auto title loan, or vehicles purchased for business use, or vehicles with "cross collateralized" loans. Chapter 13 can be used strategically to modify an underwater car or truck loan with a very high interest rate into a loan that can be paid in smaller monthly payments, at a lower interest rate, perhaps over a longer period of time, thus saving thousands of dollars. That is a very good reason for choosing Chapter 13.

Assuming the vehicle and the loan meet the eligibility requirements, the "cram down" process works as follows. The total outstanding balance of the vehicle loan is divided, like Gaul, into two parts: a secured part and an unsecured part. The amount of the secured part is the value of the vehicle when the Chapter 13 case is filed. Determination of value often is a mysterious and inscrutable process. For this purpose, the value of the vehicle is approximately what that vehicle would sell for in a car retailer's show room, which is higher than Kelly Blue Book trade-in value. The amount of the unsecured part is the difference between what was owed and the secured part. The secured part of the amount owed is paid over the term of the Chapter 13 plan (generally five years) with interest, also calculated pursuant to an inscrutable and mysterious bankruptcy process that generally works out to be a much lower rate than the interest rate built into the original vehicle loan. Advantage debtor. The unsecured part of the amount owed is lumped in with all the debtor's other unsecured debt and paid over the term of the plan based upon the debtor's "disposable income." As was the case with the "stripped off" mortgage, this only makes economic sense if the disposable income being paid to creditors is a small fraction of the unsecured debt that is owed. If the Chapter 13 plan calls for the payment of 100% of unsecured debts, then the same amount of vehicle loan will be paid, plus a fee to the Chapter 13 Trustee and a fee to the bankruptcy lawyer. Again, the "cram down" is only successfully executed if all the payments required to be made under the plan are made. Statistically, completion of all plan payments is unlikely to occur.

Here's an example: The Smiths bought a new Toyota Corolla on January 2, 2018, trading in their old Honda Civic and taking on a new loan from Toyota. On December 20, 2020, the Smiths filed a Chapter 13 bankruptcy. The car was then worth $17,000 but they owed $25,000 on the car loan which still had three years left. The car loan amount seems high, probably because the Smiths "rolled in" to the new Toyota Corolla loan the outstanding balance of the old Honda Civic loan which likely exceeded the trade-in value of the Civic. When the Chapter 13 case was filed, the Toyota Corolla had been owned by the Smiths for more than 310 days, so the car loan was eligible for "cram down." Under their Chapter 13 plan, the Smiths proposed to pay the secured portion of the car loan ($17,000, the value of the car) over five years (instead of the three remaining on the car loan) at a bankruptcy interest rate of 6% (instead of the 18% interest rate in the car loan). As a result, the proposed Chapter 13 car loan payments were much more affordable than the Corolla loan payments. The remaining $8,000 unsecured portion of the Corolla loan ($25,000 - $17,000) was lumped in with the Smith's $80,000 credit debt and $32,000 medical debt. The total $120,000 of unsecured debt would be paid over the five-year term of the plan. Based on the Smiths' $10,000 of "disposable income," after paying their secured debts, the amount the Smiths would pay to unsecured creditors was minimal. The car loan "cram down" will work out very well for the Smiths assuming they can complete all their plan payments.

### *Differences In Dischargeability*

Another reason to prefer Chapter 13 to Chapter 7 is that certain debts are not dischargeable in Chapter 7 but are dischargeable in Chapter 13. There are very few of those kinds of debts. The most significant is a debt for a property obligation that arose during a divorce. This does not include alimony or child support. The obligation to pay alimony or child support is not dischargeable in any kind of bankruptcy. Congress hates deadbeat dads. But, if, for example, a car had been jointly owned during a marriage and one ex-spouse was awarded ownership of the car in exchange for paying the other ex-spouse $1,000, that $1,000 property obligation could be discharged in a Chapter 13 case, but not in a Chapter 7 case. For the most part, knowledgeable divorce attorneys do not allow this opportunity to arise. They craft divorce agreements with every obligation deemed to be non-dischargeable support obligations and not dischargeable property obligations. It bears repeating that to have the property obligation discharged in Chapter 13, the Chapter 13 plan must be completed, and a discharge of unpaid debts must be received.

### *Longer Application Of The Automatic Stay*

Besides alimony and child support, there are a few other debts that are not dischargeable in either Chapter 13 and Chapter 7, including recent income tax obligations and student loans. Under certain circumstances, despite those debts being non-dischargeable, it might be beneficial to choose to file Chapter 13 to pay the non-dischargeable debts in a Chapter 13 plan.

For example, a debtor who was being persecuted by collectors for a non-dischargeable student loan debt might choose to file Chapter 13 to trigger the application of the automatic stay to stop those collection efforts. The debtor's Chapter 13 plan would propose to pay as much on the student loans as the debtor's "disposable income" allowed. If that amount was less than what the student loan collectors wanted, too bad for the student loan collectors. By using Chapter 13, the debtor could keep his student loan collectors at bay. They would be prevented from calling, writing, or suing to collect the debt. Unfortunately, that respite would be temporary. At the end of the Chapter 13 plan, the collection efforts would restart. If the Chapter 13 plan payments were small, the debtor might owe more in student loans after the conclusion of the Chapter 13 plan than he owed before. What does the debtor do then? File another Chapter 13 case.

### *"Co-debtor Stay"*

Unlike Chapter 7, Chapter 13 has a "co-debtor stay" which extends the automatic stay to prevent collection efforts against someone else who was also liable for a debt during the term of the Chapter 13 case.

For example, parents are often called upon to co-sign or guarantee a car loan for a child, usually to obtain a better rate of interest on the car loan than the child could obtain on its own. Parents are co-debtors on those car loans. If the car loan was not paid, the lender could attempt to collect against the child and against the parent who co-signed or guaranteed the car loan. If the car loan was not paid and the child filed Chapter 7, the child's obligation would be discharged, but the parent would still be liable for the car loan (unless the parent also filed Chapter 7). If the car loan was not paid and the child filed Chapter 13, the car lender would be prohibiting from trying to collect the car loan from the child and the parent during the term of the Chapter 13 case. The co-debtor stay of Chapter 13 gives the parent a break from collection efforts during the child's Chapter 13 case. However, once the child's Chapter 13 case ends, the car lender could pursue collection against the parent for any unpaid portion of the car loan, even if the unpaid portion had been discharged (or crammed down!) in the child's Chapter 13 case.

### *Ease Of Dismissal And Conversion*

There may be strategic reasons to file a case in Chapter 13 knowing that the case might be dismissed or converted later to Chapter 7. It is quite easy in most jurisdictions to dismiss a Chapter 13 case after it has been filed. In contrast, it is difficult and often impossible to dismiss a Chapter 7 case once it has been filed. Similarly, it is quite easy in most jurisdictions to convert a Chapter 13 case to a Chapter 7 case, but much more difficult, and often impossible, to convert a Chapter 7 case to a Chapter 13 case.

As a result, there could be circumstances in which a bankruptcy case needed to be filed quickly, say to implement the "automatic stay" to stop a collection lawsuit or to stop a wage garnishment, but there were still certain "unknowns" at the time, such as the valuation of particular assets or whether particular exemptions might apply. The "unknowns" could make it impossible to know which bankruptcy chapter would be better at the time the case needed to be filed. Chapter 13 gives the debtor more options. Filing in Chapter 13 would implement the automatic stay and stop the lawsuit or garnishment. If it became clear later that Chapter 7 was the better option, the case could then be converted to Chapter 7 simply and easily. In contrast, if the case were filed in Chapter 7 assuming a low asset valuation or available exemption that later turned out to be wrong, the debtor likely would be unable to convert the Chapter 7 case to Chapter 13. In Chapter 7, the asset might be lost. Moral of the story: when in doubt, file in Chapter 13.

### *Legal Fee Payment Flexibility*

Some bankruptcy attorneys prefer to file all their bankruptcy cases in Chapter 13 and later choose the better option. Another advantage of filing in Chapter 13 is that the client can pay the attorney's fees over time. With a few regional exceptions, Chapter 7 legal fees must be paid before the Chapter 7 case is filed. For clients who cannot afford to pay for Chapter 7 in advance, filing in Chapter 13 provides immediate protection from creditors, an opportunity to pay over time, and the flexibility to convert to Chapter 7 if Chapter 7 turns out to be the better option. Deferred payments may be easier for the client to make than up-front payments, but deferred payments come at a price. Attorney fees for Chapter 13 cases are higher than attorney fees for Chapter 7 cases. It is not unusual for bankruptcy attorneys to charge twice as much for Chapter 13 cases than Chapter 7 cases.

### Credit Reports

The final reason often cited for preferring Chapter 13 over Chapter 7 is that credit reports will contain a footnote indicating a Chapter 13 filing for a period of seven years, as opposed to ten years for a Chapter 7 filing. Since the footnote does not factor into the calculation of the credit score, that three-year difference is, in my opinion, immaterial.

## Advantages Of Chapter 7 Over Chapter 13

### Speed

Unless a prospective client presents the relatively limited set of special circumstances outlined above, my practice is always to prefer Chapter 7 to Chapter 13. The principal reason is speed. The typical length of a well-prepared bankruptcy case in Chapter 7 from filing the case to receiving a discharge in the jurisdictions in which I practice is approximately three months. Add to that another month of "homework" -- collecting and preparing information to be disclosed in the bankruptcy paperwork, known as a "petition." In as little as four months, a typical client can go from struggling with unmanageable debt to getting a fresh start. Why would anyone choose to spend a minimum of three years and possibly as long as six years, between preparation, confirmation, and completion of plan payments, in Chapter 13 when they could have their lives back in less than four months in Chapter 7? There are other reasons to be wary of Chapter 13.

### Sooner Access To Credit

During the period of time someone is in Chapter 13, they may have limited access to credit. Credit card issuers tend to turn their cards off, because debt incurred during the Chapter 13 case could be discharged if the debtor later converts the Chapter 13 case to a Chapter 7 case. Getting access to secured debt may also be a problem. For example, if the debtor needs a new car during the term of the Chapter 13 case, the new car loan will need to be approved by the Chapter 13 Trustee and, in some jurisdictions, by the bankruptcy court judge as well. Selling a house encumbered by a mortgage to move to a new job in a new jurisdiction can be a huge undertaking for someone in Chapter 13.

### Future Gains Do Not Go To Creditors

The amount paid to creditors in Chapter 13 generally is based upon a debtor's "disposable income" at the time the case is filed. The Chapter 13 plan will treat the amount to be paid to creditors as fixed during the term of the plan. But, what happens if the debtor performs his job well and gets a raise or a substantial bonus during the term of the plan? Who gets the benefit of the increase in income? Unfortunately for the debtor, if the debtor's gross income and, therefore, the debtor's "disposable income" goes up significantly during the term of the plan, it is possible that the Chapter 13 Trustee or an unsecured creditor could ask the bankruptcy court to increase plan payments to unsecured creditors. Similarly, if assets are inherited by the debtor during the term of the plan, that inheritance may have to go to pay unsecured creditors as well. Heads, the creditors win. Tails, the debtor loses. Why would anyone choose to risk losing future financial gains in Chapter 13?

### *Student Loan Accrual Problem*

As briefly mentioned above, Chapter 13 can provide a haven for debtors struggling with student loan collection efforts, because the application of the automatic stay when the Chapter 13 case is filed brings collection efforts to a halt. All collection efforts are prevented as long the debtor is in Chapter 13. However, even though collections efforts cease, the running of interest on the student loan continues. The ticking time bomb of accrued but unpaid interest may leave the debtor worse off at the end of the Chapter 13 case than at the beginning.

Here's how. Student loan debt is non-dischargeable, but, unlike most other types of non-dischargeable debts in Chapter 13, student loan debt has no priority of payment. In contrast, a Chapter 13 debtor with recent tax or alimony debts would pay those non-dischargeable debts before paying any credit card debts. Student loan debt is paid to the same extent that other unsecured debts, such as credit card debts, are paid. If the debtor's "disposable income" is low and only a small percentage of unsecured debts are paid in the debtor's Chapter 13 plan (and why else would the debtor be in Chapter 13 to begin with?), then only a small percentage of the student loan debt would be paid as well.

For example, if only 2% of credit card debts are paid in the debtor's Chapter 13 plan, then only 2% of student loan debt are paid. At the end of the Chapter 13 case, all unpaid credit card debt will be discharged. It does not matter how much unpaid credit card debt remains. In this example, the 98% of credit card debt remaining at the successful conclusion of the Chapter 13 payment plan will be discharged. But, student loan debt is not dischargeable. The 98% of student loan debt remaining at the successful conclusion of the Chapter 13 payment plan will not be discharged. It will remain due and payable. Even worse, the 98% unpaid portion of the student loan debt will have accrued interest during the term of the Chapter 13 case.

Here's a rough approximation of the math: a student loan debt of $50,000 with $400/month payments prior to bankruptcy, might only be paid $8/month (2%) in the Chapter 13 plan. That leaves the debtor with an additional $392/month the debtor can spend on food, clothing, and shelter. That's great. But, the $392/month that is not being paid on the student loan debt continues to accrue interest. At the end of a five-year Chapter 13 plan, the debtor might owe $60,000, which is $10,000 more student loan debt than the debtor owed before filing bankruptcy. Unless Congress changes the law, there may be no alternative for that debtor to avoid collection efforts once the Chapter 13 case ends but to file another Chapter 13 case again as quickly as possible.

 CHAPTER 7

Chapter 7 is by far the fastest, easiest, and cheapest bankruptcy option. As a result, Chapter 7 is the most popular choice. Sometimes referred to as "straight bankruptcy" or "liquidation," Chapter 7 is what most people mean or think of when they refer to bankruptcy.

The "deal" in Chapter 7 is that you get to "discharge," that is, eliminate, your liability for paying, most, if not all, of your unsecured debts, such as credit card and medical debts, while keeping all your income in the future. Unlike the other types of bankruptcy, Chapters 11, 12 and 13, described above, there is no repayment plan in Chapter 7. The downside of Chapter 7 is that you are limited in what you can keep. You must give up all your assets that are not specifically made "exempt" from creditors under state law or, where applicable, federal bankruptcy law.

How good the "deal" in Chapter 7 is for you will depend upon the availability of exemptions to protect the property you own. If you have no nonexempt assets, then you can keep everything you own in Chapter 7. Fortunately for most people, all their assets are exempt. Chapter 7 requires them to give up nothing. Most people get to eliminate all their unsecured debts, keep 100% of their income and keep 100% of their assets. Pretty good deal.

The "deal" in Chapter 7 is so good that Congress limits the number of people who may qualify. The next section will address whether you are eligible to file in Chapter 7.

# CHAPTER 6

## Do You Qualify To File Bankruptcy In Chapter 7?

 INTRODUCTION

There are three ways for an individual to qualify for Chapter 7. First, their debts are primarily non-consumer debts. This applies mostly to sole proprietors with business debts. For individuals with primarily consumer debts, to qualify for Chapter 7, they must either have a gross income that is lower than the state median gross income for their household size or they must "pass" the Means Test.

Individuals who do not qualify for Chapter 7 likely will be eligible to file bankruptcy in Chapter 13. The results of the Means Test largely will determine the portion of their gross income that will go to pay creditors in Chapter 13.

 QUALIFYING BY HAVING PRIMARILY NON-CONSUMER DEBT

Individuals with primarily non-consumer debt qualify for Chapter 7. What is a "non-consumer" debt? A "consumer" debt is any debt incurred by an individual primarily for personal, family, or household purposes. Consumer debts include home mortgages, car loans, and credit card debt incurred for household purposes. Debts that are not consumer debts are non-consumer debts. Generally, these are business debts, such as money owed to suppliers for inventory, equipment leases or for rent of commercial space.

Congress made a policy decision that people who are in business for themselves, who incur mostly business debt, should have an easier time discharging all their debt, both non-consumer and consumer, in bankruptcy through Chapter 7. Why? Presumably to make it easier for small businessmen, whose businesses had failed, to clear the decks and start again, although business failure is not a requirement. Does that make sense? Who knows? Congress makes mistakes. Barry White's birthday still is not a national holiday.

The business debt must be debt incurred by an individual operating a small business, known as a "sole proprietorship." If the individual does business through an entity, such as a corporation, an LLC or a partnership, the debt incurred by the entity does not count as non-consumer debt for qualification purposes. The entity is separately eligible to file in Chapter 7, but the owner of the entity cannot become eligible to file in Chapter 7 based on debt incurred by the entity, with one important exception.

Many small business owners are co-debtors or guarantors of debts incurred by their entities. In fact, small business owners almost always are co-debtors or guarantors of debts incurred by their entities. American Express, for example, will insist upon it. By itself, the entity generally will not be considered credit worthy. By co-signing or guaranteeing a debt, both the entity and the owner of the entity will be liable for the debt. If the entity fails to pay, the creditor can collect against the owner. Co-signed or guaranteed debt of a business entity does count as non-consumer debt of the individual co-signor or guarantor for qualification purposes. If you have guaranteed the debt of your LLC, that personal guarantee is non-consumer debt that would count towards your qualification for Chapter 7.

It is not widely known, but income taxes owed to the Internal Revenue Service or state taxing agencies are considered to be non-consumer debts for qualification purposes. Tax debts count as non-consumer debts regardless of how the tax debts arose or whether the tax debts are dischargeable in bankruptcy. Recently incurred income tax debts, for example, cannot be discharged in bankruptcy. Despite their non-dischargeability, tax debts are non-consumer debts and could qualify an individual for Chapter 7. Once in Chapter 7, all the individual's unsecured debts, both consumer and non-consumer, could be discharged.

What does "primarily" mean? In most of the country, if the total dollar amount of non-consumer debt is $1 more than one-half of the total dollar amount of all debt (including both consumer plus non-consumer debt), then the debts are "primarily" non-consumer debts. But, bankruptcy judges are idiosyncratic. In some parts of the country, bankruptcy judges consider "primarily" to mean both more than half in dollar amount as well as more than half in number of separate debts. That is a minority view, but it could be the official position in your bankruptcy district.

Example: Your debts include a home mortgage of $300,000, medical debt owed to the local hospital of $20,000, personal American Express credit card debt of $45,000, and $375,000 owed to vendors and suppliers of your restaurant business (a sole proprietorship) that failed due to Covid-19 shutdowns. The total debt is $740,000, of which $375,000 is non-consumer debt. Since more than one-half of the total debt is non-consumer, you would qualify for Chapter 7 in most districts. In a district that also required more than one half in number of the debts to be non-consumer debts to qualify as "primarily" non-consumer debts, you also would have to show that the $375,000 of non-consumer debt was owed to more than three creditors, e.g., vendors and suppliers of your failed restaurant business. If the debts were primarily non-consumer debts, then all $740,000 of debt would be dischargeable, not just the $375,000 of non-consumer debt.

# QUALIFYING BY HAVING SUFFICIENTLY LOW INCOME (BELOW MEDIAN INCOME)

If your consumer debt exceeds your non-consumer debt, which normally is the case, then your income will determine whether you qualify to file bankruptcy in Chapter 7. There are two ways to qualify for Chapter 7 based upon income. The first is to be below median income. The second is to "pass" the Means Test, that is, to have sufficiently low income that creditors would not be paid a meaningful amount in Chapter 13.

The income being examined is not just the income of the person considering filing bankruptcy. It also includes the income of the filer's spouse and possibly others who live in the same household. That income then gets compared to the income of households of comparable size.

If your household income is under the median income for a household of comparable size, then you qualify for Chapter 7. If your household income is over the median income for a household of comparable size, you may still qualify for Chapter 7 if you pass the Means Test, which also takes into consideration household size and household income. Consequently, both "tests" require a determination of household size and household income.

## What Is Your Household Size?

If you live by yourself, answering this question is easy. You are a household of one. If you are married and your spouse lives with you, answering this question also is easy. You are a household of two. You are a household of two regardless of whether both spouses file or only one spouse files. Same household size. If you and your spouse have two children and they both live with you, still easy. You are a household of four. For most people, household size is straight forward. But, like children, not all households are easy.

What about separated or divorced parents sharing custody of children? Are roommates or unmarried boyfriends and girlfriends living together a household of one or two? What about an elderly parent who is being cared for by an adult child in the adult child's home? Are unemployed adult children temporarily living with their parents while looking for employment included in the household? Determining the size of those households is more difficult.

There are three different approaches taken by bankruptcy courts around the country to determine household size:

*"Heads On Beds"*

The "heads on beds" approach uses the U.S. Census Bureau definition of a "household" in physical terms -- how many people occupy the housing unit? Under this approach, it does not matter what relationship the people in the housing unit have to each other. This approach generally results in larger households which usually is more favorable to debtors.

*"IRS Dependency"*

The "IRS dependency" approach limits household size to include only spouses and other individuals that can be claimed as dependents for federal income tax purposes. This approach generally results in smaller households which usually is less favorable to debtors.

## *"Economic Unit"*

The "economic unit" approach includes all individuals living in the same housing unit who act together economically. Under this approach, a household will include spouses and individuals who are financially dependent on the prospective filer, individuals who financially support the prospective filer, and individuals whose income or expenses are significantly comingled or interdependent with the prospective filer.

Of the three approaches, the "economic unit" approach makes the most sense. When a prospective client comes in to see me, I will ask how many people live in their house, what their ages and relationships are, whether they share expenses, and whether they share bank accounts.

Roommates generally are each considered to be a household of one, because roommates have no legal responsibility to support each other and, apart from sharing the rent, cable bill and some other household expenses, their finances generally are kept separate. Roommates ordinarily do not maintain joint bank accounts. There is no expectation that roommates will be together for very long.

For more complicated household situations, you should consult an attorney familiar with local bankruptcy law. Local approaches vary. For example, a household consisting of an unmarried couple with a child belonging to both parents, who maintain one joint bank account and share their income and expenses, would constitute a household of three in one of the states in which I practice and a household of two in the other. The first state considers the unmarried couple's dependence upon each other and the economic interrelatedness of their relationship to constitute a household of three. The second state generally considers unmarried people to be roommates who, apart from the child, have no legal responsibility for each other. In the second state, whichever member of the couple filed along with their child would constitute a household of two.

Whether the couple and their child constitute a household of two or three can make a huge difference in qualifying for Chapter 7. If they were considered to be a household of three, both adults' incomes would be included in household income even if only one were filing. If they were considered to be a household of two, only the filer's income would be considered.

## ❦ What Is Your Household Income?

As just mentioned, anyone who was excluded from being considered a member of the household for purposes of determining household size would have their income excluded for purposes of determining household income. So, for example, a roommate's income would not be included in household income because a roommate is not considered part of the household in determining household size.

Normally, anyone who is included in the household will have their income included in household income, at least to the extent that they contribute toward paying household expenses. Consider the situation of adult children, that is, children above the legal age of "majority." Once the child hits that age, 18 in Connecticut, 21 in New York, the parents generally have no legal responsibility for the child. What if adult children are living at home because they cannot afford to support themselves? In most states, adult children will be included in household size and their income will be included in household income to the extent that the adult children contribute to household expenses. Typically, adult children living with their parents contribute very little to household expenses.

As more people get included in household size, the potential for household income rises. But, as household size increases so does the median income. People qualify for Chapter 7 if their household income is below the median income for a household of comparable size. The larger the household size, the higher the median income threshold for qualification for Chapter 7. In other words, the larger your household size, the higher your household income can be and still qualify for Chapter 7.

For example, the median income for a household of one in Connecticut currently is just over $69,000. The median income for a household of four in Connecticut currently is just over $130,000. It should be easier to qualify for Chapter 7 as a household of four than a household of one, except that with the higher household size, there may be more contributors to household income. A single person earning $75,000/year would not qualify for Chapter 7 as a household of one. The $75,000 income would exceed the median income for a household of one of $69,0000. If the same person married someone with no income and two children, the same person with the same income would qualify as a household of four. The $75,000 income would be under the median income for a household of four of $130,0000. The same person who married someone with an income of $60,000 and two children would not qualify for Chapter 7, because, as a household of four, their combined income of $135,000 would exceed the median income for a household of four of $130,0000.

The determination of household size is made by the person filing bankruptcy (or their attorney) in the bankruptcy filing, known as a "petition." That determination could be challenged by the U.S. Trustee. A division of the U.S. Department of Justice, the Office of the U.S. Trustee plays a role in all bankruptcies to ensure that all bankruptcy laws are followed. One of their responsibilities in Chapter 7 cases is to review the basis on which the filer, known as the "debtor," claims to be eligible to file Chapter 7.

The U.S. Trustee could argue that the debtor does not qualify for Chapter 7 because the debtor's household income exceeds the median income for a household of comparable size. That challenge could happen if the U.S. Trustee thought the actual household size was smaller than what the debtor claimed or if the actual household income was higher than what the debtor claimed, perhaps because some or all of the income of others residing in the household should have been included.

If, upon reviewing the petition, the U.S. Trustee has a concern about eligibility based upon household size or household income, an attorney or financial paralegal for the U.S. Trustee will send the attorney for the debtor a series of questions regarding the debtor's household size and household income. If the answers do not convince the U.S. Trustee that the information contained in the petition is accurate and that the debtor really is eligible for Chapter 7, the U.S. Trustee could file a motion with the bankruptcy court challenging the debtor's eligibility. The bankruptcy court judge would then decide whether the debtor is eligible for Chapter 7.

Recently, I represented a couple who filed bankruptcy in Chapter 7. In addition to the couple, their household consisted of an adult child who was attending college and another adult child who was living at home and working part-time. In Connecticut, children attending college full-time generally are considered part of the household. Although they are "adults" under the law, children in college are dependent upon their parents for support. What about the other adult child who was not in college? The other adult child was living at home with her parents and was dependent upon her parents for support. Connecticut considers such children to be part of the household. The household size was four. The U.S. Trustee was not concerned with household size. What the U.S. Trustee inquired about was the household income. Their concern was whether the adult child who was working part-time was contributing to household income or should have been contributing to household income. Had that adult child's contribution of income been high enough, the household income would have exceeded the median income for a household of four and the couple would not have qualified for Chapter 7. Fortunately, I prevailed in convincing the U.S. Trustee that the adult child was not and should not have been contributing enough to household income to disqualify the parents.

Why does the U.S. Trustee care? The U.S. Trustee acts as the bankruptcy police to ensure that debtors who can pay creditors do not receive complete debt relief in Chapter 7. Instead, debtors with the ability, or the "means," to pay at least some of what they owe, should file in Chapter 13, which requires a debt repayment plan. By challenging eligibility for Chapter 7, the U.S. Trustee is, in effect, saying to the debtor, you have the means to pay your creditors. You should be paying creditors in Chapter 13.

Usually, the U.S. Trustee will not challenge a debtor's eligibility for Chapter 7 unless it appears that the debtor will be able to make a meaningful payment to creditors in Chapter 13. In the prior example, had the adult child's income been included and had that income combined with the parents' incomes exceeded the median income for a household of four by $5, the U.S. Trustee would not have challenged the debtors' eligibility for Chapter 7 in court. There would be no point in "forcing" the debtors into Chapter

13 if all the creditors would receive in Chapter 13 was $5. That would not represent a meaningful recovery to creditors. On the other hand, if the adult child had an income of $20,000, all or a large part of which should have been included in household income, then creditors would receive a meaningful payout in Chapter 13. In that situation, the U.S. Trustee would challenge the debtors' eligibility for Chapter 7 to force them to file in Chapter 13.

Congress enacted the median income "test" as an objective, relatively simple, way to determine whether a debtor has the means to repay creditors. As with all "one size fits all" tests, the outcomes are not always fair. People are not all the same. To add some fairness and to take into consideration more issues that might affect a particular debtor's ability to pay creditors, Congress enacted the Means Test.

 ## WHAT IS INCOME FOR BANKRUPTCY PURPOSES?

Income plays a critical role in determining whether someone qualifies for Chapter 7 by being under median or by passing the Means Test. Up to now, we have been loosely goosey with what "income" means. Income for bankruptcy purposes may not necessarily mean what you think "income" means outside the bankruptcy context. When you think of income, you may think of take-home income, after deductions for taxes and health insurance. When you think of income, you may think of annualized income on a W2 or tax return. Income in bankruptcy world is different. How bankruptcy math calculates income is special. This next section will explain what your income is for bankruptcy purposes. We will start with something bankruptcy world calls "current monthly income."

## ❦ What Months Are Included?

"Current monthly income" is the average monthly income from all sources that you receive during the six-month period ending on the last day of the calendar month immediately preceding the month in which your bankruptcy case is filed. So, if your bankruptcy case is filed in November, the six months that count for computing bankruptcy income are the six months of May through October. It does not matter what you earned before May or what you earn in November. If you file in November, your income for bankruptcy purposes only takes into consideration what you received in May through October. To determine your annualized income, take the total six-month income, divide by six to get the average monthly income, and then multiply the average monthly income by 12.

If you are on a salary and earn the same amount every month, this computation regimen will not matter. You could take any month and multiply by 12. But, for people with uneven monthly income, this computation regimen may produce surprising results. It is important to get it right. For example, if you received a large bonus in May, your total income for the six months of May through October will be higher than your total income for the six months of June through November. Your total income for the year will be the same, but bankruptcy math does not look at total income for the year. It looks at income in six-month periods. The average monthly income of May through October when multiplied by 12 may exceed median income while the average monthly income of June through November when multiplied by 12 may be below median income. So, you may not be eligible for Chapter 7 if you file in November, but, if you wait one month to file, you would be eligible for Chapter 7 if you file in December. All because the bonus income from May drops out from the income calculation by filing in December.

Since you normally have some freedom to choose when you will file bankruptcy, you can use the six-month period calculation to your advantage. If you expect your income to be unusually high in December, maybe because you expect to receive a large Christmas bonus in December, you will want to file in (or, preferably, before) December because income received in the month of filing is not included in determining "current monthly income." Bankruptcy math stops in (or before) November. If you received a bonus in December and your December income was high enough, you might qualify for Chapter 7 with a December filing, but you might not qualify with a January filing because the December income would be included in a January filing.

If you are self-employed or earn income though sales commissions or over-time, you may have more control over when your income is earned than someone on straight salary. You might be able to qualify as being under median by working and earning a little less during an upcoming six-month period than you might have earned during a six-month period earlier in the year. People filing due to job loss or Covid-related business decline typically show more recent income declines. You lose your income; you need to file bankruptcy. If your income is close to median income and thus at risk of not qualifying, waiting an additional month to file may allow you to include a month in which your income is much lower than an earlier month.

Is it possible for someone whose income is well over median to qualify for Chapter 7 by taking a vacation for six months? Probably not. The U.S. Trustee also brings challenges to eligibility for Chapter 7 if the filing is "abusive." Bankruptcy is for honest but unfortunately debtors. If it appears that the debtor deliberately tanked his or her income and then resumed work shortly after filing, the U.S. Trustee might challenge the filing as being "abusive" and seek to have a bankruptcy court judge dismiss the case.

## ❧ What Is Included In "Income"?

"Current monthly income" includes virtually all gross income, including gross wages from employment, most unemployment compensation, private pension payments (from a former employer), alimony and child support.

"Income" for bankruptcy purposes is gross income, the top line on a paystub, not what is taken home after deducting taxes, health insurance and other withholdings, usually the bottom line on a paystub. For most people, gross income is their annual salary. Most people who have an annual salary of $65,000 will have a gross income of $65,000. But not always. It is possible to have an annual salary of $65,000 but have a higher gross income of say $70,000. That can occur when an employer "grosses up" the employee's wages for certain expenses that are then deducted from the paycheck.

For example, a salesperson with an annual salary of $65,000 who also receives a travel allowance of say $5,000, will receive a paystub showing gross income of $70,000. The salesperson's gross income is $70,000 even though the travel allowance merely reimburses the employee for travel expenses the employee has already incurred and paid, even though the travel allowance is deducted from the employee's paycheck, and even though for Social Security and federal income tax purposes, the salesperson's W2 will report gross income of only $65,000. Having a paystub gross income of $70,000 could prevent the salesperson from qualifying for Chapter 7 if the relevant median household income threshold was $68,000. The median income "test" is a very mechanical computation. The good news is that it still may be possible for the salesperson to qualify for Chapter 7 by passing the Means Test. The Means Test has the flexibility to allow the salesperson to deduct and explain that the travel allowance was not actually gross income that was received by the salesperson. It merely reimbursed the salesperson for travel expenses.

Social Security benefits, including Social Security disability benefits, are not included in "income" for bankruptcy purposes. Social Security benefits receive enormous protection from creditors both inside and outside bankruptcy. Congress made a policy decision to ensure that people have enough money to live on in retirement.

"Income" for bankruptcy purposes includes any amount you receive on a regular basis that goes to pay your household expenses or the household expenses of someone who is dependent upon you. Payments such as alimony, maintenance, and child support, which are regularly received for support to pay household expenses, are included in income. Some less obvious payments may also get included. Parents often will assist an adult child who is dealing with unmanageable debt by paying the child's mortgage, cable television bill or similar expenses. If those support payments are "regular," that is, made every month, then the support payments must be included in income for bankruptcy purposes. In contrast, occasional gifts from parents that may be used to pay the same expenses are not "regular" and thus are not included in income. Plan accordingly. This is another area where the median income "test" is very mechanical, but the Means Test provides more flexibility to deduct some child support payments.

## ❧ What About Income From Self-Employment?

For people who receive paystubs, determining income is straightforward. Gross income from wages is determined prior to deductions and withholding. But, what about people who are self-employed, whose income comes from 1099s, or from the operation of a sole proprietorship where they pay themselves out of profits. What constitutes their bankruptcy income? Is self-employment income for bankruptcy purposes determined before or after deductions for business expenses?

Unfortunately, there is no clear answer. There is a better answer, but not every bankruptcy jurisdiction has adopted it. The approach of most bankruptcy courts, and to me the correct approach, is that gross income from self-employment is determined after deducting all cash-related expenses directly related to earning the income.

For example, if you are self-employed in the business of designing websites, your gross income for bankruptcy purposes should consist of all the revenue you receive from customers, reduced by all your cash expenses directly related to operating your business and earning the income, such as the annual license fee for Microsoft and Adobe software, the lease of commercial space, the cost of newspaper ads, etc. Your income for bankruptcy purposes should be close to the income shown on your tax return as being derived from your business, with an important exception. Bankruptcy world generally does not allow deductions for non-cash expenses, such as the depreciation of a car or the portion of your home you use as a home office. Those expenses may count as deductions for income tax purposes, but they generally are not allowed as deductions for bankruptcy income purposes. The calculation of income from self-employment for bankruptcy purposes differs among bankruptcy courts, so seek local counsel. Once again, even if business expense deductions were not allowed in the calculation of bankruptcy income, which prevented the self-employed person from qualifying for Chapter 7 under the median income "test," the self-employed person might qualify under the more flexible Means Test where the business expense deductions might be allowed. Gross income for the self-employed is calculated before deduction for quarterly estimated tax payments. However, tax payments are allowed as deductions on the Means Test.

## ❦ How Is Average Current Monthly Income Calculated?

For people with paystubs who receive about the same gross wages each pay period, calculating the average monthly income for the last six months is simple. Just remember that there are 52 weeks in a year, not 48, so some months may have more pay periods than others. For people with paystubs whose gross wages vary each pay period, the best practice is to collect every pay stub for the last six months prior to the month of filing, add up all the gross wages and divide the total by six.

In every Chapter 7 case, the Chapter 7 Trustee will ask for "proof" of income, but, curiously, paystubs for only the last 60 days generally are requested. Since only the last two or three months of paystubs are turned over to the Chapter 7 Trustee, a forgetful, careless, or less than honest debtor could underestimate the first few months in the six-month period, which may have been the months with the extra pay periods. Underestimating gross wages to be under median is not foolproof, however. There is a risk that the U.S. Trustee will audit the case and request copies of every paystub received during the relevant six-month period. If gross wages have been underestimated, the case will be dismissed.

People with self-employment income calculate their average monthly income for the last six months using actual monthly income and expense information for the period, usually provided by Quickbooks or similar accounting software. The bankruptcy petitions of self-employed people receive much greater scrutiny from the Chapter 7 Trustee and the U.S. Trustee. Expect that your attorney will request monthly profit & loss statements for every month in the year of filing and for any months during the prior year that are within the relevant six-month period. You likely also will be asked for profit & loss statements for the two prior calendar years as well as balance sheets for the month prior to the date of filing and the prior two calendar years. Your tax returns may contain sufficient annual profit & loss and balance sheet information. If your case is audited by the U.S. Trustee, you may be asked to provide further detail to substantiate particular items of income and/or expense.

The median incomes by household size for every state are revised every six months on April 1 and November 1. They can be found on the website for the U.S. Trustee at https://www.justice.gov/ust/means-testing. Scroll down to "Data Required for Completing the 122A Forms and the 122C Forms." Select the most recent time period on the top of the drop-down list and click "Go". This will bring you to another page. Scroll down to "Median Family Income Based on State/Territory and Family Size" where the median incomes are available for download.

To determine whether you qualify for Chapter 7, you would multiply your average monthly income by 12 and compare the result to the median income for households of comparable size in your state. If your annualized gross income is lower than the median, you qualify for Chapter 7. No further financial analysis is required. Passing the Means Test is not necessary. On the other hand, if your annualized gross income is above the median household income for comparable household size, the second way to qualify to file bankruptcy in Chapter 7 is to pass the Means Test.

QUALIFYING BY PASSING THE MEANS TEST

## What Is the Means Test?

The idea behind the Means Test is simple: People with the "means," that is, the ability, to pay creditors, should not receive a complete discharge of all their debts in Chapter 7. Instead, people with the means should have to pay some or all of what they owe creditors over time, based upon their ability to pay, in Chapter 13. Fundamentally, the Means Test is a compromise enacted by Congress that reflects the tension between debtors, who view complete debt forgiveness as a human right, and creditors, who view debt forgiveness as a privilege that should be granted sparingly and with their permission. Like all legislative compromises, the Means Test is inherently arbitrary. It works well in many, but not all, cases. Some of its inclusions seems counterintuitive, others counterproductive. The Means Test itself will determine whether a debtor is eligible for Chapter 7. A variation of the Means Test will determine how much "disposable income" a debtor will be required to pay creditors in Chapter 13. Although simple in concept, calculations under the Means Test can be quite complex.

## How Does The Means Test Work?

The Means Test starts with current monthly income, which is the same current monthly income as described above. Against that income, the Means Test then applies certain expense deductions to determine whether the debtor has sufficient income remaining to pay creditors a meaningful amount compared to what the creditors are owed.

Unlike income, which is the "real" income actually received by the debtor, the Means Test uses deductions for most living expenses that are "fake." Not fake in the sense that they are imaginary, but fake in the sense that the deductions are not the debtor's actual living expenses. Instead of actual living expenses, the Means Test uses deductions for living expenses that are based upon allowances for living expenses that the IRS uses in considering offers in compromise. Why did Congress choose the IRS living allowances over actual living expenses? For objectivity, simplicity, and ease of administration. On the positive side, everyone who lives in the same geographic area receives the same living expense deductions for certain categories, such as food, clothing, housing, and car ownership. By opting for "objective" measures, Congress spared bankruptcy judges from having to determine whether it was reasonable for someone to pay $500 for a winter coast and someone else to pay $500/month for their cat. That makes administering the Means Test much easier. On the negative side, it may pose a problem for people in particular circumstances. There is no "standard" deduction on the Means Test for private Russian language lessons for a child in a family whose relatives all live in Russia. Should the debtor be using those funds to pay creditors? How does a court decide?

The Means Test is not entirely inflexible. In addition to the "standard" living expense deductions, there are a few deductions allowed under the Means Test for actual, provable expenses incurred by the debtor in certain categories, including payments on secured debts, such as car loans and mortgages (if they exceed the IRS living expense allowances), payments on certain priority debts, such as tax claims and child support obligations, childcare, certain dependent care, withholding taxes, health care and term life insurance. There are other possible deductions for actual, provable expenses incurred by the debtor, but subject to a "cap," in a few more categories, such as extra food expense required by someone with celiac disease. If you take these non-standard deductions, be sure to have "proof." You can expect that the U.S. Trustee will audit your case and will demand fairly extensive proof that you are entitled to the claimed deductions. It is the job of the U.S. Trustee to police bankruptcy cases to ensure that people who claim eligibility for Chapter 7 are, in fact, eligible. The U.S. Trustee takes that responsibility seriously.

While simple in theory, the Means Test can be extraordinarily complicated in practice. Often, I cannot be sure during an initial consultation whether a prospective client will pass the Means Test. It may require a fair amount of detailed financial and living expense information from the prospective client and a fair amount of analysis to make a correct determination. Even lawyers who provide initial consultations for free typically charge for a Means Test analysis.

In most cases, however, based upon a prospective client's gross income and how close the prospective client's gross income is to median income, I can make a fairly good estimate of the likelihood of passing the Means Test. For example, if the prospective client's gross income is $200,000 and the applicable median household income is $100,000, it is highly unlikely that the prospective client will pass the Means Test. For less obvious variances, the smaller the household size, the greater a prospective client's income can be above median and still pass the Means Test. For example, a prospective client in a household of one might pass the Means Test with a gross income that was up to 10% above median income while a prospective client in a household of four would not pass the Means Test with a gross income that was $1 above median income. That's just how bankruptcy math works. It may also depend upon the living allowances the IRS provides in the areas in which I practice. Passing the Means Test may also depend upon whether the prospective client has a few of what I call "wildcard" Means Test deductions.

The "wildcard" deductions allowed under the Means Test are deductions one ordinarily would not think would apply. For example, there are separate deductions for mortgage arrearages and recent delinquent income taxes. Take two identical families with identical income and expenses, except that one family regularly made monthly mortgage payments and annual tax payments and the other family did not. Most people would consider the first family as having done the "right" thing, paying their obligations on time. The Means Test provides an extra deduction for mortgage arrearages and recent tax debts. The amount of the deduction is roughly the combined amount of both amounts owed divided by 60. If the mortgage arrearage was high enough and the recent tax debt was high enough, the extra deduction might be the difference between passing and failing the Means Test. The family that did the "wrong" thing, not paying their obligations on time, would have a significant advantage in qualifying for Chapter 7, and having all of their unsecured debts discharged, over the family that did the "right" thing.

Does it make sense for Congress to effectively encourage people who are struggling with unmanageable debt, who might have to file bankruptcy, to not pay their mortgage and, to a lesser extent, their taxes? No, it does not. Most likely, Congress did not intend to create that perverse incentive, but Congress did, and Congress has not corrected the problem over the last 15 years.

While I am prohibited from advising clients to incur additional debt prior to filing bankruptcy, I am not prohibited from explaining how the Means Test and bankruptcy math work. If incurring a tax debt is a strategy that might enable you to qualify for Chapter 7, keep in mind that recent tax debts are not dischargeable. Not paying your taxes is a double edge sword. The extra tax debt might provide an extra deduction to help you pass the Means Test, but the extra tax debt will have to be paid with interest and penalties. On the other hand, a mortgage arrearage could be discharged in Chapter 7 and could disappear along with the house when the house gets foreclosed in the future.

## ❧ The Means Test And "Abusive" Filings

As mentioned previously, the U.S. Trustee can challenge a bankruptcy filing as being "abusive," that is, it would be an abuse of bankruptcy law to allow the debtor to receive a discharge in Chapter 7, because of something "wrong" the debtor has done (such as earning too much income or not providing proof for the extra deduction for special food needed for celiac disease). In general, choosing to pay some expenses over others, even though that choice could mean the difference between passing and failing the Means Test, is not considered an "abuse." At least if the choice is not too obvious. It is not unusual for someone dealing with unmanageable debt to pay the electric bill or the food bill instead of the mortgage or tax bill. By paying for electricity and food instead of paying the mortgage or taxes, an arrearage might arise that could generate an additional Means Test deduction. It is extremely difficult to prove a debtor deliberately manipulated the system by not making mortgage or tax payments to qualify for Chapter 7. In challenging Chapter 7 filings as being "abusive," the U.S. Trustee tends to focus more on the manipulation of income for qualification purposes than the manipulation of expenses (at least until the U.S. Trustee reads this book).

Here is what you should be aware of. If your income seems to have been unusually low during the six-month qualification period, expect an inquiry from the U.S. Trustee. If you were unemployed when you filed your case, but you are employed at the time of the Meeting of Creditors (about 30 days after filing), and your new annual salary would have disqualified you from Chapter 7, expect an inquiry from the U.S. Trustee. So, if you expect to have a new job at a higher salary after filing, it might not be a bad idea to plan to start that new job after the Meeting of Creditors. The likelihood of an inquiry from the U.S. Trustee following the conclusion of the Meeting of Creditors is much lower.

Even if you have income remaining after applying the "standard" and "wildcard" deductions, it is still possible to pass the Means Test if the remaining income available to be paid to creditors is so small relative to how much is owed that creditors would not receive a meaningful payment in Chapter 13. "Meaningful" in bankruptcy world is smaller than you think. Do not expect this formula to save you.

If you fail the Means Test, because the test shows that you have the means to pay creditors at least some of what they are owed, the amount by which you fail the Means Test is a good approximation of the final amount you will have to pay creditors in Chapter 13. Not a precise determination but a good approximation. The Means Test runs slightly differently to determine "disposable income" payments to creditors in Chapter 13. You will have the opportunity to argue before a bankruptcy judge that the amount of money you spend on Russian language lessons for your child, for example, really is a necessity that should not instead go to paying your creditors.

Also note that just because you fail the Means Test does not mean that you must file in Chapter 13. Filing in Chapter 13 always is a choice. You may have a better bankruptcy option or a better non-bankruptcy option than filing in Chapter 13.

It goes without saying, but I will say it anyway, that finding a knowledge bankruptcy lawyer who can guide you through the minefield of the Means Test is highly recommended. Paying for a Means Test analysis is advised. On the few occasions when prospective clients have come in for an initial consultation having run the Means Test on their own beforehand, the results were always wrong.

## ARE YOU ELIGIBLE TO RECEIVE A DISCHARGE?

## Have You Filed Bankruptcy Before?

The whole purpose of filing bankruptcy is to discharge unsecured debts. Ordinarily, it would make no sense for someone to file bankruptcy if they were ineligible to receive a discharge. If you have previously received a discharge in bankruptcy, you will not be eligible to receive another discharge in bankruptcy for some period of time. The exact period of time will vary depending upon the prior and current chapters of bankruptcy. If you have not filed bankruptcy before and received a discharge, this section will not apply to you.

## ❦ How Long Between Successive Chapter 7 Filings?

The eligibility limitation that most often arises for someone considering filing in Chapter 7 is having previously received a Chapter 7 discharge. If you received a discharge in a Chapter 7 case filed less than eight years before the filing of the new case, no discharge will be available in the new Chapter 7 case. You cannot receive another discharge in Chapter 7 unless the new case is filed eight years or more after the filing date of the prior case.

## ❦ How Long Between A Chapter 7 Filing And A Prior Chapter 13 Filing?

The less common eligibility limitation for someone contemplating filing in Chapter 7 is having previously received a Chapter 13 discharge. With some limited exceptions, there is a six-year filing to filing limitation. If you received a discharge in a Chapter 13 case filed less than six years before the filing of the new Chapter 7 case, no discharge will be available in the new Chapter 7 case. You cannot receive a discharge in Chapter 7 unless the new case is filed six years or more after the filing date of the prior Chapter 13 case.

## ❦ What If Your Spouse Previously Filed, But You Did Not, And You Both Want To File Now?

Both spouses are not required to file bankruptcy in any chapter just because one spouse wants to file. Both spouses can file jointly at the same time or each can file separately, usually at different times. Normally, there is a cost savings in filing one joint case for both spouses at the same time. The eligibility limitations apply separately to each spouse even if one joint case is filed. So, if one spouse had previously filed and received a discharge too recently to be eligible for another discharge, if a new joint case is filed, only the spouse who had not previously filed would be eligible for a discharge. One joint case could be filed, but only one spouse would be eligible for a discharge. It would make more sense to wait until the eight or six years had passed before filing a joint case for both spouses.

## 🕊 Do You Always Need A Discharge?

In general, people file bankruptcy to discharge unsecured debts. But not always. Here is one situation in which someone might file bankruptcy even though no discharge was available. As mentioned above, it may be possible to use Chapter 13 to "strip off" a wholly unsecured mortgage lien. Mortgage strip offs are not allowed in Chapter 7. In most jurisdictions, courts will allow a debtor to strip off a wholly unsecured mortgage lien even though the debtor is not eligible to receive a discharge in Chapter 13. The debtor does not need a discharge to have the wholly unsecured mortgage stripped off. Usually, these cases are brought by people who have just finished a Chapter 7 case in which all their unsecured debts were discharged. Why not just file one case in Chapter 13? The debtor may have had too many unsecured debts to be eligible. There is an unsecured debt limit in Chapter 13. Without the prior Chapter 7 filing, the debtor would have had too many unsecured debts to qualify for Chapter 13. Once the unsecured debts are discharged and eliminated in Chapter 7, the debtor can satisfy the unsecured debt eligibility limit of Chapter 13. The absence of a discharge in the subsequent Chapter 13 case is irrelevant. The debts were already discharged in the Chapter 7 case. The debtor immediately files the Chapter 13 case solely for the purpose of stripping off the wholly unsecured mortgage lien. The filing of a Chapter 13 case immediately following the close of a Chapter 7 case is known as a "Chapter 20." Stripping off a wholly unsecured mortgage lien is a good reason to file a Chapter 13 case even though no discharge is available. It is harder to find a good reason to file a Chapter 7 case if no discharge is available.

## What If You Had Previously Filed Bankruptcy But Did Not Receive A Discharge?

If you have filed bankruptcy in the past, but did not receive a discharge, you are eligible for a discharge without any waiting period. The discharge eligibility limitations only apply if you previously received a discharge. Why would someone file bankruptcy and not receive a discharge? Usually because the case was dismissed for failure to provide all the required documents. If a recently filed bankruptcy case was dismissed for other reasons, there may be other restrictions against re-filing, but for shorter time periods.

## Other Limitations On Repeat Filings

If a case previously filed in any bankruptcy chapter was dismissed by the bankruptcy court for willful failure to abide by its orders or for failure to appear in court in furtherance of the case, then the filer would be ineligible to file another case again in any bankruptcy chapter for 180 days following the dismissal date. It is often difficult to know whether a dismissal is based upon a willful failure to abide by orders of the bankruptcy court. The bankruptcy court might not make a specific finding of willfulness when the dismissal is ordered. To be on the safe side, if you previously filed a bankruptcy case and it was dismissed by the court, wait six months from the date of dismissal to refile a new case.

In addition, if your previous bankruptcy case was dismissed at your request following the filing of a motion by a creditor--usually a mortgage lender--for relief from the automatic stay, then you would be ineligible to file again in any bankruptcy chapter for 180 days following the dismissal date. This rule is designed to deter repeated filings for the purpose of delaying mortgage foreclosure. So, if you filed bankruptcy to stop the foreclosure of your house and then asked the court to dismiss the case after the mortgage lender had asked the bankruptcy court for permission to restart the foreclosure case, and the bankruptcy court then dismissed your case, you cannot immediately refile. You must wait at least six months from the dismissal date to file bankruptcy again. Why would someone do that? Usually, to try to stop the foreclosure again.

Congress and bankruptcy court judges hate people using the bankruptcy courts just to postpone mortgage foreclosures. Filing bankruptcy triggers the application of the automatic stay which brings the foreclosure case to an immediate halt regardless of what stage the foreclosure case is in, including right before the sale of the house. If you plan on filing bankruptcy just to stop foreclosure, be aware of another limitation, this time not on discharge eligibility, but on the application of the automatic stay. If you had filed bankruptcy in any chapter within the prior twelve months and that case was dismissed, then the automatic stay will go into effect when a new Chapter 7 case is filed, but the automatic stay will only remain in effect for thirty days from the day the new Chapter 7 case is filed, unless the court extends the automatic stay. So, if you previously filed bankruptcy to stop foreclosure and the case was dismissed and you want to file bankruptcy again to stop the foreclosure case again, you will only get the benefit of the automatic stay for 30 days. You can stop the foreclosure case for 30 days. After that, the automatic stay ends and the foreclosure case can start again. For real gluttons for punishment who had two or more bankruptcy cases dismissed within twelve months before the new Chapter 7 case is filed, the automatic stay would not go into effect at all. The bankruptcy court would have to impose the automatic stay for a reason other than delaying the mortgage foreclosure case. Good luck with that. Hopefully, I have dissuaded you from filing bankruptcy just to postpone foreclosure.

Since there is almost no chance that you have previously filed bankruptcy (because had you previously filed, you would already know how fast and easy bankruptcy is and would not be reading this book), you may be wondering about other eligibility requirements. There is one more to be aware of. The next section looks at where you can file bankruptcy.

 ## WHERE CAN YOU FILE BANKRUPTCY?

If you have been living in the same state your entire life, there will not be an issue as to the state in which you can file bankruptcy. But, if you have moved recently and want to file in the state you left or the state you moved to there could be an issue. Where you can file your bankruptcy case is known as "venue."

Most people file bankruptcy in the state and, within the state, in the bankruptcy district and, within the district, in the bankruptcy division, in which they reside. Some states have more than one bankruptcy district and division. Each district and division are responsible for a different geographic part of the state. As a rule, if you have resided in a bankruptcy district/division for at least the last 91 days or a majority of the last 180 days, you can file in that district/division.

For bankruptcy venue purposes, residence means a permanent residence, such as a home, as distinguished from a mere stopping place for the transaction of business or pleasure, such as a hotel. Some people have more than one residence at the same time. They might own a primary home in one state and a vacation home in a different state. By having two permanent residences, they could choose to file in either state.

If you have recently moved to a new state, normally you would need to wait 91 days before you could file in the new state. That's not always true. In some states, like Connecticut, it has been possible to file cases after being in the state for only one day. I am not sure I would risk filing a case after only one day of residence, but I have seen it done. Once you have resided in the new state for 91 days, you would no longer be eligible to file in the old state.

If you have recently left a state, it would still be possible to file in the old state for 90 days after leaving. You could live in the new state for 89 days and still be eligible to file in the old state. The major drawback of filing in the old state is that you may have to return to the old state for the Meeting of Creditors, which is held approximately 30 days after the filing date. Due to Covid-19 social distancing requirements, many Meetings of Creditors currently are being held telephonically, so you could "attend" the meeting via telephone from the new state.

The more significant risk of filing in the old state is that by filing in the old state you agree to resolve any disputes that arise during the bankruptcy case in the bankruptcy court located in the old state. By filing in the old state, you "confer jurisdiction" on the bankruptcy court in the old state. Disputes are rare in Chapter 7 cases, but they do arise.

For instance, I once received a call from a client of a local bankruptcy "dabbler." The client was living in Utah. He had filed a Chapter 7 case in Connecticut immediately before moving to Utah. By filing his case in Connecticut, the client had "conferred jurisdiction" to resolve disputes on the bankruptcy court in Connecticut. One of his creditors filed an adversary proceeding with the bankruptcy court in Connecticut seeking to deny the discharge of that creditor's debt. The "dabbler" (who by that time had given up his bankruptcy practice) suggested to his client that a letter from me to the creditor would make the adversary proceeding go away. It was not that simple. The adversary proceeding could evolve into full-blown litigation with discovery, depositions, collecting evidence and, eventually, a trial, all of which would take place in the district in which the case was filed – Connecticut. If the creditor wanted to move ahead, there was no way to stop him. A letter from me was highly unlikely to change the creditor's mind about challenging the dischargeability of his debt. The client might have to spend a great deal of time (and expense) in Connecticut defending the adversary proceeding. Strategically, it would have been far better to have filed the case in Utah after the client moved there. The angry creditor would have been much less likely to travel from Connecticut to Utah to file and conduct an adversary proceeding. Never hire a "dabbler."

There are other possible bases for venue besides residence, including your domicile, which could be different from your residence, if, for example, you were in the military, as well as the location of your principal place of business or principal assets. Ordinarily, in Chapter 7 cases there are no reasons to select a bankruptcy court or a bankruptcy judge other than the one closest to you. In other chapters, there could be a reason to seek a court that had issued more favorable opinions on a particular issue that you were concerned about. That is why most large Chapter 11 cases are filed in Delaware and the Southern District of New York.

Residency also affects which exemptions you may be entitled to use and which assets you may be able to keep in Chapter 7. That is our next topic.

# CHAPTER 7

## What Can You Keep In Bankruptcy?

One of the main fears people considering bankruptcy have is losing their house, their car or other property. Like the fear of the abominable snowman and shape-shifting aliens, that fear is mostly unfounded. Filing bankruptcy does not mean that you must give up everything you own. Congress does not want you to be homeless, destitute, living on the street or living in my conference room after filing. Congress wants you to be able to continue to live a productive life. You start fresh, not from scratch. Towards that end, bankruptcy laws allow most people to keep everything they own, including their house, car, and other assets. How that comes about requires some explaining. Like everything else in bankruptcy world, numerous rules and specialized vocabulary words complicate matters.

 EXEMPTIONS

When you file a bankruptcy case in Chapter 7, a Trustee is automatically appointed to administer your bankruptcy "estate," which consists of any money or other property you own that could be sold to pay your creditors. That property is known as "property of the estate." Basically, property of the estate consists of everything you own, and every possible interest in property you may have, that you cannot keep. The rules governing what property you can keep are called "exemptions." When you file bankruptcy, you are required to list each item of property you own in your bankruptcy schedules. You must also indicate the statutory exemption that protects each item. "Exempt property" is the property you can keep during and after bankruptcy. "Nonexempt property" is the property that the Trustee may sell to pay your creditors. Property that is not listed in the schedule of bankruptcy assets is automatically nonexempt and could be lost to the Trustee.

Exemptions play an important role in all bankruptcy chapters. In Chapter 7, exemptions help determine which property you can keep. In Chapter 13, exemptions help determine how much you may have to pay your unsecured creditors.

Every state has its own set of exemptions that protect your property from creditors whether you file bankruptcy or if a creditor has sued for collection in state court and is trying to collect a judgment against you. A few states have particular exemptions that apply only in bankruptcy. Congress created a separate set of federal bankruptcy exemptions. Some states require their residents to use only their state exemptions. California is one such state that does not allow its residents to use the federal bankruptcy exemptions, but, instead, offers two sets of state exemptions. Nineteen states and the District of Columbia allow their residents to choose between their state's exemptions and the federal bankruptcy exemptions. You select the one set of exemptions that better protects your property. You cannot mix and match some exemptions from the state set and other exemptions from the federal set. States that currently allow residents the choice between state and federal exemptions include Alaska, Arkansas, Connecticut, District of Columbia, Hawaii, Kentucky, Massachusetts, Michigan, Minnesota, New Hampshire, New Jersey, New Mexico, New York, Oregon, Pennsylvania, Rhode Island, Texas, Vermont, Washington, and Wisconsin.

For example, if you live in Florida, you can only use the Florida state exemptions. But, if you live in New York, you can choose either the New York state exemptions or the federal bankruptcy exemptions, depending upon which set of exemptions offers greater protection for the type of property you own.

If you file a joint bankruptcy case with a spouse, both of you must use the same exemptions. Nothing precludes from you and your spouse from filing two separate cases, using two different sets of exemptions, if that better protects your property. Be aware that even if your spouse is not filing, if you live in a community property state (Alaska, Arizona, California, Idaho, Louisiana, Nevada, New Mexico, Texas, Washington, or Wisconsin), your spouse's property might be considered to be property owned by you.

Generally, the exemption laws of the state in which you reside apply. However, if you have moved within the last 2 years, the exemption laws of another state or the federal bankruptcy exemptions might apply. The topic of which state's exemption law applies is discussed later.

 ## WHAT KINDS OF EXEMPTIONS ARE THERE?

To give you an idea of what exemptions are, here is a partial list of the federal bankruptcy exemptions:

> Homestead: Real property, including houses, mobile homes, co-ops, and burial plots: up to $25,150. If husband and wife are both on the title, this amount is doubled. Any unused portion, up to $12,575, becomes a "wildcard" exemption. The homestead exemption applies to the equity in the home; that is, the fair market value of the home minus mortgages and other liens. Underwater homes have no equity to protect.

> One motor vehicle: up to $4,000 of equity per filer. Equity is the fair market value of the vehicle less the outstanding balance of the car loan.

Household goods and furnishings, including household furniture, appliances and clothing: up to $13,400 in total; but, up to $625 per item.

Jewelry: up to $1,700 in total.

Pensions and tax-exempt retirement accounts (including 401(k)s, 403(b)s, profit-sharing and money purchase plans, SEP and SIMPLE IRAs, and defined benefit plans): unlimited. IRAs and Roth IRAs: up to $1,362,800.

Un-matured life insurance policy cash surrender value: up to $13,400.

Personal injury recovery: up to $25,150 for bodily injuries, plus lost earnings payments. No exemptions for pain and suffering or for pecuniary loss.

Social security, veterans, unemployment benefits and public assistance payments: unlimited.

Tools of the trade: up to $2,525 in total. "Tools of the trade" are the things you use to perform your job.

Wildcard exemption: $1,325 plus any unused portion of the homestead exemption up to $12,575. The wildcard exemption can be used to protect any other property.

State exemptions can be found via an Internet search for something like "[state] bankruptcy exemptions." Note that exemptions change over time and websites are not always updated to present the latest version of state exemptions.

## EXEMPTIONS MAY BE LIMITED OR UNLIMITED IN AMOUNT

Some exemptions protect the entire value of the asset. Other exemptions only protect the value of the asset up to a certain dollar amount. For example, Connecticut protects bridal jewelry of unlimited value. The federal bankruptcy exemption protects jewelry of all types but only up to $1,700. Connecticut protects "tools of the trade" of unlimited value. The federal bankruptcy exemption protects "tools of the trade" up to only $2,525. So, if you lived in Connecticut and only had a $10,000 engagement ring and a $10,000 Mac computer you used in your web design business, you probably would select the Connecticut exemptions which would allow you to keep the engagement ring and the Mac computer.

 ## WILDCARD EXEMPTIONS

While most exemptions protect specific types of property, some states and the federal bankruptcy exemptions have a general-purpose exemption, called a "wildcard" exemption, that can be used to protect any property. The unused portion of most exemptions is lost if not used to protect the specific asset. The wildcard exemption is a maximum dollar amount that can be used to protect any asset as well as the value of assets that exceeds the specific exemption dollar limit. If the motor vehicle exemption is not enough to protect the entire value of your car, you can use the wildcard exemption to cover the excess.

For example, suppose you own a $4,000 drone in a state that does not have a specific exemption protecting drones, but does have a wildcard exemption of $5,000. You can use $4,000 of the wildcard exemption and apply it to protect the drone. You get to keep the $4,000 drone. If you also owned a car with $5,000 of equity but the state motor vehicle exemption was limited to $4,000, you could use the $1,000 remaining from the wildcard exemption to protect the $1,000 excess equity in the car. You get to keep the $5,000 car.

 CAN YOU KEEP YOUR HOUSE?

A house usually is the most important asset most people own and the asset most people want to keep in bankruptcy. Whether you can keep your house or, more accurately stated, whether a "homestead" exemption exists to protect your equity in your house, requires answering the following questions.

## What Is Your House Worth?

An on-line valuation, such as Zillow.com or Realtor.com, may be considered adequate in many jurisdictions to determine the value of a house, especially if the valuation results in house equity that is far below the available homestead exemption. But, if it appears that the amount of house equity is close to or slightly above the available homestead exemption, or if you believe the on-line valuations significantly over-value your house, because they do not consider the poor condition of your roof, your outdated kitchen, your broken septic system, or the fact that your house was built on an ancient Indian burial ground, you might want a better valuation. A local real estate broker often will provide a current market analysis ("CMA"), also known as a broker's price opinion ("BPO"), for free or for a small fee. The broker's valuation is considered more reliable than an on-line valuation because the broker visits your house. The broker also has a better sense of the comparability of houses currently on the market and houses that were recently sold. If valuation is critical to being able to keep a house and there is doubt as to value, then getting the house appraised by a licensed real estate appraiser is worth the additional expense.

## 💌 Who Owns The House?

Homestead exemptions generally are available to the persons who are on the deed or title to the house and who either live in the house as their primary residence or have a dependent who lives in the house, usually because of divorce. For example, if two spouses live in a house, but only one spouse is on the deed to the house as the owner of the house (ignore community property states), then the spouse who owns the house can only take advantage of one homestead exemption, $25,150 if the federal homestead exemption applies. If both spouses are on the deed to the house as the owners of the house, then the homestead exemption in most states and the federal homestead exemption is doubled, currently to $50,300 for the federal homestead exemption. Note, if both spouses were on the deed, both spouses would not have to file bankruptcy for two homestead exemptions to be available. If only one spouse was on the deed to the house and the spouse who was not on the deed was filing bankruptcy, then no homestead exemption would be needed. The filing spouse would not need an exemption to protect property the spouse does not own. It is rare, but not unheard of, for elderly parents and their children to all be on the deed to a house. A homestead exemption could be available for each of those persons even if only one of them is filing bankruptcy. They all may have to be living in the house for multiple homestead exemptions to be available. Due to the primary residence requirement contained in most homestead exemptions, protecting a vacation property usually is not possible with the homestead exemption. A wildcard exemption could protect a vacation property with little equity.

## 🕊 How Much Is Owed On The House?

The homestead exemption protects the equity a homeowner has in the house, not the value of the house. The equity is the difference between the value of the house and the total of all liabilities legally attached to the house, known as "liens." Because most people considering bankruptcy usually have little equity in their houses, keeping a house in bankruptcy usually is not a problem.

The liens on a house include all mortgages, judgment liens (also known as judicial liens) and statutory liens. How do you know if your house has any liens? Land records list every lien that has been recorded against your house. They usually are maintained in the local town or county clerk's office. Land records are increasingly also available on-line. Deduct the total of the current amount owed on all the liens attached to the house from the value of the house to determine the equity in the house.

## ❤ Determining House Equity

Start with the outstanding principal balance on all mortgages on your house, plus any mortgage arrearages for unpaid principal, interest, late fees, legal fees, escrow deficiency, etc. You could call your mortgage lender and ask for a "payoff" amount to determine this number. Next, if you have lost a collection lawsuit and your home was "liened" by the judgment creditor, then the amount of that judgment, plus interest, if interest was awarded, gets deducted from the value of the house. You could contact the lawyer for the creditor for the exact amount owed on the judgment lien. Some liens arise by state law because of the non-payment of certain taxes and fees, usually real estate taxes and sewer taxes. These liens, known as "statutory liens," arise automatically by statute and do not require a court to authorize them. You could contact the local tax assessor for amounts owed on any statutory liens. Deduct the total amount owed on all liens attached to the house from the house's fair market value to determine how much equity you have in the house.

In general, it does not matter that a mortgage or other lien is owed by someone other than the person filing bankruptcy. For example, both spouses may be on the deed as owners of the house, but only one spouse is on the mortgage. Often, a non-working spouse whose "credit" was not needed for obtaining a mortgage is not "on" the mortgage, meaning the non-working spouse has not signed the mortgage or is otherwise not obligated to pay it, say as guarantor. Regardless of who is "on" the mortgage, the mortgage is a lien against the house and reduces the fair market value of the house in determining the house's equity. Even though the non-working spouse is not on the mortgage, the non-working spouse could claim a homestead exemption. Because both spouses were on title, most exemptions would be doubled, again even though only one spouse was on the mortgage and only one spouse was filing.

## ♥ Homestead Exemption Example

Your house is valued by Zillow.com at $350,000 and by Realtor.com at $300,000. On-line valuations can vary that much. The valuation depends upon the selection of houses the computer algorithm considers to be "comparable" houses. Unless you had a strong feeling about which of the two was more accurate, use the average -- $325,000 as the fair market value of the house. If you and your spouse are both on the deed to the house and are living in the house (i.e., not separated or divorced), then in most states and with the federal exemptions you would be entitled to two homestead exemptions. In some states, you would only get one homestead exemption regardless of the number of people on the deed, but the homestead exemptions in those states usually are exceptionally large. In this example, two spouses are on the deed. This house has two mortgages, both of which are "current," meaning that monthly payments have been made in full and on time. No arrearages are due on either the first mortgage or the second mortgage/HELOC. The principal amount outstanding on both mortgages totals $260,000. In addition to the two mortgage liens, a judgment creditor put a $15,000 lien on the house after he won a collection case against one of the spouses. The total amount owed (or "liened") on the house is $275,000 ($260,000 + $15,000). The equity in the house is $50,000 ($325,000 - $275,000).

Is the $50,000 equity protected by available homestead exemptions? Check to see what homestead exemption is available in your state, whether the federal bankruptcy homestead exemption is available and whether the available exemption applies to more than one person on the deed.

In Florida, assuming the house was the primary residence, the spouses were Florida residents and had lived in Florida for at least 3-1/2 years, the almost unlimited Florida homestead exemption would protect the equity in the house. In New Jersey, the state homestead exemption would not be sufficient to protect the $50,000 equity, but the federal homestead exemption, which can be elected by New Jersey residents, would be sufficient to protect the $50,000 equity. With both spouses on the deed, the $25,150 federal homestead exemption becomes $50,300 which is sufficient to protect $50,000 of house equity.

Recall that in this example the value of the house was determined by averaging two on-line valuations. What if the average of the two on-line valuations was $350,000? If the house value was $350,000 instead of $325,000, there could be almost $25,000 of nonexempt house equity. This is an instance where it would be advisable to pay for a CMA or, perhaps, even an appraisal for a valuation closer to $325,000. You would want to be sure that the amount of equity you were trying to protect was within the available homestead exemption.

If the appraisal indicated the house had a value of $400,000, because a $100,000 kitchen remodeling was recently completed or the house was within walking distance of a church, among other reasons, then the nonexempt equity might be too high for you to file in Chapter 7.

## ❧ Should You Keep Your House?

People usually want to keep their houses during and after bankruptcy, but not always. If the value of the house is significantly below the total amount owed on the outstanding balances of mortgages and other liens, then keeping the house may not make economic sense. Keeping a house whose liabilities exceed the value of the house (known as an "underwater" house or a house with "negative" equity) is like buying a house for more than it is worth. Admittedly, it is painful to give up a house and move, but keeping the albatross of a house with negative equity does nothing to enhance a "fresh start." Especially, if bankruptcy provides a "jet out of jail free" card.

As part of a Chapter 7 filing, the debtor can "surrender" the underwater house to the mortgage lender and have the amount by which the mortgage liability exceeds the value of the house (known as the "deficiency") discharged. Surrendering a house in bankruptcy does not transfer the title to the house. The debtor remains the legal owner of the house until the mortgage lender does something to take title. Usually, the mortgage lender will foreclose to take title. Compare the same situation outside of bankruptcy (excluding deed of trust states where mortgages are "non-recourse"). If a house is foreclosed and sold to pay off the outstanding mortgage and related fees, any remaining deficiency would be a personal liability of anyone who signed the mortgage (technically, the note part of the mortgage financing). A discharge in Chapter 7 eliminates that deficiency. The deficiency is discharged regardless of when the bankruptcy case is filed. Bankruptcy could be filed before the foreclosure case has commenced or after the foreclosure case has ended and the house sold.

The ability to file bankruptcy and discharge the liability for any future mortgage deficiency provides homeowners with the ability to "strategically default" in the future. In states like New York, it takes, on average, three years to evict a homeowner from a house once the homeowner defaults on a mortgage. If the homeowner had already filed bankruptcy in Chapter 7, the homeowner could live, on average, for three years without making a mortgage payment before being evicted. That could provide plenty of time to look for a new job in a different state and the funds to move. The ability to strategic default is not available in every state, but where it is available, it can be extremely valuable.

## 🦋 How To Keep A House In Bankruptcy – Reaffirming A Mortgage

If the house is not surrendered to the mortgage lender in bankruptcy, in most states, liability for the full amount owed on the mortgage will not be discharged. The homeowner must remain personally liable in a process known as "reaffirmation." The homeowner's personal liability on the mortgage is reaffirmed. In the future, if the house is foreclosed and the value of the house is less than what is owed, the homeowner will be personally liable for the deficiency by reaffirming the mortgage.

In a few states, including Connecticut, thanks to favorable state statutes and judicial opinions, instead of reaffirming the mortgage, debtors have the option of keeping their homes provided the mortgages continue to be paid. This option is known as "retain and pay." The enormous advantage of retain and pay over reaffirmation is that by not reaffirming, by not having personal liability for the mortgage amount owed, the homeowner can strategically default on the mortgage at any time in the future, as described above. If the house is foreclosed, the homeowner will only lose the house. The homeowner will have no additional liability for the deficiency.

The downside of not reaffirming the mortgage is that the mortgage lender will not report mortgage payments to the credit reporting agencies. The mortgage generally gets reported as having been discharged in bankruptcy. The homeowner's credit score will not increase as a result of timely mortgage payments being made in the future. This is less of a disadvantage than it might at first seem because mortgage lenders frequently fail to report mortgage payments by borrowers who have filed bankruptcy in any chapter even when the mortgages are reaffirmed. On balance, where available, the ability to strategically default on a mortgage after bankruptcy far outweighs the benefit of the mortgage payments being reported to the credit reporting agencies.

Whether the homeowner chooses to reaffirm the mortgage or to retain and pay the mortgage, if the homeowner wants to keep the house, the homeowner should be current on the mortgage at the time the Chapter 7 bankruptcy case is filed. If there were a mortgage arrearage at the time the Chapter 7 was filed, the mortgage lender would have the option of foreclosing on the house. By filing a bankruptcy case, the application of the automatic stay would prevent the foreclosure case from starting immediately, but it would not postpone foreclosure for very long. The mortgage lender could wait a few months until the bankruptcy case ended. Or, if it were impatient, the mortgage lender could file a motion asking the bankruptcy court judge to lift the automatic stay. Once the bankruptcy case ended or the automatic stay was lifted, the mortgage lender could proceed with foreclosure.

Although they could foreclose if there were an arrearage at the time of filing, in practice, most mortgage lenders do not foreclose. Instead, they tend to offer Chapter 7 filers mortgage modification options. Mortgage lenders generally prefer to have performing mortgages on their books than foreclosed houses in their inventory. If the homeowner can afford to make mortgage payments, restructuring the mortgage is a better option for the lender. But, that option is up to the mortgage lender. If there is a mortgage arrearage when the case is filed, the mortgage lender could choose to foreclose.

For homeowners who want to keep their house but are behind on monthly mortgage payments and cannot catch up on the payments before filing bankruptcy, filing in Chapter 13 would be a better option than filing in Chapter 7. Chapter 13 provides the homeowner with more time to catch up on past due mortgage payments while staying current on regular monthly mortgage payments. Although Chapter 13 can keep a homeowner in a house, if the value of the house has fallen below the outstanding mortgage balance, keeping the house may not be the smartest economic decision.

## ❤ Avoiding Judgment Liens

Receiving a discharge in Chapter 7 does not let the homeowner keep the house for free. Even if the homeowner's personal liability is discharged by retaining and paying, the mortgage lien "survives" or "rides through" bankruptcy. If the mortgage is not paid following discharge, the mortgage could be foreclosed. Judgment or judicial liens, which arose from a court order following a collection lawsuit and which were recorded on the land records, are treated differently than mortgage liens. Judgment liens survive bankruptcy and remain on the land records unless they are removed during bankruptcy.

A judgment lien can be "avoided," that is, removed, from the land records if the judgment lien "impairs" the homeowner's homestead exemption. The computations can be quite difficult. In a simple example, assume a house worth $300,000, subject to a $250,000 first mortgage and a $10,000 judgment lien. The available homestead exemption is $50,000. The equity in the house is $40,000 ($300,000 - $250,000 - $10,000 = $40,000). The $10,000 judgment lien "impairs" the $50,000 available homestead exemption by $10,000. In this example, the full amount of the $10,000 judgment may be "avoided" and removed from the land records. Following the issuance of a discharge in bankruptcy, the judgment lien would no longer be a cloud on title to the house and liability to the creditor for the $10,000 amount of the lien would be discharged. The avoidance of the judgment lien requires the filing of a motion with the bankruptcy court. If contested, the avoidance motion would be decided by the bankruptcy court judge after a hearing. Whether a judgment lien on your house can be avoided and what the process will cost are questions you would want to discuss with a knowledgeable bankruptcy attorney.

# CAN YOU KEEP YOUR CAR?

Next to losing a house, losing a car is most people's biggest fear about bankruptcy. That fear is completely unfounded. In my practice, I have never had a client lose a car or decide against filing bankruptcy in Chapter 7 because there was a chance that they would lose a car. Whether you can keep a car or, more accurately, whether an exemption exists to protect your equity in the car, requires answering the following questions.

## ❦ What Is Your Car Worth?

The value of a car can be estimated by going to the websites of the NADA Official Used Car Guide and Kelley Blue Book and inputting the make, model, year, mileage, and options of the car. If that valuation seems too high based upon the condition of the car and there is too much car equity to protect with the available state or federal exemptions, you could obtain a more accurate appraisal from Carmax or other used car dealer.

## ❦ Who Owns The Car?

Exemptions are only needed by the owner of a car. So, you need to check to see who is on the title to the car. If your spouse alone is on title to the car, then your spouse owns the car and you do not need to protect the car in your bankruptcy. If you and your spouse are both on title to the car, then you may only need to protect one-half of the value of the car (community property states may differ). In my experience, prospective clients often do not know which spouse is on title or whether the car is owned jointly.

## ❦ How Much Is Owed On The Car Loan?

Normally, the outstanding balance owed on a car loan is disclosed on the monthly statement. Or, you can ask the car lender for a "payoff letter" showing the amount owed. The payoff letter may contain pre-payment penalties, so it may be higher than the amount shown as owed on the monthly statement. The higher the amount owed, the less equity to protect. It does not matter whether the person filing bankruptcy is on the car loan or that another person alone or with the debtor is on the car loan. The existence of the car loan reduces the car's equity by the amount of the loan regardless of who is liable for the loan. If there is no car loan, the value of the car is the car equity.

## Is The Car Equity Less Than The Available Exemptions?

The car equity is the difference between the value of the car and what is owed on the car loan. Compare the car equity with the available motor vehicle and wildcard exemptions.

## Car Exemption Example

Car is valued by the average of KBB.com and NADA.com at $25,000. The outstanding balance of the car loan is $22,000. The remaining $3,000 of equity can be protected by the $3,500 motor vehicle exemption in Connecticut, the $4,550 motor vehicle exemption in New York and the $4,000 federal bankruptcy motor vehicle exemption.

Notice that a car worth as much as $25,000 can be kept by someone in bankruptcy. It does not matter how much the car is worth. What matters is the car's equity. That may seem counter intuitive. Why should a debtor filing in Chapter 7 be able to keep an expensive car? The answer is that the car has little value to the debtor's creditors. The equity in the car is what would be available to creditors if the car were sold after repaying the car loan. If the $25,000 car were sold, $22,000 would go the car lender to pay off the car loan. Only $3,000 would be left to pay creditors. Since $3,000 is less than the motor vehicle exemption available in Connecticut and New York, as well as most other states, and the federal bankruptcy exemption, the debtor can keep the car in bankruptcy.

## ❦ What If The Car Equity Is Slightly Above The Exemption Level?

Some states and the federal bankruptcy exemptions have a "wildcard" exemption that can be used to protect property that either is not specifically protected or has a value above the specific exemption limit. If the car in the previous example was worth $30,000 instead of $25,000, the car would have $8,000 of equity instead of $3,000. In that situation, the debtor would need a "wildcard" exemption in addition to the motor vehicle exemption to protect the car. Using the federal exemptions, the motor vehicle exemption would only protect $4,000 of car equity, so $4,000 of the "wildcard" exemption would be needed to protect the full $8,000 of car equity.

## ❦ What If The Car Equity Exceeds Available Exemptions?

If the car equity exceeds available exemptions, then the car could be taken by the Chapter 7 Trustee and sold. After the expenses of the sale, the debtor would receive the amount of exemptions that had been used to protect at least some of the equity of the car, and creditors would receive the remainder of the proceeds.

## ❧ Car Exemption Example, Continued

Car is valued by the average of KBB.com and NADA.com at $30,000. The outstanding balance of the car loan is $22,000. The car's equity is $8,000. The motor vehicle exemption available in the state of Connecticut currently is $3,500 and the maximum wildcard exemption is $1,000. Connecticut is a state in which debtors may select the federal exemptions instead of the state exemptions. The federal exemptions include a motor vehicle exemption of $4,000 and a wildcard exemption potentially as high as $12,575, which is more than enough to protect the car's equity. But, the Connecticut homestead exemption is much higher than the federal homestead exemption. Because only one set of exemptions can be selected, if a debtor needs the Connecticut homestead exemption to protect equity in a house, the debtor might be stuck with the less generous Connecticut motor vehicle exemption to protect the car.

Using the Connecticut exemptions, the debtor could protect a maximum of $4,500 of car equity (the $3,500 motor vehicle exemption plus the $1,000 wildcard exemption). Since the car equity was $8,000, $3,500 of car equity would be nonexempt ($8,000 - $4,500 = $3,500). In theory, the Chapter 7 Trustee would sell the $30,000 car, repay the $22,000 car loan, give the debtor his $4,500 exemptions and have $3,500 left to pay creditors. In practice, the Trustee might not be very anxious to sell the car. Maybe the car cannot really be sold for $30,000. And there will be fees associated with the sale. After expenses, maybe the sale of the car nets only $28,000. Now the amount available for creditors drops to $1,500. Out of that $1,500, the Chapter 7 Trustee will have her own fees and expenses. The amount finally available, after all expenses and fees, to pay creditors might not be meaningful.

As a result, most Chapter 7 Trustees will not "administer estates," that is, take and sell the debtor's property for the benefit of creditors, unless the expected amount available to pay creditors is above a threshold of several thousand dollars. "Several" is likely to be higher for Chapter 7 Trustees in Maryland than in Mississippi, but there is a threshold level below which it is not economical for Chapter 7 Trustees to administer estates. So, just because there is some unprotected equity does not necessarily mean that the property will be lost in bankruptcy. A car typically must be worth significantly more than available exemptions to make it worthwhile for the Chapter 7 Trustee to sell the car. That is another reason why debtors rarely lose their cars in bankruptcy. To get a better idea of how much nonexempt property a debtor in Chapter 7 can keep, consult a knowledgeable local bankruptcy attorney.

In general, only one car can be protected with one motor vehicle exemption. If a debtor owns two cars, each worth $2,000, in most jurisdictions only one motor vehicle exemption can be used to protect one car. If the motor vehicle exemption were $4,000, only $2,000 could be used to protect one car. The other car would need a wildcard exemption for protection, but the likelihood that a Chapter 7 Trustee would attempt to sell a nonexempt car worth $2,000 is small. Some jurisdictions have allowed an exception to the one-car/one-exemption rule where a second car served a specific need that was different from the first car, such as an all-terrain vehicle used for business and an electric car used for commuting.

Note that if two cars were owned, but the outstanding balance of one car loan exceeded that car's value, that car would have no equity and no need for protection with exemptions. The other car with equity could be protected with the motor vehicle exemption. Also note that if two spouses file a joint case, the one-car/one-exemption rule still applies. Joint debtors in most jurisdictions cannot "stack" two motor vehicle exemptions and use the total exemption to protect total car equity. For example, if one spouse owns a car worth $6,000 and the other spouse owns a car worth $2,000, both cars could not be protected with two $4,000 motor vehicle exemptions, even though together the couple has $8,000 of car equity and $8,000 of available car exemptions. The $2,000 car equity would be fully exempt, and the $6,000 car equity would have $4,000 of exempt equity and $2,000 of nonexempt equity unless a wildcard exemption were available to protect the $2,000 of car equity. Similarly, if one spouse alone owned both cars, only one car could be protected by one motor vehicle exemption, even if both spouses filed. The other car would be nonexempt unless a wildcard exemption were available.

To illustrate how frequently bankruptcy rules change, and the need to stay abreast of changes, in the time between my finishing writing this book and my approving the pre-publication "proof," the Connecticut state legislature passed a new motor vehicle exemption. As of October 1, 2021, the Connecticut exemptions will protect up to two motor vehicles with an aggregate equity value of $7,000.

# STATEMENT OF INTENTION

If your car is not subject to a loan, whether you can keep the car or not in bankruptcy is simply a matter of comparing the fair market value of the car to the available exemptions. But, if your car is subject to a loan secured by the car, that is, the car is collateral for the loan, then you must notify the car lender about your "intention" with respect to the car. Notification is made by filing a form, known as the "Statement of Intention," with the bankruptcy court with your other bankruptcy documents. In most bankruptcy jurisdictions there are three options for the "intention" to take. In some jurisdictions, there are four options.

## ❦ Reaffirm

The first "intention" option is to keep the car and to "reaffirm" the car loan. This means that you will have the same liability for the car loan after bankruptcy that you had prior to bankruptcy. If the car has equity, that probably is not an issue. You would want to keep the car and continue paying off the car loan. But, if there is no car equity, that is, more is owed on the car loan than the car is worth, then keeping the car and reaffirming the car loan may not be an attractive option. The downside of reaffirming a car loan is that if, for some reason, you stopped paying the car loan in the future after bankruptcy and the car was repossessed, you could be liable for the full amount of the car loan. If after repossessing and selling the car, the car lender was still owed money, because the proceeds from the sale of the car were less than what the lender was owed on the car loan, by reaffirming the car loan in bankruptcy you will be liable for that deficiency. Again, if there is car equity, that risk is probably small and worth taking. The greater the car equity, the smaller the risk. But if the car loan already is upside-down, that is, more is owed on the car loan than the car is worth, then the risk of having a liability for a future deficiency may not be a risk worth taking.

In addition to indicating an intention to reaffirm on the Statement of Intention, reaffirming the car loan requires the execution of a reaffirmation agreement, usually prepared by the lender, which is either signed by the debtor's attorney as being in the best interest of the debtor or approved by the bankruptcy court judge after a hearing. Reaffirming an upside-down car loan can be problematic because doing so is rarely in the debtor's best interest.

## Surrender

The second "intention" option is to give the car back to the lender, known as "surrender." Most people want to keep their cars. But, if the car is worth less than amount owed on the car loan, there can be a significant economic benefit to surrendering the car to the lender. Afterall, in a perfect world, you would never pay more for a car than the car was worth. That is what reaffirming an upside-down car loan is. Outside bankruptcy, if you were to return a car prior to the end of the loan term, you likely would trigger penalty fees. In bankruptcy, the penalty fees are just additional unsecured debt that will be discharged with all your other unsecured debt. Bankruptcy is a golden opportunity to relieve yourself of an unattractive car loan.

### How Will You Get Around Without Your Car?

Maybe you can borrow a car from a friend or family member or buy a cheap clunker or even use Uber or Lyft. Finding a replacement for your car may be difficult, but it is not forever. Once bankruptcy is over and your credit score has rebounded, you will be able to buy a car with a loan that does not exceed the value of the car at an interest rate that is likely to be much lower than the interest rate on your current car loan. "Surrendering" a car in bankruptcy does not automatically transfer title to the car to the lender. The lender must take possession of the car. I recommend that clients contact the lender and plan to return the car, usually to the appropriate local dealer, prior to filing. All car lenders have excellent mechanisms in place to repossess cars after filing.

## Redeem

The third "intention" option is to "redeem" the car. This option allows you to purchase your car from the lender at its market value. For example, if the car is worth $5,000, but it is subject to a loan of $10,000, usually because a prior car loan was rolled into the current car loan, the redemption option allows you to purchase your car from the lender for $5,000. Economically, that is an extremely attractive option. Practically, however, unless you have a generous friend or family member willing to advance the funds, financing the purchase price to redeem the car is a major obstacle. There are lenders who specialize in financing the redemption of cars in bankruptcy, including BankruptcyDrive.com and 722 Redemption Funding. In my experience, in the limited number of times where redemption was considered, the specialized lender financing was still too expensive. The monthly payments under the proposed redemption loan were barely less than the payments under the existing car loan. Apart from the difficulty of arranging financing, the other problem with redeeming a car in bankruptcy comes when the lender disputes your $5,000 car valuation. If there were a disagreement over the valuation of your car, a bankruptcy judge might end up having to determine its value. As a result, the legal cost of redeeming the car could be significant.

## ✔ Retain and Pay

The fourth "intention" option, known as "retain and pay," was supposedly written out of the Bankruptcy Code in 2005, but still survives in some jurisdictions. It allows you to retain ownership of your car and to continue to pay your car loan without agreeing to be personally liable for the car loan. By retaining and paying instead of reaffirming, you avoid any liability for a future deficiency. If you fail to continue to make car loan payments in the future and your car is repossessed and sold, your liability would be limited to losing the car. The lender could not pursue you for the difference between what was then owed and what the repossessed car sold for.

For retain and pay to be available as an option for you, two things must be working in your favor: (1) a favorable state law or judicial decision in your bankruptcy jurisdiction, and (2) you must be current on your car loan. You cannot owe the car lender money at filing. The favorable state law or judicial decision is needed to counteract the effect of filing bankruptcy on the car loan. Most car loans treat filing bankruptcy as an event of default, like the event of default that arises when the required car loan payments are not made when due. Most events of default entitle a car lender to repossess the car. Favorable state law or a favorable judicial decision can "override" the filing of bankruptcy being an event of default. For example, some states have a law that says that if a borrower is current on the car loan, the car lender cannot repossess the car just because the borrower filed bankruptcy. But, the second condition must also be present. The borrower must be current on the car loan for the state law to apply. Assuming both conditions are met, a car loan does not have to be reaffirmed. The retain and pay option is not one of the three options provided on the Statement of Intention form. It must be selected as "Other" and explained on the form.

You would need to consult a knowledgeable bankruptcy attorney to learn whether retain and pay is an option in your jurisdiction.

In jurisdictions in which retain and pay is not an option, the equivalent result may be accomplished by indicating an intention to reaffirm the car loan on the Statement of Intention but then failing to follow through on that intention, for example, by failing to execute or deliver a separate reaffirmation agreement required to reaffirm the car loan. You would end up without liability in the future for a deficiency, but you would risk repossession. If the car loan was significantly upside-down, that could be a risk worth taking. The lender likely would prefer to have you continue to make car loan payments on the $10,000 car loan instead of repossessing the car worth $5,000.

The downside of retain and pay is that the car lender likely will not report future car loan payments to the credit reporting agencies, which means that your future car loan payments will not help rebuild your credit score. The car loan likely will be treated as having been discharged in bankruptcy.

Chapter 13 might be a better option than Chapter 7 where the outstanding balance of the car loan is significantly higher than the value of the car. As mentioned earlier, if the car was purchased more than 910 days before filing and a host of other requirements were satisfied, the car loan could be "crammed down" to the value of the car in Chapter 13.

 CAN YOU KEEP A LEASED CAR?

Leased cars are treated a little differently in bankruptcy than cars with loans. A leased car can never be part of your "bankruptcy estate" because you do not own the leased car; the leasing company owns the car. It does not matter what a leased car is worth. No exemption is needed to keep it. As long as the monthly payment on the lease is not ridiculously expensive, you can keep the leased car, if you want to. If the leased car were a Maserati and the monthly lease payment was $5,000, the U.S. Trustee might object to your Chapter 7 filing as "abusive" in that the $5,000/month going to the Maserati dealer could otherwise go to pay your creditors. Except in this rather unusual circumstance, the decision to keep the leased car is up to you. You have the choice to either "assume" or "reject" the lease. That choice is indicated on the Statement of Intention form.

## ❧ Assume The Lease

If you choose to assume the car lease, you will be liable for all its terms and conditions. You will have the same car lease liability after bankruptcy as you had before bankruptcy. If you go over the allowed mileage, if you wear out the tires, or if you destroy the cupholders, and if the lease imposes penalties for those infractions, you will be liable to pay those penalties at the end of the lease. Bankruptcy will not relieve you from the obligation to pay those future penalties if and when they arise. If you "assume" the lease, you will be liable for those penalties after bankruptcy.

## ❧ Reject The Lease

Would you prefer to return the leased car? You might not want to keep the leased car if the monthly lease payments were more than you could afford. You might not want to keep the leased car if you knew you would be way over the allowed mileage at the end of the lease or if the cupholders already were damaged. In those circumstances, you might want to "reject" the lease and return the car. If you reject the lease, you could be liable for lease penalties as well as an early termination fee along with any lease payments owed at the time of filing, but that entire liability could be discharged in Chapter 7. So, relieving yourself of a disadvantageous car lease in Chapter 7 could be enormously beneficial to your future monthly cash flow. But, you will need some other form of transportation. Again, try to borrow a car, buy a clunker, or use Uber.

Homes and cars are the items people are most concerned about losing in bankruptcy. Some of the other major items of property and particular issues that could arise with respect to keeping them are discussed below.

 HOUSEHOLD ITEMS

Household goods, furniture and apparel are generally fully exempt under most state exemptions and the federal bankruptcy exemptions. Most household items are of such limited value that they would hardly be worth the trouble of selling by the Chapter 7 Trustee. Jewelry generally receives some protection between specific and wildcard exemptions. In my practice, it is exceedingly rare for clients to lose household items in bankruptcy because the available exemptions were less than the value of the items. Generally, any item of significant value that could have been sold was already sold long before a client comes in to see me.

Be aware that some debts incurred to purchase household items may be treated differently in bankruptcy than other unsecured debts. People often purchase household items using credit cards. Under some circumstances, the furniture, jewelry, electronics, or other household items purchased with the retailer's credit card could be collateral for the retailer's credit card debt, just as cars are collateral for car loan debt. In other words, it is possible that certain store credit card debts that you thought were unsecured actually are secured by the items the cards were used to purchase. For example, if you were asked to sign extensive paperwork at the upscale furniture store when you bought a dining room set using the store's credit card, it is likely that you agreed to give the dining room set as collateral for the debt. In that situation, the furniture store credit card debt would be secured by the dining room set. If you did not pay the debt, the furniture store could repossess the dining room set. Other household goods retailers may have you sign a magic screen when you use their credit card without explaining that every item you purchase using their credit card becomes collateral for their debt.

For those store credit card debts to be secured debts, however, the purchase transactions must comply with all the particulars of state law for having validly executed, enforceable security interests. If the purchase transactions comply with state law, the furniture, jewelry or 64-inch TVs would be collateral for the debts, subject to repossession if the debts were not paid, just as your car is subject to repossession if you fail to pay your car loan. If the debts were secured debts, in most bankruptcy jurisdictions, when you file bankruptcy you would have the same three "intention" options available as you had with your car loan: (1) surrender (return) the property to the retailer and eliminate any further liability; (2) redeem (purchase) the property for its fair market value, which is likely to be less than the outstanding debt; or (3) reaffirm the debt and continue to pay it, generally as it had been paid prior to bankruptcy.

Here's a bankruptcy secret. In practice, most of these debts are treated as unsecured debts, even if it is possible that the retailers did comply with all the state law requirements for having secured debts. Most retailers will not attempt to repossess their "collateral." The cost of sending out a truck and a crew to repossess a used dining room furniture set almost always exceeds the proceeds the retailer would receive from selling the repossessed furniture. So, if you are willing to risk repossession by treating the store credit card debt as unsecured, the risk of repossession being small (at least until retailers read this book), the store credit card debt is likely to be discharged in Chapter 7 and you will get to keep the furniture.

One of the things that makes practicing bankruptcy law interesting is that bankruptcy rules frequently are double-edged swords. Rules that can hurt debtors in one situation can be used to help debtors in another situation. Here, for example. You might not think that treating furniture store credit card debt as secured could ever be preferable to treating the debt as unsecured and fully dischargeable. You would be wrong. Recall that eligibility for Chapter 13 was based, in part, upon being below two threshold debt limits: one for secured debts and one for unsecured debts. If you wanted to be in Chapter 13 and happened to be over the unsecured debt limit but not the secured debt limit, you might want to treat the furniture store credit card debt as secured to qualify.

 ## PROPERTY THAT CAN BE HARD TO KEEP IN CHAPTER 7

It is easy for most people to recognize that their house, car, and household furniture are items of property that they own that must be exempted in order to be kept in bankruptcy. There are several other assets, however, that people do not always recognize as items of property they own that must be exempted. Those other assets are often overlooked and can inadvertently be lost in bankruptcy, especially for people filing bankruptcy without an attorney. Keeping the assets listed below may be difficult in Chapter 7. If the assets are identified in advance as assets that cannot be exempted and kept in Chapter 7, Chapter 13 may be a better option.

## ❧ LLCs And Other Business Entities

People often do business through an entity, such as a limited liability company or corporation ("LLC"), which they alone own. When they file bankruptcy individually, they may believe that their personal filing is separate from, and therefore has no consequences for, their entity. That belief is only partially correct. Any debt owed by the entity would not be affected by the individual's filing. To the extent that the individual had liability for the entity's debts, as guarantor or co-signor of the entity's debt, the individual's liability could be discharged in the individual's bankruptcy, but the entity's liability for the entity's debts would remain. What people often fail to consider properly is that the entity is an asset they own. Like all assets, unless an exemption is available to protect it, the entity could be lost in bankruptcy.

Most of the time, the entity will be a personal services business with little or no value apart from the individual performing the services. For example, a tutor or web designer may use an LLC to limit liability. The LLC will have few, if any, assets other than perhaps a computer or a website. All the value in the LLC is the individual providing the tutoring or web design services. No one would want to buy the LLC without the tutor or the web designer. Neither the entity nor the entity's assets could be sold by a Chapter 7 Trustee. If the tutor or web designer filed Chapter 7, the entity would not be affected. That is the normal situation.

Occasionally, however, I will observe a Meeting of Creditors in which an individual, who filed bankruptcy without an attorney, discloses that he owns an LLC through which he operates his business, say a motorcycle repair business. The motorcycle repair business owns equipment and tools worth tens of thousands of dollars. The individual believes he has no problem. Only he filed bankruptcy. The LLC did not file bankruptcy. The individual does not own the equipment and the tools, the LLC does. The individual could not be more wrong. The individual owns the LLC. The LLC is an asset of the individual. If the LLC has more assets than liabilities, then the LLC is an asset with value. If that asset is not disclosed and exempted, the asset could be lost to the Chapter 7 Trustee and sold to pay the individual's creditors.

The way in which the value of the LLC is realized is as follows. When the individual files his bankruptcy case, the LLC, which the individual alone owns, becomes part of his "bankruptcy estate" whether the LLC is disclosed as an asset or not. The Chapter 7 Trustee, who is appointed to administer the individual's bankruptcy estate, will "stand in the shoes" of the individual as the sole owner of the LLC with the ability to manage the LLC, including the ability to liquidate the LLC. The Chapter 7 Trustee could sell the motorcycle repair business assets, pay off all the business's debts, and use the remaining proceeds to pay the individual's creditors.

But wait, there is more. It can get even worse. If it appears that the LLC has positive value, that is, the value of the LLC's assets exceeds its debts, the individual might need the permission of the Chapter 7 Trustee to continue to operate the motorcycle repair business after filing bankruptcy. If the LLC has valuable assets, the Chapter 7 Trustee might prefer to close the business rather than risk losing any asset value. If the business continued to operate, the equipment and tools could be lost or damaged. The business might incur additional expenses. A customer might be injured in the garage. The Chapter 7 Trustee might prefer to eliminate the risk of loss by shutting down the business.

The individual saved a few thousand dollars by filing bankruptcy without an attorney, but at an exceedingly high cost. A knowledgeable attorney would have identified the LLC as an asset of the individual. Chapter 13 might have been a better option had exemptions not been available to protect the LLC. Alternatively, some planning might have solved the problem. It might have been possible to liquidate the LLC and turn all the LLC assets and liabilities into assets and liabilities of the individual. The LLC does not have a "tools of the trade" exemption, but the individual does. By liquidating the LLC, the individual might have been able to keep all of motorcycle repair assets in Chapter 7.

What if LLC has some valuable assets, but the LLC itself has debts that exceed the value of the assets? I saw a dentist recently who owned an LLC through which he provided dental services. The LLC owned equipment, including chairs, lights, cabinets, an X-ray machine, and other diagnostic equipment, and had "good will" in the form of a customer list. It is possible that another dentist might want to buy that practice. The LLC thus had some value. Offsetting that value, however, were debts of the LLC including credit card debts, an SBA loan and money owed to vendors. The LLC's debts far exceeded the value of the LLC's assets. If the dentist individually filed Chapter 7, the entity would not be lost to the Chapter 7 Trustee. The dentist would be able to keep the entity because the entity had no "equity" value. The LLC could not be sold. No one would want to buy a dental LLC whose debts exceeded its assets. Even if the LLC's assets were sold separately, the proceeds of the asset sales would first be applied to the LLC's debts before any excess could be used to pay the dentist's personal creditors. Since the LLC's debts exceeded its assets, there could be no proceeds left for the dentist's personal creditors. Technically, the Chapter 7 Trustee would "abandon" the LLC asset back to the debtor, because the LLC asset had no value to the debtor's bankruptcy estate.

It is worth pointing out that in the above illustration, although the dentist could keep the LLC, the dentist most likely would not be able to continue to operate the LLC even after the dentist's Chapter 7 bankruptcy had ended and all the dentist's personal debts were discharged. The discharge the dentist receives will not discharge the LLC's debts. The dentist's personal liability as guarantor of the LLC's debts will be discharged. Creditors of the LLC could not try to collect the LLC's debts against the dentist. But creditors of the LLC could and likely would continue to collect their debts against the LLC. In the example, the LLC did not file Chapter 7, only the dentist filed Chapter 7. Even if the LLC had filed Chapter 7, however, it would make no difference. The entity still would be liable for the entity's debts. Entities are not eligible for a discharge in Chapter 7. Unless the dentists could negotiate some sort of debt repayment plan with the LLC's creditors, eventually the LLC's creditors would obtain a judgment against the LLC and seize the assets of the LLC. In the meantime, the dentist would be spending a fair amount of time and money defending the LLC against the LLC's creditors in court. In this type of situation, it is usually preferable for the dentist to close the LLC, work for someone else for a period of time or move to a new location and "start fresh" with a new practice.

## ❧ Tax Refunds

Unrepresented debtors, and even debtors with inexperienced attorneys, make mistakes with tax refunds. Identifying the potential problem requires a little explaining. If you file your tax return on April 14th and, based upon that tax return filing, you are entitled to receive a tax refund, that right to receive a tax refund would be an asset of yours. If you were to file bankruptcy the next day, on April 15th, you would be required to list the tax refund you expected to receive as an asset on your bankruptcy schedules. Like all assets, you would need an available exemption to protect and keep the tax refund. The only exemption that might be available to protect the tax refund would be a wildcard exemption and it might not be enough to fully protect the tax refund. The nonexempt portion of the tax refund would be lost. That result was straight forward. Let us make the example harder.

What if you file bankruptcy on January 12th? What happens then? Is the tax refund you might be entitled to for the prior year an asset? On January 12th, most likely you will not have filed your tax return for the prior year. The tax return is not due until April 15th. Even if you wanted to file your tax return for the prior year on January 12th, it might not be possible. You might not have received your W-2 or other information that would allow you to complete a tax return on January 12th. Notwithstanding that you have not filed a tax return for the prior year and may not know if you are even entitled to receive a tax refund for the prior year on January 12th, if you file bankruptcy on January 12th, the entire tax refund for the prior year that you receive when you file your tax return would be an asset. Your entitlement to a tax refund for the prior year actually arose at the end of the day on December 31st. The tax refund for the prior year is an asset of yours on January 12th even though you may have no idea how much, if any, of a tax refund you will receive. You may not know if you are entitled to receive a tax refund or how much the tax refund will be until you file your tax return on April 14th. If you do not exempt the tax refund when you file bankruptcy on January 12th, you could lose the tax refund whenever you receive it. If you file your bankruptcy case on January 12th, your Meeting of Creditors will take place at the end of February. At that meeting, the Chapter 7 Trustee will make a point of telling you that you must give him a copy of the tax return when you file it, and you must turn over the nonexempt portion of the tax refund when you receive it. That is bad, but it can get even worse.

What if you file bankruptcy on November 1st? What happens then? Is the tax refund for the current year an asset on November 1st? The current tax year will not end for another two months. The tax return for the current year is not due until April 15th of the following year. Could you have to turn over a tax refund for the current year even though the current year has not ended? Believe it or not, you could have a tax refund asset on November 1st of the current year. Here is how. If in each of the prior two years you received a tax refund of $6,000 because you were significantly over withheld and this year you have approximately the same income, withholding and dependents as the prior two years, you could have "accrued" 10/12 of the $6,000 expected tax refund for the current year on November 1st. You should expect the Chapter 7 Trustee to demand that you turn over approximately $5,000 (10/12's of $6,000) of your tax refund when you receive it in April or May of the following year. The Chapter 7 Trustee would demand the $5,000 even though the tax year had not ended on November 1st. And he would be entitled to it because you "accrue" the tax refund ratably as the year progresses. On November 1st, you would have accrued 10/12 of the tax refund for the year. Unless you had an available wildcard exemption, the nonexempt portion of the tax refund would be lost. At the Meeting of Creditors, the Trustee will make a point of telling you that you must give him a copy of the tax return when it is filed, and you must turn over the nonexempt portion of the refund when you get it. This is a hard case. There are things that could happen after November 1st that might affect the amount of the tax refund. The Trustee would not be entitled to $5,000 if the tax refund ended up being a lot less than $6,000, but the Trustee could be entitled to more, say $8,000 if the refund ended up being say $12,000. Typically, Trustees will not claim a portion of a tax refund before October because of the uncertainty about the tax refund accruing during the rest of the year. If you file bankruptcy late in the year and you regularly receive a large tax refund, there likely will be some significant portion of your tax refund that will be lost unless there is an available wildcard exemption to protect it.

The failure to understand that tax refunds accrue ratably during the year and could result in a tax refund asset prior to the end of the year is a mistake that gets made a lot. Even by attorneys who have filed bankruptcy cases before. They are only likely to make that mistake once. There is some planning that might solve the problem. I have my clients exempt the greatest possible tax refund based on tax refunds received in prior years. If the client expects to receive a large tax refund that cannot be fully exempted, it may be possible to change the tax withholdings before filing bankruptcy so that the actual tax refund is lower than in previous years. Lower tax refund means less tax refund that must be exempted. It may also be possible to wait to file the bankruptcy case until after the tax refund has been received and spent (on items that do not constitute fraudulent transfers).

## ❤ Property Held By Someone Else In Your Name

Another category of assets that gets overlooked and not protected are assets that are held or managed by someone else in the name of the individual who is filing bankruptcy. The best example of this is the joint bank account. If your name is on the title of a bank account, you own that account, at least in part, if not in whole. The extent to which you will be deemed the owner of money on deposit in a bank account titled in multiple parties' names will depend upon state law. Typically, there is a good chance that a judgment creditor of yours could reach (i.e., seize) all the money in a bank account jointly owned by you, even if none of the money in the account was either earned by you or deposited into the account by you. If a judgment creditor could reach (i.e., seize) the funds outside of bankruptcy to satisfy a judgment against you, then a Chapter 7 Trustee will be able to reach those funds to the same extent in bankruptcy, unless an exemption were available. If the money in the joint bank account was not yours, you might not care, but the joint account owner to whom the money belonged might not be thrilled to learn that all their money was lost to your creditors (either outside or in bankruptcy).

Joint bank accounts with spouses generally are no more of a problem than individual bank accounts because the person filing bankruptcy monitors the account and understands how much money is likely to be in the bank account on the day their bankruptcy case is filed and, therefore, what exemptions will be needed to protect the funds.

The problematic accounts are joint bank accounts held and managed by elderly family members. Putting a younger relative on a bank account as co-owner allows the younger relative to manage the account in case the elder family member becomes incapacitated. In the ordinary course of events, owning a joint bank account this way is perfectly fine elder planning. But, if the younger relative gets into financial trouble, the joint bank account becomes a target for the younger relative's creditors outside bankruptcy and the Chapter 7 Trustee in bankruptcy.

The younger relative may not even know that he or she is the co-owner of a bank account that needs to be protected. If they know they are on the joint bank account, they may not know how much money is in the account. The better way to handle the bank account for the elderly family member is to give the younger relative a power of attorney on the bank account to handle the elderly family member's financial affairs in the event of their incapacity. Having a power of attorney is completely different than being on the title of the bank account as a co-owner. There is no need to protect the power of attorney. It has no value.

The mistake that arises in bankruptcy is that these accounts are often overlooked. If the bankruptcy case has already been filed when the account is discovered by the Chapter 7 Trustee, it may be too late to solve the problem, unless exemptions are still available. In some states, it may be possible to prove that none of the money in the joint account ever belonged to the debtor and, therefore, should not be available to judgment creditors of the debtor or the Chapter 7 Trustee. At a minimum, the resolution of that issue, likely before a judge, will involve a lot of legal work, the cost of which could exceed the amount of money in the joint account.

Some advance planning might solve the joint bank account problem. I have my clients investigate whether they possibly could be the co-owner of a bank account with an elderly relative or anyone else. If they are, it may be possible to take the client off as co-owner of the account. If the funds in the account never belonged to the client, removing the client as a co-owner generally is not considered a fraudulent transfer.

A similar problem can arise with people who own a partial interest in family real estate. Unless the ownership interest is small and exemptions are available, the problem is difficult to solve. Simply transferring the real estate interest out of the debtor's name before filing would be considered a fraudulent transfer and reversed. The debtor might be able to sell the interest for fair market value, which would not be considered a fraudulent transfer, and then spend the proceeds before filing (on items that do not themselves constitute fraudulent transfers). In any event, it is far better to be aware of potential problems that might exist than to file bankruptcy without knowing.

## 🕊 Property Held In Your Name For The Benefit Of Someone Else

A related problem is property you own on behalf of someone else. You know you have legal title to the property, but you consider someone else to be the real owner of the property.

This is the problem of a car titled in the name of a parent. The parent has legal title to the car, but the child uses the car and pays for the upkeep of the car and the car loan. The parent is on title to the car because it was cheaper for insurance reasons, the child was too young to obtain financing for the car, or for other reasons. The car may be kept by the child in a state that is not the state in which the parent lives.

In general, if a car is titled in your name, you own the car even though your child is 100% responsible for the car loan and/or maintaining the car. The car does not belong to the child. If you do not have an available exemption to protect it, you could lose the car in bankruptcy. A standard motor vehicle exemption might not be available if you were not using the car.

To avoid this problem, it might be possible for the parent to sell the car to the child for fair market value. The parent could then spend the proceeds before filing (on items that do not themselves constitute fraudulent transfers).

What if the car could not be sold to the child, the parent had to retain ownership of the car and had no available exemptions to protect the car? In that case, the Chapter 7 Trustee could claim that the car was nonexempt property of the parent's bankruptcy estate. The Chapter 7 Trustee would want to sell the car and pay creditors. It might be possible to challenge a Chapter 7 Trustee's characterization of the parent as owner of the car by arguing that the parent merely held "bare legal title" for the child. The parent was the "legal" owner, but the child was the "equitable" owner. If the parent only held the car "in constructive trust" for the benefit of the child, then the car would not be considered part of the parent's bankruptcy estate. The parent would have a better chance of prevailing on this argument if the child originally had paid for the car. The bankruptcy judge might have to render a decision on this issue and that extra legal process will be expensive.

How likely the parent is to prevail on this issue will depend upon the law of the state in which the bankruptcy case is filed. Some states have more "expansive" law on "equitable" vs. "legal" ownership and the concept of a parent holding title for a child in "constructive trust." Other states will take a more literal, name on title means ownership, approach. A knowledgeable bankruptcy attorney will know how favorable the law of the particular state is on the "constructive trust" defense. Although federal bankruptcy law determines what property constitutes "property of the estate," state law determines who owns the property. Once again, "uniform" bankruptcy laws can produce different results in different states.

## ❧ Trusts

Trusts are legal devices used primarily for estate planning purposes and, to a lesser extent, for asset protection purposes. Because bankruptcy requires you to list all the property in which you have an interest and any exemptions that might apply, it is necessary to know whether you have an interest in a trust when you file.

### *Trust Beneficiary*

If you are the beneficiary of a trust, your interest in the trust, for bankruptcy purposes, will coincide with what a creditor of yours could collect from the trust with a judgment from a state law collection lawsuit. For example, if the trust pays you $15,000 every year and you had not yet received the $15,000 from the trust when your bankruptcy case was filed but you were entitled to receive it, the $15,000 likely would be part of your bankruptcy estate. A judgment creditor likely could reach the $15,000 under the laws of most states. You would need an available wildcard exemption to protect it. On the other hand, if the trust pays you $1,000,000 when you turn 31 years old and you are 22 years old when you file bankruptcy, the $1,000,000 likely would not be part of your bankruptcy estate. You had no right to receive the $1,000,000 when you filed bankruptcy. A judgment creditor likely could not reach the $1,000,000 in most states.

### Irrevocable Trusts

The other way you could have an interest in a trust is as the grantor of the trust. An "irrevocable trust" is a trust to which you convey property without retaining the ability to have the trust reconvey the property back to you. The property is irrevocably owned by the trust. If you conveyed property to an "irrevocable trust" long enough before filing bankruptcy that the conveyance could not be considered to be a fraudulent transfer, and if the conveyance was executed by a competent trust attorney in compliance with all relevant statutes, then there is a particularly good chance that neither the trust nor the property that was conveyed to the trust belongs to you. Although you were the grantor of the irrevocable trust, neither the trust nor the property conveyed to the trust would be part of your bankruptcy estate. If you were also the beneficiary of the irrevocable trust, you could have an interest in the irrevocable trust as a beneficiary, as explained in the preceding paragraph.

### Revocable Trusts (Living Trusts)

A "revocable trust" is a trust to which you convey property while retaining the ability to have the trust reconvey the property back to you. The property is owned by the trust, but you could get the property back if you wanted it back. Bankruptcy mistakes tend to be made with revocable trusts and, in particular, revocable trusts known as "living trusts."

Living trusts are popular estate planning tools used to keep property out of the state probate system. Living trusts can save the legal expense of probate and, perhaps, estate taxes. For example, a couple might transfer ownership of their home to a living trust so that when they both die ownership of the house would automatically pass to a beneficiary named in the trust, usually a child. Without the living trust, upon their deaths, the couple's house would pass to an heir mentioned in their wills. The process of transferring the house from the couple's estate to the heir would be administered by a probate judge. Putting the house in a living trust avoids probate. Typically, living trusts are revocable. The grantor can change its mind at any time, revoke the transfer to the trust and get the property back. The couple in the example could change their minds and have the living trust reconvey ownership of the house back to the couple. Why would the couple want the power to reconvey ownership of the house out of the trust and back to them? Having the power to revoke the transfer allows the couple to regain ownership of the house and to sell it, perhaps with greater tax benefits than would be available to the living trust if the living trust were to sell the house.

The bankruptcy problem with revocable trusts, in general, and living trusts, in particular, is that the property in a revocable trust will become part of the grantor's bankruptcy estate. Even though the grantor transferred ownership of the property to the revocable trust, the property will be considered property owned by the grantor. Here's how. The grantor has the power to revoke the transfer of property to the revocable trust. When the grantor files bankruptcy, the Chapter 7 Trustee "steps into the shoes" of the grantor. The Chapter 7 Trustee acquires the grantor's power to revoke the transfer of the property into the revocable trust and executes that power. In effect, any property transferred to a revocable trust by a grantor becomes property of the grantor's bankruptcy estate.

There are two mistakes often made in bankruptcy regarding revocable trusts. The first is not recognizing that a trust is revocable and therefore that the property in the trust will become property of the grantor's bankruptcy estate. The second is not understanding that because the trust is the legal owner of the property, certain exemptions may not be available to protect the property even though it comes into the grantor's bankruptcy estate. For example, if the couple who had transferred ownership of their house to their living trust later filed bankruptcy, their house would come into their bankruptcy estates but would not have the protection of the homestead exemption in most states because the trust owned the house. The couple did not own the house. Exemptions are only available to individuals. The living trust owned the house. The living trust did not file bankruptcy and, even if it had filed, it has no exemptions. The couple potentially has exemptions, but they did not own the house when they filed. The house comes into their bankruptcy estates because the Chapter 7 Trustee revokes the transfer. The couple might be able to use a wildcard exemption, but not the homestead exemption in most states. With proper planning, it may be possible to avoid this mistake by revoking the transfer and dissolving the trust before filing bankruptcy. The couple would then own the house when they file bankruptcy.

## Lawsuits

Do you have any reason to sue someone for money? As they say on late night TV, "Have you been injured in a car accident?" or "Have you taken the following drugs?" and "You may be entitled to compensation." Are you even thinking about suing someone in the future? Well, forget about collecting very much, if anything, from those lawsuits in the future if you file bankruptcy. You may be entitled to compensation, but your chances of receiving the compensation after filing bankruptcy are slim.

Any claim you may have against someone for an accident, personal injury, employment discrimination, failed business deal, or anything else, must be disclosed and protected with available exemptions or lost in bankruptcy. The lawsuit does not have to be filed when you file bankruptcy. Any possible potential lawsuit that you have the right to bring at the time you file bankruptcy, even if it the lawsuit has not been filed by the time you file bankruptcy, must be listed in your bankruptcy schedules, and protected with available exemptions. Otherwise, any recovery will be lost. Like other assets, the right to bring a lawsuit is an asset that must be disclosed and exempted, or it may be lost to creditors.

You may be inclined to ask, "How will anyone know if I fail to include a potential lawsuit in my petition? What if I wait two years after the bankruptcy is over to start the lawsuit?" The answer is that every defendant you file a lawsuit against in the future will check to see if you have ever filed bankruptcy. If you have and if it appears that the claim you are suing for may have arisen before you filed bankruptcy, then the defendant will argue that you are not entitled to bring the lawsuit. The lawsuit belongs to your bankruptcy estate and can only be brought by your bankruptcy estate. You lost the ability to bring the lawsuit by failing to list it as an asset in your bankruptcy petition. If the cause of action entitling you to file the lawsuit arose before you filed bankruptcy, the defendant will prevail.

What happens to the lawsuit if you cannot bring it? If a lawsuit you were entitled to commence prior to filing bankruptcy has merit and value, the Chapter 7 Trustee will pursue the lawsuit on behalf of your creditors. This could happen long after your bankruptcy case has closed, provided the cause of action arose before you filed bankruptcy.

For example, assume you had been injured in an automobile accident prior to filing. You had some pain. You went to see a doctor. He took some x-rays. It was not clear what the extent of the injury was, whether the pain would last very long or whether surgery was needed. You were out of work for four months and are now back to work on a part-time basis. The medical expense debt you incurred due to the loss of income is unmanageable. You are considering filing a personal injury lawsuit. You also are considering filing bankruptcy. Whether you file the personal injury lawsuit by the time you file bankruptcy, you have the right to bring the lawsuit. The potential personal injury lawsuit must be listed in your bankruptcy documents and protected, or you will lose it. In most jurisdictions, there are very few exemptions available to protect a recovery from a personal injury lawsuit.

If the potential personal injury lawsuit is not listed and the personal injury case is brought after the bankruptcy case has closed, the defendant in the personal injury case will argue that the lawsuit is not your case to bring but instead belongs to your bankruptcy estate. The Chapter 7 Trustee might then step in and pursue the case for the benefit of your creditors. If you failed to disclose the existence of a possible cause of action in bankruptcy, it is possible that you will be denied any recovery from the personal injury lawsuit even if some exemptions were available and even if the recovery exceeds 100% of what you owed your creditors. You get punished for not disclosing your potential lawsuit. And it could get even worse. By failing to disclose your potential lawsuit, your bankruptcy discharge could be revoked. Deliberating failing to disclose assets can have harsh consequences in bankruptcy.

In my practice, when I see a prospective client who has a personal injury claim, I always recommend consulting a personal injury lawyer for an estimate of how large the potential damages might be and how long it might take to receive them. If the recovery is large enough and the timing short enough, I recommend pursuing the personal injury lawsuit first. Bankruptcy might not even be needed. In many cases, however, the injuries are too minor, the time until a recovery would be received too long, and the debt too unmanageable to wait. The prospective client sacrifices the potential recovery on the personal injury case but gets immediate debt relief. Whether the Chapter 7 Trustee will pursue the personal injury case on behalf of creditors is something the Trustee will investigate and determine.

## ❦ Property You Are Entitled To Receive But Do Not Yet Have

People who file bankruptcy are required to list every item of property in which they have a legal interest. It is often hard to know or hard to remember that you have an interest in certain types of property that have not been received at the time you file bankruptcy. Although easy to overlook, if these items of property are not listed in your bankruptcy schedules and exempted, they could be lost. Here are some examples:

- Tax refunds, discussed earlier.
- Bonuses or commissions earned but not paid before you file bankruptcy.
- Vacation or severance pay earned but not paid before you file bankruptcy.
- Inheritance or proceeds of a life insurance policy left to you, but not yet received, from someone who died before you file bankruptcy.
- Claims made but not yet paid on a homeowners insurance policy for property damaged before you file bankruptcy.
- Accounts receivable for goods sold or services performed by your sole proprietorship before you file bankruptcy.
- Certain Property You May Receive Within 180 Days After You File

In general, property you acquire after the day you file bankruptcy is not property of your bankruptcy estate. You get to keep everything you acquire after the filing date. There are two main exceptions for property that if acquired (or if you became entitled to acquire) within 180 days (roughly 6 months) after the filing date, would become part of your bankruptcy estate.

### Divorce

The first exception is for property (not including alimony or child support) you receive from a property settlement agreement or divorce decree that goes into effect during the 180-day period after filing. The timing of a property settlement agreement or divorce decree should be within your control, so this exception should rarely occur.

### Inheritance

The second exception is for property you inherit or death benefits or life insurance policy proceeds that you become entitled to during the 180-day period after filing. You acquire the rights to inheritance or life insurance when someone dies. Should someone die within 180 days of your filing a bankruptcy case, anything you would inherit directly or through insurance would become part of your bankruptcy estate. You do not have to receive the property or life insurance during the 180-day period. It is sufficient that the person who has left you something just die during the 180-day period for the property to become part of your bankruptcy estate. Your bankruptcy case may have closed by the time someone dies. It does not matter. If someone dies during the 180-day period, you must notify your bankruptcy attorney and the Chapter 7 Trustee. Your case will be reopened. Unless there are available exemptions, and usually there are not many, the inheritance or life insurance proceeds will go to your creditors whenever you receive them. You might receive them long after the 180-day period has ended. If the inheritance or life insurance proceeds were large enough to pay off 100% of your debts plus fees and expenses of the Chapter 7 Trustee, the remainder would go to you.

With some planning, the loss of inheritance and life insurance can be avoided. Provided they have the mental capacity, the person leaving you the inheritance could change their will and/or insurance policy to leave the inheritance to someone else. Once the 180-day period has ended, the person could change their will and/or insurance policy back to leave the inheritance to you.

I explain the risk of losing an inheritance and the solution to every client. As far as I am aware, no client has ever had someone change their will or life insurance policy to protect against the risk of loss during the 180-day period. The cost of making the change always outweighs the perceived risk. Still, every two years or so, a client contacts me to inform me that someone had died within the 180-day period and left them money, which then goes to their creditors.

 KEEPING NONEXEMPT PROPERTY

As a rule, you need exemptions to protect property from being sold for the benefit of creditors in Chapter 7. If no specific exemption is available, or if the value of the particular asset exceeds the available exemption, the asset, or the excess value of the asset, is nonexempt. The general rule does not always apply. Even if you have nonexempt property, you do not automatically lose the property. There are a few reasons why the Chapter 7 Trustee may not want to sell the property even though it is nonexempt.

First, you and the Chapter 7 Trustee may have different opinions regarding value. For example, an autographed copy of Barry White's debut LP record album "I've Got So Much To Give" may be extremely valuable to you (and me) but not to many other people. There may be a wide divergence of opinion regarding the value of that album. It may take a fair amount of time and effort for the Chapter 7 Trustee to find a buyer willing to pay top dollar for the album. A specialized autographed record album auction may only be held once a year in a distant state. The Trustee will have to safeguard the record album until the auction takes place. The expense of holding the album and transporting the album, as well as the expense of the auction, will reduce the amount received from the sale. Auction fees can easily exceed 15% of the sales price. Finally, the Chapter 7 Trustee receives a fee for distributing money to creditors, which further reduces the net proceeds available to creditors from the sale of the album.

As a result, the expected net proceeds from the sale of the Barry White album and any other nonexempt assets of the debtor must be high enough for creditors to receive a meaningful recovery or the Trustee will not bother administering the debtor's bankruptcy estate. In some jurisdictions, Trustees will not administer an estate if the nonexempt assets appear to be worth under $5,000. You can safely assume that an autographed copy of Barry White's debut LP record album "I've Got So Much To Give" will not sell for more than $5,000. So, even if it were nonexempt, it is unlikely that you would lose the album in bankruptcy. You are "never, never gonna give up" that Barry White album. The Chapter 7 Trustee will "let the music play." That album will remain "the first, the last, [your] everything."

Furthermore, if the nonexempt property appeared to have a value close to the Trustee's threshold for estate administration, the Trustee typically would offer to sell the nonexempt property back to the debtor at a discount that approximates the expenses of the sale. The Trustee would rather sell the Barry White autographed album back to you than at auction if the expected net proceeds to the Trustee were about the same. The Trustee likely would offer to sell the Barry White album to you for 80% of the expected auction sales price (before the auction house's commission). Trustees have an interest in administering bankruptcy estates and closing bankruptcy cases as quickly as possible. If the Trustee must wait several months to realize proceeds at auction, the discount he offers you may be even larger.

Admittedly, it would be unfortunate to lose your autographed copy of Barry White's debut LP record album "I've Got So Much To Give" in Chapter 7. If the Chapter 7 Trustee valued the album at $7,500 and offered it to you for $5,000 to save the time and expense of waiting for the autographed album auction, it might be difficult to come up with the $5,000. Trustees typically will want the money within 45 days. Nevertheless, if you had $50,000 of unsecured debts, paying $5,000 to the Chapter 7 Trustee to, in effect, "settle" the $50,000 debt would be a great deal. It is unlikely that you could settle your debts for 10% outside of bankruptcy.

 ## CHOOSING TO SURRENDER NONEXEMPT PROPERTY

Sometimes, it makes sense to choose Chapter 7 even though you know you will lose nonexempt property. Sometime, the "cost" of surrendering nonexempt property in Chapter 7 is cheaper than paying creditors outside of bankruptcy or paying creditors pursuant to a plan in other bankruptcy chapters. Giving up nonexempt property may be your best economic alternative.

For example, I have represented several clients who needed debt relief following the loss of a business-related lawsuit. The damages they were ordered to pay left them with debts that were unmanageable. One such client owed a judgment creditor over $1 million. In addition to her house, which was fully exempt under the homestead exemption, the client owned a vacation cabin worth $100,000. No exemptions were available to protect the cabin. She earned over $250,000/year. How could she qualify for Chapter 7 with a gross income that high? Her non-consumer debt exceeded her consumer debt. Her $1 million business debt, which was non-consumer debt, exceeded the total of her home mortgage, car loan and credit card debt.

Although she had to give up the nonexempt vacation home worth $100,000 in Chapter 7, that cost was cheaper than the alternatives. In Chapter 13 or Chapter 11, she would have paid creditors at least $100,000 in "disposable income" each year for five years, a total of $500,000. Outside of bankruptcy, she faced being persecuted by the business judgment creditor for $1 million for the rest of her life. In effect, she settled her $1 million business judgment debt and her credit card debt in exchange for her vacation home. By surrendering the $100,000 nonexempt vacation home in Chapter 7, the client effectively settled her debt for less than 10% of what she owed in less than six months. Not a bad deal.

 FRAUDULENT TRANSFERS – GIVING AWAY NONEXEMPT PROPERTY TO KEEP IT FROM CREDITORS

At this point you may be wondering whether there is something you could do prior to filing bankruptcy to keep nonexempt property from winding up in the hands of the Chapter 7 Trustee for the benefit of your creditors. My clients regularly ask whether they can give away property that they will not be able to keep in bankruptcy before they file.

For example, one client asked whether it would be permissible to give away a valuable harp she no longer played to her sister who enjoyed playing the harp. Another client wanted to take his name off the title to a car that was titled in his both his name and his son's name. The son paid the insurance, the car loan, and the maintenance on the car. A third client wanted to sell his interest in his house, which he owned jointly with his wife, to his wife for $1. Unfortunately, those transfers will not succeed in keeping the nonexempt property away from creditors.

When you give away property or sell property for less than it is worth, while you are insolvent, that transfer is known as a "fraudulent transfer" or a "fraudulent conveyance." The transfer can be reversed by a Chapter 7 Trustee. If you are considering bankruptcy, you almost always are insolvent. Taking your name off a vehicle title or deed is really a gift of your half of the property to the other joint owner. It makes no difference whether you plan on reversing the transfer after bankruptcy.

The transfers are not "fraudulent" in the criminal sense, at least not ordinarily. Many fraudulent transfers are made by people who had no idea the transfers were improper or could be reversed. By the way, fraudulent transfers are not just a bankruptcy problem. Fraudulent transfers can also be reversed by judgment creditors outside of bankruptcy if the creditors are aware of the transfers. Fraudulent transfers are considered improper because they deny creditors property that could be used to pay creditors what they are owed. When you give away property or sell property for less than what it is worth, you are keeping property away from creditors that could be used to satisfy their judgments.

What if you gave your harp to your sister many years ago as a birthday present, could the Chapter 7 Trustee reverse the gift when you file bankruptcy? The answer depends upon when you made the gift. The "look-back" period for reversing a fraudulent transfer varies by state but is generally four to six years prior to when your bankruptcy case is filed. So, to keep the transfer of the harp or the car from being reversed by the Chapter 7 Trustee, you would have to wait perhaps as long as six years from the date of the transfer to the date you file bankruptcy. Very few people considering bankruptcy can wait that long. If you file bankruptcy only two years after giving the harp or the car away, the Chapter 7 Trustee would demand the person to whom the property was given return it to the Trustee for sale to benefit your creditors. If you had sold the harp or the car for less than what they were worth, the Chapter 7 Trustee would demand the difference from the buyers. Again, this assumes you were insolvent when the transfers were made.

## How Will The Chapter 7 Trustee Find Out?

If you sell or give away property during the two-year period immediately before you file, you must disclose the transfer in your bankruptcy paperwork. At the Meeting of Creditors, which is held under oath under penalty of perjury, the Chapter 7 Trustee will ask you whether you sold or gave away property above a certain dollar amount during the relevant state law look-back period (usually four to six years) before you filed bankruptcy.

## ❦ What If You Fail To Disclose The Transfer?

If the transfer was made with the intent to hinder, delay, or defraud a creditor or conceal property, not only would the transfer be reversed, but you could be denied a discharge entirely. Failure to disclose a transfer on the bankruptcy paperwork or at the Meeting of Creditors is some evidence that you intended to conceal the transfer, albeit evidence that could be rebutted by other evidence of neglect, carelessness, or stupidity on the part of you or your attorney. Transfers that result in the denial of a discharge are relatively rare. More common are innocent transfers to family members made for less than fair market value that may be reversed by the Chapter 7 Trustee.

An excellent example of a fraudulent transfer often made without any intention of being concealed but overlooked, because it comes as a complete surprise to most clients and some attorneys, is paying college tuition for an adult child. An adult child is a child who is above the age up to which parents are legally responsible for supporting a child. This problem tends to arise with people who had enough resources to comfortably pay not only their own debts but their children's college tuition as well, until something unexpected happened to make their debts unmanageable.

## ❦ The College Tuition Fraudulent Transfer

Imagine the owner of a restaurant business that lost money due to Covid-19 pandemic shutdowns in 2020 and 2021. Out of his savings from when the restaurant was profitable, the restaurant owner paid his daughter's $65,000/ year tuition to Harvard for those two years. Imagine he files Chapter 7 at the end of 2021 to discharge $1 million in restaurant-related debt he personally guaranteed. The Chapter 7 Trustee will discover the tuition payments at the Meeting of Creditors. The Trustee likely will send Harvard a letter requesting the return of those two years' worth of tuition payments on the basis that the payment of tuition to Harvard by the parent was a fraudulent transfer.

If Harvard had accepted the tuition payments directly from the parent and not the daughter/student, it is likely that Harvard would turn over the two years of tuition to the Chapter 7 Trustee. Most courts that have dealt with this issue have determined that paying tuition for an adult child is a fraudulent transfer because parents have no legal obligation to pay tuition for other adults and because the parent receives nothing of value in return for paying the tuition. The child receives an education, which may or may not be worth $65,000/year in the case of Harvard, but the parent receives nothing. Had the daughter paid the tuition or had the parent been ordered by a court to pay the tuition, which may happen in divorce, the outcome could be different.

If it wanted to, Harvard could fight the Trustee in court. Harvard might have a defense to the fraudulent transfer claim. Harvard could argue, for example, that the parent was not insolvent when the tuition payments were made. If the parent was not insolvent when the tuition payments were made, the tuition payments would not be fraudulent transfers. Despite the possibility of there being a defense, Harvard is more likely to turn over the tuition payments to the Chapter 7 Trustee than it is to challenge the Trustee in court. Paying lawyers to fight the Chapter 7 Trustee in court is time consuming and expensive.

Paying tuition and receiving nothing in return while being insolvent is a fraudulent transfer. If the daughter had graduated from Harvard and received a diploma before the bankruptcy case was filed, the parent might not care. Harvard would be out the tuition, not the parent. The turnover by Harvard of the tuition payments to the Chapter 7 Trustee would not cost the parent anything. But, what will happen to the daughter in the future if she needs a transcript from Harvard to apply to law school? The answer is unclear. Harvard turned the tuition over to the Trustee. Harvard might claim the tuition was still owed. Harvard might demand payment of the tuition before releasing the daughter's transcript. If Harvard claimed the daughter still owed the tuition, the daughter might have to file her own bankruptcy to discharge the tuition debt. Once the daughter filed bankruptcy and discharged the tuition debt (which is not a student loan), Harvard could not refuse to release the transcript.

On the other hand, if the daughter had not yet graduated from Harvard and received her diploma when her parent filed bankruptcy, a bigger problem arises. If the daughter is still attending Harvard when Harvard turns over the tuition to the Chapter 7 Trustee, the daughter will owe two years of tuition. The daughter may not be able to complete her coursework without paying the tuition. It is possible that Harvard will not award the daughter a diploma if the tuition is not paid and the coursework completed.

Colleges are working to avoid this fraudulent transfer problem by setting up mechanisms to take tuition payments directly from students, not their parents, even if the parents are funding the payments. The transfer of funds would be from the parent to the student and then from the student to the college. The fraudulent transfer part would then be between the parent and the adult child. The Chapter 7 Trustee could try to recover the tuition payments from the adult child, but few adult children will have the funds to repay the fraudulent transfers. The Chapter 7 Trustee will not be able to collect from Harvard because the transfer of money from the student to Harvard was not a fraudulent transfer. The student did receive something of value from Harvard.

## ❦ Can You Solve A Fraudulent Transfer Problem?

It may be possible to "solve" some fraudulent transfer problems by reversing the transfer prior to filing bankruptcy. The debtor would get the property back but would then own nonexempt property. Whether getting the harp back from your sister or putting your name back on the title to your son's car undoes the fraudulent transfer will depend upon state law and bankruptcy court decisions in your jurisdiction.

Reversing the transfer is not always possible. If your sister or son were themselves insolvent when the transfer was reversed, the transfer of the property back to you could be a fraudulent transfer with respect to creditors of your sister or your son. The harp or car was property your sister or son owned that could have gone to pay their creditors.

If reversing the fraudulent transfer was not an option, then the only "cure" would be to wait out the look-back period. If you gave your sister the harp two years ago and the state law look-back period was four years, you would have to wait two more years to file bankruptcy. Once the full, four-year look-back period had expired, the Chapter 7 Trustee would not be able to reverse the fraudulent transfer and get the harp. Probably. There is always an exception. A good rule to follow is that fraudulent transfers should always be avoided. There is some legitimate planning you can engage in prior to filing bankruptcy that could minimize the amount of nonexempt property you have when you file bankruptcy.

 # WHAT PLANNING CAN YOU DO TO MINIMIZE NONEXEMPT PROPERTY?

## ❧ Exemption Planning

If you cannot give away your nonexempt property without the transfer being treated as a fraudulent transfer and reversed, is there anything else you can do to keep nonexempt property out of your bankruptcy estate? This topic is known as exemption planning. A full discussion is quite complicated and beyond the scope of this book. I will try to provide a simple, Readers Digest, version: a little planning is ok; a lot of planning looks bad and could be problematic. Here are some guidelines.

### Sales At Fair Market Value

Remember the nonexempt harp mentioned above? You could not give the harp to your sister without the gift being reversed as a fraudulent transfer, because you received nothing of value in return from your sister. With gifts, nothing of value ever is received in return. Gifts always are fraudulent transfers. One way to avoid the gift as fraudulent transfer problem is to sell the harp for what it is worth, its fair market value. The way the harp is sold, and the identity of the purchaser, will provide some indication of whether the sale was for fair market value. Sales at auction to unrelated parties are most indicative that the sale was at fair market value. A sale to your sister would come under greater scrutiny. You would want "proof" from other sources that the price your sister paid for the harp was its fair market value. Closed auction prices from sales on eBay, for example, provide good "proof" of value.

### Pay Living Expenses

The sale at fair market value solves the gift problem, but it merely transforms a nonexempt harp into cash that also is nonexempt. Unlike the harp, however, the cash can be used in a way that is not a fraudulent transfer. The most common way is to use the cash proceeds from the sale of the harp for normal, day to day living expenses. That is the most common method of "exemption planning." The proceeds from the sale of the nonexempt harp can be used, for example, to make regular monthly mortgage, cable TV and electric bill payments. The reason paying regular monthly bills is not a fraudulent transfer is because you receive equivalent value in exchange for the payments. You pay $100 for groceries or for cable TV and you receive $100 worth of groceries or cable TV in return. You could even use the proceeds from the sale of your nonexempt harp to pay your bankruptcy lawyer. Again, you receive equivalent value in return. I once had a client who sold a nonexempt boat and used to proceeds to pay me. It was a small boat.

### Avoid Pre-payments

There are, as you might expect, limits on how the proceeds from the sale of nonexempt property can be spent prior to filing. You may not pre-pay expenses. If you pay an expense before it arises, by paying a bill before it becomes due, you are creating a pre-payment. That pre-payment is an asset you would have to list and exempt in your bankruptcy schedules or lose. If you had sold your harp and prepaid your cable TV for the next year, you would have converted one nonexempt asset into another nonexempt asset.

Some pre-payment assets are obvious, such as prepaying one-years' worth of cable TV. Other prepayments can arise inadvertently. I once had an initial consultation in April with a prospective client who waited until October to file bankruptcy in Chapter 7. At the end of August, the client paid an entire year's worth of daycare tuition for her pre-school child. The daycare tuition was normally billed monthly. By prepaying the monthly tuition for the entire year, the client had inadvertently created a daycare tuition prepayment asset. Had I known about the prepayment, the prepayment might have been listed as an asset and exempted, if exemptions were available. In this case, I was unaware that the prepayment had been made and there were no available exemptions anyway. Had the daycare tuition been charged on an annual basis due in August and not been refundable for any reason, the payment might not have been a prepayment. Unfortunately, this daycare tuition was due monthly, not on an annual basis. The client had merely prepaid a year's worth of monthly daycare tuition payments in August. The prepayment was a nonexempt asset. By prepaying the daycare tuition before it was due, the client inadvertently had done the equivalent of giving her sister a nonexempt harp.

The Chapter 7 Trustee sent the day care center a letter demanding the return of the then unused portion of the prepayment. In theory, the daycare center could have challenged the characterization of the payment as a fraudulent transfer and fought to keep the money. Doing so would have meant going before a judge and incurring considerable legal expenses. Instead, the daycare center turned over the remaining prepayment to the Chapter 7 Trustee. At that point, my client did not owe the daycare center any money for prior tuition, but the prepayment for future tuition was lost. The day care center then sent my client another bill for tuition for the remainder of the year. Since she wanted to keep her child in the daycare center, my client had to pay the tuition bill a second time. The daycare tuition prepayment was inadvertent, but there was no way to "fix" the problem once the case was filed.

### Converting Nonexempt Property Into Exempt Property

In addition to using the proceeds from the sale of the nonexempt harp to pay current living expenses, it also might be possible to use the proceeds to buy property that has a specific exemption available to protect it. This is known as converting a nonexempt asset into an exempt asset. Most bankruptcy courts will allow some degree of converting nonexempt assets into exempt assets, even if the conversion is done relatively shortly before filing. For example, the nonexempt harp might be sold, and the proceeds of the sale used to buy tools of the trade, where a specific tools of the trade exemption was available to protect that kind of property.

This type of exemption planning can even be used by a prospective bankruptcy filer to buy a house before filing and thereby convert nonexempt cash into a house protected by the homestead exemption. A pretty significant chunk of cash that otherwise would be nonexempt and lost to creditors could be converted into a house completely exempt from creditors. That may seem unfair to creditors, but courts recognize that people in bankruptcy need a place to live and liberally allow the conversion of nonexempt assets into houses protected by the homestead exemption. This type of exemption planning is allowed even on the "eve of filing." Some courts in states that have exemptions protecting annuities liberally allow similar "eve of filing" conversions of nonexempt cash into exempt annuities. Check with a knowledgeable bankruptcy attorney to see if that type of exemption planning is allowed in your jurisdiction.

The risk in engaging in too much exemption planning is that you may look less like an honest person who suffered an unexpected setback and more like a dishonest person just trying to get out of paying creditors. If your situation looks "abusive," the filing could be challenged, and the bankruptcy court judge could deny your discharge. Perhaps by design, there are no hard and fast rules governing exemption planning. If there were, people would always go right up to the line. Nevertheless, what follows is a list of exemption planning practices that tend to be allowed in most bankruptcy jurisdictions. Caveat: there is no guarantee they will work in your jurisdiction.

- Make your yearly retirement plan contribution.
- Repay any retirement plan loans.
- Catch up on tax payments if you have been under-withheld.
- Get needed medical or dental treatments, where non-refundable payment for the treatment is required in advance even though the treatment may not be performed immediately, like braces.
- Repair a leaky roof or septic system or make other necessary household repairs, but be aware that repairs could increase the value of your house beyond the available homestead exemption.
- Repair or tune-up a car, or buy needed tires, but be aware that repairs could increase the value of your car beyond the available motor vehicle and wildcard exemptions.
- Pay non-dischargeable priority debts, such as back alimony and child support and recent income taxes.
- Pay arrearages on secured debts, such as a home mortgage or car loan.

If you engage in any kind of prebankruptcy exemption planning, make sure that all required disclosures are made. It is far better to disclose the sale of nonexempt property on the Statement of Financial Affairs and in the Meeting of Creditors along with an explanation of how the proceeds from the sale were used -- to pay living expenses or to purchase exempt property, than to conceal what you did. Honesty goes a long way in bankruptcy.

## WHICH STATE'S EXEMPTION LAWS APPLY?

If you have lived in one state continuously for the two years prior to filing bankruptcy, then there is no question about which state's exemption laws apply. Your exemptions be those of the state in which you have been living and, if that state is one of 19 states plus the District of Columbia that currently provide the option of using the federal bankruptcy exemptions, you could select the better for you between that state's exemptions and the federal bankruptcy exemptions.

What if you moved within the last two years and have lived in more than one state during the two years prior to filing? Which state's exemption laws apply? Remember that some states have far more generous exemptions than others. To keep people from moving to the states with the best exemptions, Congress established a set of rules. If you have lived in more than one state within the last two years, a series of questions must be answered to determine which state's exemption laws apply.

## ❧ Question 1: Have You Been "Domiciled" In The Same State Continuously For Two Years Or More Prior To Filing Bankruptcy?

Notice that this question asks about "domicile," not "residence." There is a big difference. Residence is where you happen to be living on more than a temporary basis. Domicile is where you reside and intend to stay for an indefinite period of time. A person can have only one domicile at a particular time, even though he or she may have several residences. For most people, their domicile state will be the state where their principal residence is located. For example: You own a home in Washington state, but you are in the military currently stationed at a base in Alabama. You may be a resident of both states, but your domicile is Washington. You do not intend to stay in Alabama.

If you have been domiciled in the same state continuously for two years or more prior to filing, that state's exemption laws will apply. That will generally be the state in which the case will be filed. That state may give you the option of using the federal bankruptcy exemptions. For example: If you have lived continuously for three years in Florida, Florida's exemption laws will apply. Florida does not offer the option of using the federal exemptions. Whatever exemptions Florida law provides will protect your property in bankruptcy. If you have lived continuously for three years in Connecticut, Connecticut's exemption laws will apply. But, unlike Florida, Connecticut law allows the choice between Connecticut exemptions and federal bankruptcy exemptions. You could select the exemptions that offered your property the best protection.

If you were domiciled in two states during the past two years, the next question will apply. Notice that you could have lived temporarily in two states without having a domicile in two states. If you were on assignment for work for two months or if you were visiting your parents for the summer, you might have been "resident" in two states within the past two years, but you were not "domiciled" in two states during the past two years. You had to have intended to stay in both states to have domiciles in both states. Normally, that means you had a job and a house in one state and then moved to a new state for a new job and bought a new house.

## ❧ Question 2: If You Were "Domiciled" In More Than One State During The Two Years Prior To Filing Bankruptcy, Where Did You Reside The Most During The Six Months Immediately Preceding The Two-Year Period?

If you have been domiciled in more than one state during the two-year period immediately preceding the bankruptcy filing, the applicable state exemption laws will be those of the state in which you resided the most time during the six months immediately preceding the two-year period, in other words, between 24 and 30 months prior to filing.

This is confusing, so here are a few examples to make sense of it. The Smiths lived in Missouri their wholes lives until moving to New York one year ago. The Smiths have lived in New York for more than 91 days, so they can file their bankruptcy case in New York, but the Smiths have not lived continuously in New York for the two years prior to filing, so New York exemption law does not apply. We must see where the Smiths lived in the six months prior to the last two years. Since the Smiths have only lived in

New York for the last year and lived in Missouri their whole lives before that, it is clear that they lived in Missouri for the six months prior to the last two years. Missouri exemption law would apply even though the Smiths live in New York and file bankruptcy in New York.

What if the Smiths worked for a company that liked to move its employees around a lot? IBM was famous for frequently moving its employees. There was a joke at one time that IBM stood for "I've Been Moved." What if the Smiths had been domiciled in both Missouri and Kansas in the six-month period prior to the two years before filing bankruptcy? Again, to be domiciled, they had to have intended to stay in both states during that six-month period, so this is unlikely to happen, but it could and surprisingly it does. The Smiths bought houses, enrolled their kids in schools and intended to stay in both states until they moved. The Smiths could have had a home in one suburb of Kansas City and moved to another suburb of Kansas City not far away, but in another state. Which state's exemption law applies – Kansas or Missouri? The answer is the state in which the Smiths lived the most. They will have lived in either Kansas or Missouri for a majority of the six months prior to the two years prior to filing bankruptcy. Whichever of those states they lived in the most during the six-month period is the state whose exemption laws apply. In most cases, but not all. I never told you bankruptcy would be easy, just easier than you think.

## ❦ Question 3: Does The State Whose Exemption Laws Apply Allow Its Exemption Laws To Apply Outside The State?

There are a few states that do not allow their exemption laws to apply "extraterritorially," that is, outside their state. It turns out that Kansas is one such state. If the Smiths had lived in Kansas for the majority of the six-month period prior to the two years prior to filing, that is, between two and two and one-half years before filing, Kansas exemption law would apply. However, Kansas exemption law says that only people residing in Kansas can use Kansas exemptions. The Smiths now live in New York. They are not residents of Kansas. Kansas exemption law prohibits people living in New York from using Kansas exemptions. Kansas exemption law applies, but the Smiths cannot use it. What can the Smiths do? Besides finding a particularly good bankruptcy lawyer.

Fortunately, Congress planned for this contingency. If you are not eligible to claim the exemption laws of the state whose exemption laws should apply, you may claim the federal bankruptcy exemptions. This can even get more complicated because it turns out that a few states have some exemptions that are available to people living outside the state and some other exemptions that are not available to people living outside the state.

The reason Congress enacted these seemingly crazy two-year and six-month rules was to deter people from moving from states with stingy exemption laws to states with generous exemption laws. The homestead exemption, which protects a house, is the one exemption most people move to take advantage of. Florida and Texas are states with extremely generous homestead exemptions. What if you had $1 million in cash? Could you buy a home in those states and protect the home from creditors using the state homestead exemption? Not immediately. You would have to buy the house and wait 1,215 days (about 3 years, 4 months) to file bankruptcy in order to be able to take advantage of the state's homestead exemption law. Prior to 1,215 days, the homestead exemption would be limited to approximately $150,000 of house equity.

Notice that none of these rules prevents exemption "planning." You can move from state to state to take advantage of one state's more generous exemptions. You can move to Connecticut to take advantage of Connecticut's unlimited bridal jewelry exemption. The only catch is that you must be domiciled in Connecticut for at least two years to be eligible to use Connecticut's exemptions. To take advantage of Florida' generous homestead exemption you would have to wait approximately 3-1/2 years.

# CHAPTER 8

# What Happens To Your Debts?

What happens to your debts in bankruptcy? Are they all discharged? Are any debts not discharged or non-dischargeable? The treatment of debts in bankruptcy depends upon the type of debt.

#  SECURED DEBTS

Secured debts, that is, debts that are secured by collateral, do not get discharged in bankruptcy. The debts do not disappear. You do not get a free house or a free car in bankruptcy.

As part of the legal process for having collateral secure a debt, the lender will "perfect" its security interest in the property and thereby obtain a "lien" on the property. The way the lien arises will vary depending upon the type of property and state law. For example, in some states to perfect its security interest in a car, the car lender will stamp the car's title with the word "lien." In other states, the car lender will take and hold title to the car until the car loan is repaid in full.

The expression in bankruptcy world is that "liens ride through bankruptcy," which means that liens are unaffected by bankruptcy. If a car has a lien, because it is collateral for a loan, before bankruptcy, the lien will remain on the car after bankruptcy.

One possible exception is if the lender made a mistake. If the lender failed to properly "perfect" its security interest in the collateral, a Trustee in bankruptcy has the power to "avoid," that is, remove, the lien from the collateral. If the lender makes such a mistake, the lien will be removed, the property will no longer be collateral for the debt and the debt will become unsecured. The debt will become the equivalent of credit card debt. There are both positive and negative consequences of that happening. As you might expect, secured lenders have exceptionally good lawyers who rarely make that mistake. So, it is highly unlikely that any of your secured debts will become unsecured, but it occasionally happens. Most famously, it was revealed in General Motor's bankruptcy that lawyers had failed to properly perfect a security interest in the auto manufacturer's property.

The secured debts most people owe are home mortgages and car loans. As described in more detail above ("What Can You Keep In Bankruptcy?"), except in the unusual situation in which continuing to pay the secured debt is uneconomical and the house or car is "surrendered" to the lender, most people will keep their house or car and continue to pay the loans.

In most bankruptcy jurisdictions, to keep your house or car, you are required to "reaffirm" the secured debt. Reaffirming the debt means that you will be personally liable for the debt just as you were prior to filing bankruptcy. The positive side is that you get to keep the property. The negative side is that to the extent the property is later foreclosed or repossessed, you will be personally liable for any deficiency, that is the difference between what you owe at that time and the value of the repossessed collateral that secures the debt.

In other bankruptcy jurisdictions, because of favorable state law or judicial precedent, you are not required to reaffirm the secured debt. Instead, you can "retain and pay," that is, retain the collateral and continue to pay the secured debt. Unlike reaffirming the secured debt, with retain and pay your personal liability will be discharged but the lien will remain (the lien "rides through" bankruptcy). That means that in the future if you fall behind on car loan or mortgage payments and the collateral is foreclosed or repossessed, you will not be liable for the deficiency. The secured lender can only take the property securing the debt.

## Cross Collateralization

Home mortgages and car loans are fairly obvious secured debts. It is clear when the loans are taken out that the house or car is collateral for the loans. You may have other debts, however, that are not as obvious. The loans may appear to be unsecured but actually are secured with collateral. These "stealth" secured debts often arise with credit unions. Credit unions operate a little differently than other lenders. Credit unions typically include "cross-collateralization" clauses in all their loans. This means that the collateral provided for one loan will immediately become collateral for all other loans extended by the credit union, even loans that are typically unsecured. The covered loans may be loans that were extended in the past or loans that might be extended in the future.

For example, if you have a car loan and a credit card or line of credit with a credit union, it is possible that your car is collateral not only for the car loan but also for the credit card or line of credit. Credit cards and lines of credit normally are unsecured. But, if the car cross-collateralizes the credit card or line of credit, the credit card or line of credit will be secured debts. The bankruptcy treatment of the credit card or line of credit will now be like a car loan. Even after you receive a discharge in bankruptcy, if the credit card debt or line of credit is not repaid in full, the credit union could retain the title to the car or, perhaps, even repossess the car.

If you have any secured debts with a credit union, you need to carefully review the loan documents to see if the collateral provided for the secured loan is also collateral for any other loans you have with the credit union. In some situations, it might be preferable to file bankruptcy in Chapter 13 and treat the combined debt as being secured only up to the value of the collateral and the remainder of the debt as unsecured debt which can be discharged. Also note that your share account at the credit union (like a savings account) could be set off by amounts owed on a credit card debt to the credit union on the day of filing. If you cannot close credit union accounts prior to filing, you should limit automatic deposits and amounts on deposit at credit unions when you file.

 UNSECURED DEBTS

Most people want to keep their house and car, so continuing to be liable for secured debts normally is not an issue. Discharging unmanageable unsecured debt, that is, debts that are not secured by collateral, is the reason most people file bankruptcy. Most unsecured debts can be discharged in bankruptcy, but there are exceptions. Some unsecured debts are not dischargeable in bankruptcy. There are a few differences between Chapter 7 and Chapter 13 in terms of the kind of unsecured debts that can discharged, but not many. Debts that are not dischargeable in Chapter 7 usually are not dischargeable in Chapter 13.

### Credit Card Debt

In general, debts incurred on credit cards issued by financial institutions including American Express, Discover, Capitol One and Chase, as well as charge cards issued by stores like Walmart, Kohls and Target (which are often managed by banks such as Synchrony and Citibank), are all unsecured debts that are dischargeable in bankruptcy. Also included within the "credit card" category are personal loans and personal lines of credit issued without collateral. As mentioned earlier, charge cards from certain stores, primarily jewelry and furniture retailers, may be secured with the items purchased at those stores.

There are a few exceptions to the general rule of credit card debt being dischargeable. The non-dischargeable exceptions are for certain purchases that Congress considered to be improper. Congress wanted to provide debt relief to honest but unfortunate folks. Congress did not want to reward less-than-honest people who deliberately misuse their credit cards. Those kinds of debts are not automatically non-dischargeable. The creditor must raise the issue. If the creditor does not raise the issue, then the credit card debt will be discharged. A few types of credit card debt are presumptively non-dischargeable. This means that if a creditor raises the issue, little "proof" will be required for a court to find the debt to be non-dischargeable. Other types of credit card debt could be found by a court to be non-dischargeable depending upon how the charges were incurred, but the creditor would need more proof to convince a court those debts should be non-dischargeable.

### *Luxury Purchases*

A credit card debt owed to a single creditor for the purchase of more than $725 of "luxury goods or services" that was incurred within ninety days before filing is presumed to be non-dischargeable. "Luxury goods or services" are defined by the Bankruptcy Code by what they are not. They are not goods or services reasonably necessary for the support of the debtor and the debtor's dependents. Basically, Congress does not want people buying a Louis Vuitton handbag, Jimmy Choo shoes or a Rolex watch and then immediately filing bankruptcy to avoid paying for them.

### Cash Advances

The presumption of non-dischargeability also extends to cash advances totaling more than $1,000 from one creditor within seventy days before filing.

### Overcoming The Presumption

For the luxury purchase or cash advance debt to be non-dischargeable, the credit card issuer must raise the issue. If the debt arose within the ninety- and seventy-day periods, there is a presumption that these types of debts are not dischargeable. The debtor could try to rebut that presumption in court by introducing sufficient evidence to convince a judge that the debt was dischargeable. In practice, that never happens. Card issuers like American Express review the purchase history of bankruptcy filers. If particular purchases or cash advances appear to be within the presumption periods, the issuer will notify the attorney and, if the purchase was not reasonably necessary for the client's support, the client will agree to pay that particular charge. The cost of overcoming the presumption in court almost always outweighs the benefit. If a particular purchase or cash advance arose within the presumption periods, only that particular "bad" charge would be paid. All other credit card debt would be discharged.

Notice that this is not a particularly difficult problem to avoid. If it appears that you took a cash advance or purchased a luxury good within the statutory period, the presumption problem could be avoided entirely by waiting 71 or 91 days to file. That is a maximum waiting period of three months.

In practice, luxury purchases and cash advances are almost never an issue. Most of my clients have maxed out their credit cards and not used them at all more than 90 days before coming to see me.

### Debts Incurred By Fraud

Waiting 91 days to file does not guarantee that a creditor will not object to the discharge of a particular debt, it just means the presumption will not apply and the creditor will have a much higher burden of proof to satisfy. Without the presumption, the creditor must prove that the debt was incurred by fraud. Debts incurred fraudulently are not dischargeable in bankruptcy. Fraud, for bankruptcy world purposes, encompasses several bad acts. For example, fraud includes obtaining credit under false pretenses, by overstating income or assets on a loan application or by falsifying documents used to support the loan application.

In consumer, that is, non-business, cases, fraud normally means that the debt was incurred with no intention of being repaid. That may sound scary, but it is rarely a problem. Most of my clients were making at least minimum monthly payments regularly for years before something bad happened to make the debt unmanageable. Rarely does someone incur a credit card debt, make no payments, and then declare bankruptcy. Once again, Congress enacted a rule to deny the discharge of debt that was not honestly incurred.

I tell my clients to expect their credit card issuers to review their purchase and payment history for the six months prior to filing. If it appears that their charges spiked close to filing, the credit card issuer might suspect that the recent charges were incurred with no intention of being repaid. One indicator of no intention of repayment would an absence of any monthly payments following the spike in usage. If that sort of history is present, the creditor will send me a letter asking for an explanation. If my explanation indicates that that the client did have an intention to pay the recently incurred debt, but something unexpected interfered, such as a job loss, divorce or medical condition, the credit card issuer normally will accept my explanation and not challenge dischargeability of the debt.

It has not happened to me in a consumer case, but if the explanation was not satisfactory, the creditor could challenge the dischargeability of the debt, at least the portion that appears to have been incurred with no intention of being repaid. Ultimately, a bankruptcy judge would determine whether the debtor did or did not intend to repay the debt. Particularly good evidence that the debtor did intend to repay the debt would be a subsequent payment of the debt. It would be difficult for a court to find that a debtor who actually did repay a portion of the debt had originally incurred the debt with no intention of repaying it. So, if your credit card usage spiked recently, you might want to make some payments for some period of time before filing.

### *When Can You Stop Paying Your Credit Card Bills?*

Making some credit card payments to protect against a challenge to dischargeability for fraud is an exception to the usual rule that once you decide to file bankruptcy, it does not make any sense to continue paying credit card debt. If you were confident that the credit card was going to be discharged, making further payments would amount to throwing away good money that might be better used elsewhere. You might pay your bankruptcy lawyer instead, for example.

The computer program that manages your account at Capital One is not going to be any less angry with you for filing bankruptcy if you make one more monthly payment before filing. Discover will not give you extra credit points in the future for making the payment. So, why waste the money?

The downside of not paying credit card debt is that collectors will call and attempt to make your life a living hell unless you pay. By retaining an attorney to represent you in bankruptcy and telling the collector, you will force the collector to call the lawyer instead of you. But you will not prevent the credit card issuer from suing you to collect until you actually file your bankruptcy case. Typically, you can go at least six months without making a payment before a credit card issuer will bring a collection lawsuit. As always, your mileage may vary. It could be a few months sooner or later and it might depend upon how much is owed. If you owe $20,000 on one credit card, the odds of being sued are a little higher than if you owe $2,000 on each of ten credit cards. My advice is always to get the bankruptcy case filed within six months of stopping payment.

### Should You Pay Any Credit Cards Off Before Filing?

What about credit cards that are open at the time a bankruptcy case is filed, but have no outstanding balances? People often ask if they will be able to carry a credit card through bankruptcy if they do not have a balance owed on the card when the case is filed. My answer is to expect all credit cards to be turned off as soon as the bankruptcy case is filed. The decision to turn off a credit card is up to the issuer, who will not receive direct notice of the bankruptcy filing if the issuer is not owed any money. However, there are very few issuers of consumer credit in the United States and they monitor bankruptcy filings. In my experience, it is likely that all your credit cards will be shut down shortly after filing whether the cards have an outstanding balance or not. As a result, it does not make any sense to pay down credit cards in advance of filing to avoid listing the cards in your bankruptcy petition in the hope that they will remain active after filing. The cards are likely to be shut off anyway.

## What About The "Gap" Period Of Time Between Filing Bankruptcy And Being Offered New Credit Cards?

How does someone who needs access to credit handle that "gap" period? To bridge that gap, the short period of time following filing before the filer has access to their own credit cards again, the filer can become an authorized user on someone else's card, say a parent or close friend. Cards on which you are merely an authorized user likely will continue to work after you file. Generally, because an authorized user is not responsible for paying off the credit card, when an authorized user files bankruptcy, the credit card usually is not shut off or otherwise affected.

## When Must You Stop Using Your Credit Cards?

The flip side of not paying your creditors once you decide to file bankruptcy is that you must stop incurring new debts. If you are no longer paying your credit cards, you must stop using the credit cards. Once you have decided to file bankruptcy, incurring any further debt would, by definition, be incurring debt with no intention of being repaid. That debt could be non-dischargeable.

How would a credit card issuer know when you decided to file? One objectively determinable moment reflecting your intention to file is when you sign an engagement agreement with a bankruptcy attorney. Your bankruptcy petition will disclose when and how much your bankruptcy lawyer was paid. Using credit cards after the date on which an engagement agreement was signed is problematic. If you thought that there would be a fairly long period of time between the date you signed an engagement agreement and the date you file bankruptcy, you could continue to use credit cards for non-luxury purchases, but you should also continue to make payments, ideally in an amount as large as the recent purchases.

## ♥ Medical Debt

Like credit card debt, medical debts normally are dischargeable in bankruptcy. The potential problem with discharging medical debt is that the medical provider may not answer the phone when you call. Hospitals generally will not refuse to admit patients who have filed bankruptcy. Under the Emergency Medical Treatment and Active Labor Act (EMTALA), a hospital cannot turn you away from their emergency room. On the other hand, doctors and dentists may refuse to see you if you have discharged their debt, with the one possible exception that Medicaid may offer some protection against health care providers denying future services.

Not listing medical debts is not an option. By law, all debts must be listed in the bankruptcy petition. As a solution, in my practice, clients who are nervous about discharging medical debt are told to blame the problem on their horrible, mean bankruptcy lawyer. We have clients tell the provider that their bankruptcy lawyer made them do it -- list and discharge the debt. Despite the discharge, the clients would like to continue to see the provider and continue to make payments on the debt. Just because a debt has been discharged in bankruptcy does not mean that the debt cannot be paid. Nothing prohibits you from paying discharged debts after bankruptcy. In fact, you could pay Amex and Capital One after those credit card debts have been discharged in bankruptcy. Usually, medical providers will be delighted that you want to continue to pay the medical debt after discharge, and will work with you on a payment plan while continuing to see you.

The other consideration with medical debt is timing. To the extent that you have some control over the timing of your bankruptcy filing, you might want to wait to file until after you have incurred upcoming expected medical debts. For example, if you knew of an upcoming operation that insurance might not fully cover, you might want to wait to file bankruptcy until those medical debts have been incurred. You do not have to wait until a bill for the uninsured portion is received to discharge the debt. You just must wait until the procedure has been performed to file. Having the operation incurs the debt, not receiving the bill.

## Personal Guarantees; Co-Signing Debts For Others

What happens if you have co-signers or guarantors on your debt when you file bankruptcy and what happens to you if you are a co-signor or guarantor of someone else's debt when they file bankruptcy?

Bankruptcy only discharges the debts of the filer. Anyone who co-signed a debt for you when you file bankruptcy will still be liable for that debt after you receive a discharge. Similarly, if you co-signed a debt for someone else who files bankruptcy, you will still be liable for that debt after that person receives a discharge.

Chapter 13 has a co-debtor stay that prevents collection of a debt from a co-debtor under certain conditions, but only during the pendency of the case. Once the Chapter 13 case has ended, the creditor could resume collection efforts against the co-debtor.

## ❧ Bad Checks

If you had checks that bounced and are listed on a bad check registry, such as ChexSystems and TeleCheck, listing the systems as creditors in your bankruptcy schedule can remove you from the systems and make it easier for you to open a bank account after you receive a discharge.

#  NON-DISCHARGEABLE DEBTS

There are several different kinds of debts that are not dischargeable in bankruptcy. Some debts are not dischargeable because of the nature of the debt itself. Examples include alimony or child support obligations, student loan debt and recent income tax debt. Other debts are not dischargeable because of something that was done or not done by the debtor, such as incurring the debt with no intention of repaying it.

## ❧ Domestic Support Obligations

Debts for alimony, maintenance, or child support, which are known as "domestic support obligations" and which bankruptcy world abbreviates as "DSOs," are never dischargeable. Congress really hates deadbeat dads

302 | FRESH START

and wants them to pay their obligations. Do not even think about using bankruptcy to discharge an obligation to pay alimony or child support.

## ❧ Property Obligations

In the context of a divorce, besides support, another type of obligation may arise – a property obligation. For example, one spouse might be awarded the marital house in exchange for paying the other spouse an amount of money over time representing the value of the spouse's interest in the house. In Chapter 7, that property obligation is not dischargeable. But, in Chapter 13, property obligations are dischargeable.

How do you know if an obligation arising in the context of a divorce is a support obligation or a property obligation? Most separation and divorce agreements are clear as to whether a particular obligation is a support obligation or a property obligation. Knowledgeable divorce attorneys will try to make every single obligation imposed on the other spouse a support obligation to prevent the obligation from being discharged later by the obligated spouse in Chapter 13. Sometimes, in less carefully drafted separation and divorce agreements, it may be difficult to tell whether the obligation to pay one spouse a sum of money over time is a support obligation or a property obligation. A large body of case law has developed in bankruptcy courts distinguishing support obligations from property obligations. For example, in most jurisdictions, bankruptcy judges have held that the obligation to pay a spouse's attorney fees or a child's guardian ad litem attorney's fees are support obligations which are not dischargeable in either Chapter 7 or Chapter 13. When in doubt, consult a knowledgeable bankruptcy attorney.

## ❧ Student Loans

Bankruptcy law states that a student loan debt, including a parent's co-liability under a Parent Plus Loan, may be discharged in bankruptcy only if the repayment of the student loan debt would impose an "undue hardship" on the debtor -- the student or the student's parent. You might have thought that paying a student loan would always create an undue hardship for someone who had to resort to bankruptcy for relief from unmanageable debt. You would be wrong.

In most jurisdictions around the country, for an "undue hardship" to exist, three conditions must be satisfied: (1) the debtor cannot maintain a "minimal" standard of living; (2) additional circumstances exist to show that the debtor's financial condition is "likely to persist for a significant portion of the repayment period," and (3) the debtor made a good faith attempt to repay the loan. "Undue hardship" is thus defined so that repaying student loan debt will not be considered to be an undue hardship unless the debtor is barely above the poverty level and the debtor's prospects for ever repaying any portion of the student loan are hopeless. In other words, the debtor must be in a coma. When a prospective client walks into my office for an initial consultation, I can immediately tell that he or she will not be able to discharge a student loan.

The good news is that the law in this area is beginning to change. Some bankruptcy courts will allow a debtor to discharge some, but not all, of the student loan debt to the extent that it can be proven that paying the entire debt is hopeless. Paying some of the debt may be possible. Hopeless is a very tough standard for a debtor to meet. Even a ballerina, who incurred significant student loan debt studying dance at Juilliard and who was later paralyzed in an auto accident and unable to dance, can earn a living at a call center.

If the Department of Education were a bank, its trillion-dollar portfolio of student loans would make it the fifth-largest bank in the United States. The total student loan debt in the U.S. is so massive and so unpayable that Congress will be forced to provide some mechanism for relief in the future. Perhaps through bankruptcy, perhaps outside of bankruptcy.

For the most part, student loans cannot be discharged in any bankruptcy chapter. In Chapter 13, student loans can be a particular nightmare. How bad the nightmare, will vary depending upon the jurisdiction. In general, student loan debts are unsecured debts, just like credit card debts. But, unlike credit card debts, to the extent student loan debts are not paid in a Chapter 13 plan, they are not discharged. Unless the Chapter 13 plan calls for the payment of 100% of your debts, some portion of your student loan debt will not be paid. The unpaid portion of your student loans will continue to accrue interest during the term of your Chapter 13 plan. The lower the total percentage of your total debts that will be paid in your Chapter 13 plan, the lower the percentage of your student loan debt that will be paid and, as a result, the more your student loan debt will continue to accrue interest.

The unpaid student loan principal and accumulated interest will still be owed upon the completion of payments under the Chapter 13 plan. Again, the unpaid portion of credit card debt will be discharged. But, student loan debt is not dischargeable, so the unpaid portion of the student loan debt will remain due and payable. If the percentage of total debts paid in the Chapter 13 plan is extremely low, it is not impossible that you could owe more money in student loans after the completion of your Chapter 13 plan than you owed before filing bankruptcy.

You might have to file bankruptcy again in Chapter 13 immediately upon the closing of the first Chapter 13 case to avoid harsh collection actions as a result of being behind on the student loans. You likely would not be entitled to a discharge in the second Chapter 13 case, but it would not matter. Your other unpaid unsecured debts would have been discharged in the first Chapter 13 case. The only reason for the second Chapter 13 case would be to impose the automatic stay and to create a payment plan for the student loan debt. You could be in Chapter 13 for the rest of your life.

To remedy this nightmare, in some jurisdictions it may be possible to separately "classify" student loans, so that they are treated differently than other unsecured debts. Separate classification may allow the student loans to be paid in a greater proportion than credit card debt to avoid the problem of additional interest accruing on unpaid student loan debt. Separate classification is not available in every jurisdiction.

At the present time, bankruptcy is not the best option for student loan debt. There are better non-bankruptcy options. Many student loan lenders have deferment and forbearance options for people who are unemployed or in the military. Income based or contingent repayment plans match the required monthly payment amount to the income of the borrower. Many of these income-based repayment plans promise to cancel any remaining debt after a certain number of years if you work for qualifying governmental or charitable 501(c)(3) organizations. Unfortunately, the number of borrowers who actually receive the expected student loan debt relief is exceedingly low. For those few who are lucky enough to receive student loan debt relief under those programs, the discharge of indebtedness income that arises when debts are forgiven is no longer taxable.

## ❤ Income Tax Debts

As a rule, most debts owed to the Internal Revenue Service or to a state taxing authority for income taxes will not be dischargeable in bankruptcy. For income tax debts to be dischargeable, the following conditions must be met.

First and foremost is that a tax return for the tax year in question must have been due more than three years before the date of the bankruptcy filing. For example: A tax return for 2020 would not be due until April 15, 2021 at the earliest. If you owed income taxes for 2020, they could not be discharged unless the bankruptcy case was filed after April 15, 2024. In May of 2021, it might be possible to discharge income taxes owed for tax years up to 2017. A return for 2017 would normally be due on April 15, 2018. Three years later would be May 2021. Note, if your tax return was on extension, the three years would run from the extension date. So, if your tax return for 2017 was on extension until October 15, 2017, you would need to wait to file bankruptcy until November 2021 to discharge income taxes owed for 2017.

Second, to discharge federal income taxes, you must have filed your federal income tax return more than two years prior to the filing of the bankruptcy case. For example: A return for 2017 would normally be due on April 15, 2018. If your 2017 tax return was not actually filed until August 15, 2020, you would need to wait to file bankruptcy until September 2022 to discharge federal income taxes owed for 2017. If, however, between April 15, 2018 and August 15, 2020 the IRS filed a "Substitute for Return" for you, you probably will not be able to discharge the 2017 income taxes. Some states take the position that if you do not file your tax return on time, you can never discharge taxes owed for that tax year.

Third, and least likely to be an issue, the taxes you are seeking to discharge cannot have been assessed within 240 days before filing bankruptcy. An "offer and compromise" can affect the timing. For example: A tax return for 2017 was filed on or before April 15, 2018. It is now after May 2021, but the IRS determined that your income was higher than you claimed on your 2017 tax return and assessed taxes in a letter dated November 1, 2021. You would have to wait until August 2022 to file bankruptcy in order for the 2017 taxes to possibly be dischargeable. Taxes owed for 2017 normally would have been dischargeable by filing bankruptcy in May 2021, but the IRS assessment received on November 1, 2021 will delay the dischargeability of the 2017 taxes. The bankruptcy case seeking to discharge the 2017 taxes cannot be filed for 240 days after the assessment, around August 2022.

To determine whether income taxes are dischargeable, you would want to request and review a tax transcript from the IRS. Even if it appeared that the three conditions were satisfied, it is still possible that something you did will disqualify you from having the old taxes discharged in bankruptcy. In practice, there is no harm in taking the position that old tax debts that appear to satisfy the three conditions are dischargeable. The worst that can happen is that the IRS disagrees. If the amount in question were large enough, you might challenge the IRS non-dischargeability determination in court. Generally, the amount of tax in question will be less than the cost of having a lawyer challenge the IRS in court.

The IRS tends to play fair. Once your bankruptcy case is filed, the IRS will review your file and treat the taxes owed as discharged if the discharge is merited. Unfortunately, the IRS will not inform you of their decision. So, if you are seeking to discharge taxes, you would want to check with the IRS a month or so after your discharge has entered to see how the IRS has treated the taxes. If the IRS determined that taxes were still owed, you likely would want to enter into a payment plan at that time.

If you owe income taxes that could be dischargeable in the future, it may be advantageous to delay filing the bankruptcy case. You would have to compare the benefit of discharging the taxes against any cost or risk of delaying the bankruptcy filing. To avoid unpleasant surprises, it is a good idea to have all your tax returns filed before filing bankruptcy.

## ❧ Lawsuits – Intentional Bad Acts vs. Negligence

Claims arising out of a willful and malicious injury by a debtor are not dischargeable in bankruptcy. There is a slight difference in the meaning of those words in Chapter 7 vs. Chapter 13, but, as a rule, if you owe someone money because you intentionally did something bad, that obligation will not be dischargeable in bankruptcy. On the other hand, if you negligently did something bad, that obligation probably will be dischargeable in bankruptcy, unless your negligence was itself caused intentionally, say by being intoxicated.

For example: An orthodontist client of mine was amazed and thrilled to learn that any liability she might have had from a malpractice lawsuit that had been filed against her could be discharged in bankruptcy. The malpractice claim was based on negligence. The lawsuit against the orthodontist stopped the moment the bankruptcy case was filed. It did not matter that the malpractice case had not ended when the bankruptcy case was filed. It also would not have mattered had the malpractice case gone to judgment against the orthodontist. As long as the claim was based upon negligence, any liability for the claim could be discharged in bankruptcy.

A different situation arose with another client who was being sued for cutting down trees on an adjoining neighbor's property when her bankruptcy case was filed. Cutting down your neighbor's trees without their permission is an intentional bad act, known as a "tort." If the state court where the lawsuit was being heard concluded that the action of cutting down the trees was willful and malicious, the resulting judgment would not be dischargeable in Chapter 7. If the state tort case had already started when the bankruptcy case was filed, it is likely that the automatic stay would be lifted in order for the state court judge to complete his determination of whether cutting down the trees was willful and malicious. If the state court judge concluded that cutting down the trees was willful and malicious, then the damages imposed for cutting down the trees would not be dischargeable in Chapter 7. It is possible that the damages could be dischargeable in Chapter 13.

## ❦ Governmental Fines And Penalties

In general, fines and penalties levied by governmental units and agencies as punishments are not dischargeable in bankruptcy. In contrast, most ordinary monetary obligations owed the government, or a governmental agency, probably will be dischargeable, at least with the passage of time. To see the distinction, consider the treatment of unpaid parking tickets and tolls. If you owe a governmental unit money because you did not pay a toll, that debt likely will be dischargeable in bankruptcy. Not feeding the meter or paying a toll is a monetary obligation. On the other hand, if you received a fine or penalty for not paying the bill as a punishment, that fine or penalty likely would not be dischargeable in bankruptcy. At least not in Chapter 7. Depending upon the nature of the fine, it might be dischargeable in Chapter 13. If the fine was for a moving violation that was considered criminal in nature, it might not even be dischargeable in Chapter 13. You may need a lawyer to explain the distinctions.

## Other Bad Acts

Other non-dischargeable debts include debts that arose because of a particular bad act you committed. These include claims for fraud and false representations regarding assets and finances, obtaining debt through fraudulent representations, frauds committed while acting in a fiduciary capacity, embezzlement or larceny. Not surprisingly, if you steal money from someone, bankruptcy will not relieve you of your obligation to repay the stolen money.

## Abusive Filings

Even if no single creditor challenges the dischargeability of its debt, the bankruptcy filing itself could be challenged by the U.S. Trustee as being "abusive." This might happen, for example, if the total amount of debt relative to the filer's income seemed extraordinarily high. I once saw a prospective client who had $200,000 of credit card debt. The prospective client had not suffered a job loss, divorce, or medical condition. She had no reason to file bankruptcy other than her difficulty making payments on the debt. A credit card debt level of $200,000 is high, but perhaps not extraordinary high if the prospective client's annual income is $350,000. This prospective client never earned more than $40,000. A credit card debt level of $200,000 is extraordinarily high relative to a $40,000 annual income. Credit card issuers ordinarily do not extend that much credit to someone with that level of income. The debt might have been incurred by misrepresentation of income, that is, by fraud. The level of debt owed each particular credit card issuer might be below the threshold level at which the issuer would bother challenging the dischargeability of its debt. But, if the U.S. Trustee believed the debtor had acted improperly in incurring the debt, the U.S. Trustee might engage in further inquiry. If the debtor lacked satisfactory answers, the filing itself could be challenged as being "abusive." If the U.S. Trustee prevailed before a judge, the bankruptcy case would be dismissed, and the discharge denied.

# CHAPTER 9

## Actions To Avoid Prior To Filing Bankruptcy

By now, you should have a good idea if you qualify for Chapter 7, what you will be able to keep and what will happen to your debts. Hopefully, you have overcome any reluctance to filing. Once you decide to file bankruptcy and, in particular, Chapter 7, there are some important things to avoid prior to filing.

##  DON'T WITHDRAW MONEY FROM A RETIREMENT ACCOUNT

It takes years of hard work and regular contributions to accumulate retirement savings in a 401(k), IRA or other retirement account. While it may seem like withdrawing money from a retirement account to pay creditors might be a good idea, there are many reasons why it is not.

First, retirement accounts receive among the greatest protections from creditors of all assets either inside or outside of bankruptcy. Most tax-exempt retirement plans are fully exempt and the exemption limits on certain IRAs exceed $1 million. You will need those funds when you retire. Since you get to keep those retirement accounts before, during and after bankruptcy, it makes no sense to use them to pay creditors, particularly to pay debts that will be discharged in bankruptcy.

Second, while funds within retirement accounts are fully protected from creditors, when those funds are withdrawn and deposited into a bank account, they require a different exemption for protection. If no exemption is available, the withdrawn funds become part of your bankruptcy estate available to creditors.

Third, if funds withdrawn a retirement account are used to repay creditors in the 90 days before filing or are used to repay friends or family members in the 12 months before filing bankruptcy, those payments may be considered "preferences" that could be recouped by the Chapter 7 Trustee for the benefit of your creditors.

Fourth, if you use funds withdrawn from a retirement account to prepay future expenses before you file bankruptcy, those pre-payments may be considered "fraudulent transfers" that could be recouped by the Chapter 7 Trustee for the benefit of your creditors.

Fifth, if you end up owning assets that are nonexempt, you may be able to withdraw funds from your retirement account after filing to buy back those nonexempt assets from the Chapter 7 Trustee.

 ## DON'T TRANSFER PROPERTY OUT OF YOUR NAME OR SELL PROPERTY FOR LESS THAN IT IS WORTH

You may be considering giving away or selling for a nominal value property that you know you will not be able to keep in bankruptcy before you file. A few examples include giving away a grand piano, taking your name off the title to a car that is titled in you and your son's names, transferring a vacation cabin titled in your name to a friend for free or for $1; moving funds from your bank account into a bank account owned by someone else.

When you give away property or sell property for less than it is worth, while you are insolvent, that transfer is known as a "fraudulent transfer" or a "fraudulent conveyance." If you are considering bankruptcy, you almost always are insolvent. Taking your name off a vehicle title or deed is really a gift of your half of the property to the other joint owner. It makes no difference whether you plan on reversing the transfer after bankruptcy.

Fraudulent transfers can be reversed by a Chapter 7 Trustee and the recovered property sold for the benefit of your creditors. Fraudulent transfers are big mistakes because, had they not been made, there might have been exemptions available to protect the property.

If you sell or give away property during the two-year period immediately before you file, you must disclose the transfer in your bankruptcy paperwork. At the Meeting of Creditors, which is held under oath under penalty of perjury, the Chapter 7 Trustee will ask you whether you sold or gave away property above a certain dollar amount during the relevant state law look-back period (usually four to six years) before you filed bankruptcy.

If the transfer was made with the intent to hinder, delay, or defraud a creditor or conceal property, not only would the transfer be reversed, but you could be denied a discharge entirely. Failure to disclose a transfer on the bankruptcy paperwork or at the Meeting of Creditors is some evidence that you intended to conceal the transfer.

 ## DON'T PAY UNSECURED CREDITORS

Once you decide to file bankruptcy, it does not make any sense to continue paying unsecured creditors, like credit cards. You should continue to pay secured debts, such as home mortgages and car loans, assuming you intend to keep that property. Note that not paying unsecured creditors does not mean that you should not pay your regular monthly bills, such as the electric and cable TV bills. You should continue to pay the monthly bills. Unless they are several months in arrears, regular monthly bills are not debts. There are a few reasons not to pay your unsecured debts.

First, it may come as a surprise, but no one cares that you made unsecured debt payments up to the date of filing. Your bankruptcy case is not "helped" by making payments prior to filing. You don't get any extra credit points with creditors for making the payments and any remaining debt will be discharged in Chapter 7 and reduced or eliminated in Chapter 13 anyway. Making the payments is a waste of money. It would be better to use the money to pay your bankruptcy attorney instead.

Second, even if you pay a credit card debt down to zero, there is no guarantee that you will be able to use the credit card after your bankruptcy case is filed. Credit card issuers monitor bankruptcy filings and, in most cases, close all credit card accounts once you file, regardless of any recent payments.

Third, paying more than $600 to any one unsecured creditor in the 90 days before you file bankruptcy may be considered a "preference" that could be recouped by the Chapter 7 Trustee for the benefit of all your creditors. One of the basic principles of bankruptcy law is that all creditors are to be treated equally. Bankruptcy world considers it unfair for one creditor to receive more than another in the 90 days prior to filing.

 ## DON'T REPAY LOANS FROM FRIENDS OR FAMILY

What about repaying a debt owed to a family member or friend? Surely, repaying the emergency loan you received from grandma before filing bankruptcy must be allowed? Unfortunately, it is not. Bankruptcy law is even tougher on payments of more than $600 to any one creditor who is an "insider," which includes relatives, certain friends, and business associates. The look-back period for reversing payments to an insider extends all the way back to one year before filing instead of 90 days. If the amount were large enough, the Chapter 7 Trustee could seek to recoup the preference payment for the benefit of all your creditors, which would include the insider. It may seem crazy to you not to repay grandma before you file, but bankruptcy world wants to make sure that American Express and Discover are treated the same as grandma. It is not fair that you preferred to repay grandma over American Express and Discover.

Making a preference payment to an insider is not necessarily a problem for you, the payor. Your liability for any loan the insider may have extended to you will be discharged in bankruptcy. The preference payment is a problem for the insider, the recipient of the repayment. The insider may have to return the payment to the Chapter 7 Trustee. If the insider still has the funds and can return the payment to the Chapter 7 Trustee, the insider may not be happy to see you at Thanksgiving. If the insider no longer has the funds, the insider could be forced to file bankruptcy to discharge the repayment obligation.

Even if the Chapter 7 Trustee is realistic enough not to sue your 82-year-old grandmother for the return of the preference payment, the payment and the debt must be disclosed in the bankruptcy schedules. That means your 82-year-old grandma will learn about your bankruptcy filing. One prospective client I met with recently decided against filing bankruptcy solely to avoid her grandmother learning of her bankruptcy filing and possibly being contacted by the Chapter 7 Trustee for the return of the preference repayment.

NOTE: Nothing prevents you from repaying friends, relatives, and business associates after bankruptcy. Just do not repay them before you file.

 DON'T USE CREDIT CARDS AFTER YOU DECIDE TO FILE

Once you decide to file bankruptcy, stop using credit cards. Instead, use a debit card which withdraws money directly from your bank account. One of the reasons why a particular debt may be determined to be "non-dischargeable" is if it was fraudulently incurred. Fraud in this context means that the debtor incurred the debt with no intention of paying it. Once you decide to file bankruptcy, particularly in Chapter 7 cases, you would have no intention of paying any new unsecured debts.

Credit card companies typically review the pattern of card usage in the months immediately prior to filing. If credit card usage spiked prior to filing, the issuer may challenge recently incurred charges as having been fraudulently incurred, that is, having been incurred with no intention of being paid.

Bankruptcy law considers some debts presumptively fraudulent. If you charge more than $725 for the purchase of luxury goods or services on any single credit card within the 90 days before you file bankruptcy, or if you take cash advances that total more than $1,000 on any single credit card within the 70 days before you file bankruptcy, those particular debts are presumed to be non-dischargeable. Congress does not want people going on a spending spree before filing bankruptcy.

##  TRY NOT TO HAVE MUCH MONEY ON DEPOSIT WHEN YOU FILE

If you owe money to a bank on an unsecured line of credit or on a credit card issued by that bank, it is a good idea to have no money on deposit at that bank or to have as little money as possible on deposit. There is a risk that the bank will "offset," that is, take, the amount the bank is owed by you with the amount you have on deposit at the bank on the day of filing. There are limitations on banks acting this way, and the risk of an offset may not be huge, but why take any risk if you can avoid it. In practice, I recommend clients either close bank accounts at banks they owe money to or to have as little money on deposit as possible.

This is a "Try to" instead of a "Don't" because it is not always possible to close bank accounts prior to filing. With direct deposit of paychecks, for example, there may not be enough time to open a new bank account and change the bank with the payroll department before the case is filed, if bankruptcy must be filed quickly.

In addition to the "offset" risk, there are some banks, notably Wells Fargo, that will "freeze" money on deposit in a bank account upon filing even if the bank is not a creditor. The bank takes the position that because it does not know if the money on deposit can be exempted by the debtor, it is possible that funds on deposit are property of the debtor's bankruptcy estate and not the debtor. The bank does not want to allow the debtor to withdraw those funds and then learn later that the funds were not the property of the debtor. The bank might end up having to pay the Chapter 7 Trustee the same amount improperly withdrawn by the debtor. Courts generally have upheld the right of the bank to freeze the account. Often a lawyer's call to the Chapter 7 Trustee will result in the bank releasing the freeze. But, in the meantime, the debtor may not have access to the only funds it has. It is commonly believed that Wells Fargo will not freeze bank accounts with less than $5,000 on deposit, but it would be safer to not have any money on deposit at Wells Fargo if you could avoid it.

# CHAPTER 10

## The Bankruptcy Process

## IT'S FASTER, EASIER AND SIMPLER THAN YOU THINK

The bankruptcy process will vary depending upon the type of bankruptcy you are filing. Most filers in Chapter 7 are pleasantly surprised by how easy the process described below is. The process in Chapter 12 and Chapter 13 is similar to that of Chapter 7 with the addition of needing to propose a plan and have the plan confirmed by a judge. The process in Chapter 11 is considerably more complicated because the approval of a plan of reorganization by a certain number of creditors is also required.

 ## HIRING AN ATTORNEY

I recommend hiring an experienced bankruptcy attorney. It is possible to file bankruptcy without an attorney. You should only consider that if you are certain that you have no or little income, no assets to protect, and you have not transferred an asset for less than it was worth in at least four years prior to filing. If all those conditions do not apply, or if you are not sure, seek qualified counsel.

Bankruptcy is often called "a giant trap for the unwary." Filling out the required bankruptcy paperwork is difficult but only part of the battle. The other part is dealing with the Chapter 7 Trustee and, perhaps, the U.S. Trustee. Having an attorney with experience negotiating those troubled waters is well worth the expense.

Bankruptcy is a legal practice area that general practitioners often claim to have knowledge of along with their expertise in a multitude of other practice areas. Typically, a general practitioner will charge less than a lawyer who specializes in bankruptcy. Bankruptcy may be a "loss leader" for a general practitioner. Once you become a client, in addition to the bankruptcy, the general practitioner can sell you a will, a house closing, a divorce and, maybe someday, the Cadillac of legal fees - a personal injury lawsuit. I recommend finding an attorney with some specialization in bankruptcy even if it costs a little more. The last thing you want during the bankruptcy process is a surprise.

Finding an experienced consumer bankruptcy attorney is as simple as going to the website of the National Association of Consumer Bankruptcy Attorneys (NACBA) and using their attorney search function: https://www. nacba.org/find-an-attorney. NACBA is the only national organization of consumer bankruptcy attorneys. I am a member.

## LEGAL FEES

To give prospective clients already dealing with unmanageable debt certainty regarding the cost of filing bankruptcy, Chapter 7 legal fees typically are charged as fixed fees, as opposed to most other legal fees, which typically are charged by the hour. The fixed fee for a Chapter 7 bankruptcy filing will vary depending upon the difficulty of the case and the area of the country. The range is roughly $1,800 for a relatively simple consumer filing to $5,000 for a more complicated case involving a sole proprietor. There are other expenses of filing, including the filing fee, now $338, which goes to the bankruptcy court, and the fees for two required courses in credit counseling and personal financial management, which can cost as little as

$10 each if taken on-line. Valuations of houses, jewelry and other items of property may be required or desired, perhaps at an additional expense.

In most parts of the country, the attorney's fee must be paid before a Chapter 7 case is filed. Legal fees for other kinds of bankruptcies may, in part, be deferred and paid after filing. If you owed your bankruptcy attorney money at the time your Chapter 7 case was filed, that legal fee debt would be discharged along with your other debts. The U.S. Trustee makes a point of letting attorneys and their clients know that at the Meeting of Creditors. Some attorneys offer payment plans prior to filing. Other attorneys will not start working on a case until all fees have been paid.

Bankruptcy attorneys can quote fixed, as opposed to hourly, fees because they know how much work will be required in a particular case and how long the work will take to perform. There are matters that could arise after a bankruptcy case has been filed that typically are excluded from the fixed fee and are billed separately. The most significant is an "adversary proceeding" brought by a creditor challenging the dischargeability of its debt, generally based on some alleged fraudulent behavior. Other matters that do not routinely arise include judicial lien avoidances, reaffirmation hearings, relief from the automatic stay actions, Rule 2004 Examinations, negotiating redemptions of secured property, negotiating settlements with the Chapter 7 Trustee, and case audits by the U.S. Trustee. These matters will arise after a case has been filed and generally will be billed for separately on an hourly basis. The fees can be quite high. An attorney experienced in bankruptcy practice will be better at identifying, possibly avoiding, and, if not, handling, these matters than a general practice attorney.

Chapter 13 legal fees are always higher than Chapter 7 legal fees, because more time is required in Chapter 13 to propose, negotiate, and confirm a payment plan. The bankruptcy court must review and approve attorney fees in Chapter 13 to ensure the fees are not excessive. Legal fees typically range from $2,500 to $5,500 for what are known as "no look" fees that basically are pre-approved as being "reasonable" by the bankruptcy court. In more complicated cases, attorneys might charge by the hour. The court would have to approve those fees before the client would be allowed to pay them. As with Chapter 7, there are other expenses of filing, including the filing fee, currently $313, which goes to the bankruptcy court, and the fees for two required courses in credit counseling and personal financial management.

## ❦ How Do You Pay For Bankruptcy?

I am often asked how my clients, who already are struggling to pay their debts, can afford to pay a bankruptcy lawyer. Here are the ways bankruptcy attorneys usually are paid:

### *Stop Paying Credit Cards*

Once a decision to file bankruptcy has been made, it makes sense to continue to make mortgage and car loan payments, because the car and the house will be kept, but it makes no sense to continue to make payments on debts you expect to be discharged, like credit cards. Use the money that would have gone towards credit cards to pay your bankruptcy lawyer instead. A few months of not making credit card payments may be sufficient to pay most, if not all, of the legal fee.

## Tax Refunds

Chapter 7 bankruptcy filings tend to rise significantly between the end of March and the beginning of May after tax refunds have been received.

## Friends And Family

A sympathetic relative or friend can be a good source of funds. If the payment is a loan, it must be disclosed and discharged, but nothing prevents the loan from being repaid after the case has been filed. Repaying the loan before filing would constitute a "preference" that the Chapter 7 Trustee might seek to reverse for the benefit of creditors.

Funds received from friends or relatives could be treated as a gift, particularly if the donor is not expecting to be repaid. Bankruptcy lawyers are required to disclose the source of funds used to pay their legal fees. In this situation, the lawyer would disclose the name of the gift giver as having paid the legal fees.

## Retirement Accounts

Some retirement accounts allow withdrawals in the event of financial hardship. Others may allow the account owner to borrow funds from the account.

## Sell Nonexempt Assets

If there are assets that cannot be fully exempted and kept, those assets could be sold for fair market value, ideally to an unrelated person. Most of my clients have sold all their valuable assets long before they come to see me, but occasionally a client will own an asset that cannot be exempted and kept in Chapter 7 that can be sold to pay my legal fee.

## 🕊 Pro Bono Appointments

Many bankruptcy courts and local legal services organizations offer "pro bono," that is, for free, attorney representation. Check the websites for your local bankruptcy court and local legal services organization for information and, perhaps, an application. Typically, applicants need to be below a certain income threshold, such as the poverty level. Owning real estate may disqualify an applicant.

Why would practicing attorneys agree to represent clients for free? In general, attorneys have at least an ethical obligation to represent indigent clients in return for receiving a license to practice law (which limits competition). In some districts, the federal or state courts explicitly require attorneys to devote a specified portion of their practice to representing indigent clients. Each year, I accept ten pro bono appointments from bankruptcy courts in which I practice. Often, the pro bono representations expose me to issues that my other clients do not present.

Just because the legal fee is waived by the lawyer does not necessarily mean the entire case will be free for the client. Even though I am not being paid, the court may still require the pro bono client to pay the filing fee. My pro bono clients often have incomes just over the poverty level, which disqualifies them from having the bankruptcy court waive the filing fee, now $338. The filing fee can be paid in installments, but it still needs to be paid in full within three or four months. That has proven difficult for some clients. The fees for the two required courses are supposed to be waived by the course providers for court-appointed clients. Frequently, it is easier to just pay the small fee than to spend the time trying to qualify for a free course.

 INITIAL CONSULTATION

Most bankruptcy attorneys offer a free initial consultation. They tend to come in two varieties: (1) a meeting with an attorney who listens carefully to your situation and explains your bankruptcy options, what the bankruptcy process entails and what it will cost; and (2) an intake meeting initially with a paralegal to prepare, and perhaps even file, a barebones bankruptcy petition. The remainder of the required disclosures are provided later. My practice is to use the first type of initial consultation. The second type results in a bankruptcy case being filed faster, but filing a case quickly with incomplete information risks an unpleasant surprise surfacing later. Once a Chapter 7 case has been filed, it cannot easily be dismissed.

In the email confirming the date and time of the initial consultation, we ask the prospective client to bring with them the answers to eight questions regarding their income, assets, secured debts, unsecured debts, tax debts and residency. Attached to the email is an Initial Consultation Agreement which we ask the prospective client to review and sign at the meeting. The agreement contains disclosures which bankruptcy lawyers are required to provide prospective clients, including a stark warning from the U.S. Trustee about the penalties for not being truthful in bankruptcy and a statement that Balbus Law Firm "is a debt relief agency that helps people file for bankruptcy relief under the Bankruptcy Code" or similar words to that effect. By law, those words must be included in certain communications from bankruptcy lawyers. You'll even find them in the introduction to this book.

A typical initial consultation is described in detail in Chapter 1. In addition to explaining the prospective client's bankruptcy options, possible alternatives to filing, the bankruptcy process and the cost, I begin to investigate potential problem areas, usually dischargeability, fraudulent transfer, and preference issues. Determining whether potential problems exist and how to deal with them may require further information and analysis. I also identify timing issues that might require expediting a filing or delaying a filing. Pressure to accelerate a filing might come, for example, from imminent foreclosure, eviction, or garnishment actions. Delaying a filing might be advisable, for example, to enable the client to qualify for Chapter 7 or to give the client time to deal with nonexempt assets.

 ## ENGAGEMENT AGREEMENT

Following the initial consultation, we give the prospective client time to consider whether he or she wants to file bankruptcy and to select which bankruptcy chapter, if several options are available. If the prospective client chooses to proceed, we set up an appointment to review their case and sign an Engagement Agreement. At the second meeting, we also will give the client "homework," a detailed questionnaire that provides all the information needed to complete the bankruptcy paperwork.

The Engagement Agreement governs the responsibilities of the lawyer and the client. The major elements of a typical Engagement Agreement include:

## ❧ Scope Of Representation

The legal services that will be provided for the fixed fee and the legal services, if any, that will require an additional hourly fee.

## ❧ Client's Responsibilities

Completing the "homework;" providing other documentation, such as federal and state tax returns for the last two years, bank statements for the last six months, pay stubs for the last seven months, current mortgage, car loan and retirement account statements, copies of recorded deed, mortgages, and other liens for the house, valuations of the house, cars, and other valuable assets; taking the required credit counseling and personal financial management courses; and attending the Meeting of Creditors.

## ❧ Fees And Expenses

The amount and the timing of payment of the legal fee, the filing fee, the two required course fees, valuation fees and other possible fees and expenses.

## ❧ Term Of Engagement

How and when either party can terminate the engagement. Usually, it is fairly easy to terminate a legal representation before a case is filed. Why would a client want to terminate an engagement? Circumstances change and bankruptcy is no longer needed. Usually because a rich family member volunteers to pay the debts. Why would an attorney want to terminate an engagement? The client fails to provide the required disclosure or refuses to comply with disclosure requirements. For example, once we learn the client owns a valuable grand piano, we cannot "forget" about the piano. After a bankruptcy case has been filed, it can be extremely difficult for an attorney to withdraw as counsel. Withdrawal generally requires court approval after a hearing.

## ❧ Reaffirmations

By "reaffirming" a debt, the client agrees to be personally responsible for the debt, which otherwise would be discharged. How reaffirmations are handled varies widely among bankruptcy districts. Often, reaffirmation of a mortgage or car loan is required. Sometimes, reaffirmation is not required. There may be other debts for which the creditor requests reaffirmation. Reaffirmation of a debt can be accomplished by having the debtor's attorney declare in writing that reaffirmation is in the client's best interest or, if the attorney declines, by having a hearing to convince the bankruptcy judge that reaffirmation is in the client's best interest. Reaffirmations are routine in some districts, rare in others. The engagement agreement will explain the attorney's policy with respect to the reaffirmation of debts.

## ❤ Attorney Client Confidentiality

Like other legal representations, bankruptcy cases are governed by attorney-client privilege and rules of professional conduct regarding the confidentiality of client information. Unlike other legal representations, however, almost everything a client tells a bankruptcy attorney is disclosed, including Social Security numbers and other identifying information. The engagement agreement will attempt to explain the attorney's responsibilities for navigating this minefield.

 THE FIRST COURSE – CREDIT COUNSELING

Before you can file bankruptcy, you must complete a course provided by a non-profit credit counseling agency. It is more of a speed bump than a roadblock. Congress requires it. The credit counseling course usually is taken on-line. Telephonic options also are available. During the credit counseling course, you enter your income and expenses. Afterwards, a credit counselor may try to explain how to cut your expenses to avoid filing bankruptcy. For all my clients, that's not a possibility. Once you complete the credit counseling course, the agency will email you and your attorney a certificate of completion which must be filed with the bankruptcy petition. You cannot file bankruptcy without having taken the credit counseling course and received a certificate. The certificate may not be filed after the petition has been filed. If you do not file a petition within 180 days of completing the course, you must retake the course.

Presumably, Congress had good intentions in requiring people seeking bankruptcy relief to consider other options before filing bankruptcy. In practice, the credit counseling course comes too late for that. If another option were available, it would have been selected before bankruptcy. As a result, the credit counseling course is a useless exercise costing around $10 and consuming one hour of your life that you will never get back. I advise clients to have a sudoku puzzle handy or something else to do while they wait for the required hour of time to pass.

## FILING THE BANKRUPTCY PETITION

How long it takes a client to complete their "homework" assignment – filling out the questionnaire and providing the other required documents, is up to them. Some clients finish the paperwork in a few days. Others may take a few months. The amount of paperwork is slightly greater than the paperwork required to refinance a mortgage. That said, I require more information from my clients than the average bankruptcy practitioner. My motto is the same as the Boy Scouts, "Be Prepared." Ironically, the Boy Scouts are also in bankruptcy.

Once the client returns the "homework" and all of the other requirement documents, drafts of the bankruptcy "Voluntary Petition" and related schedules, statements and other filing documents are prepared and sent to the client for review. Only a small percentage of my clients actually read the bankruptcy documents in advance. For most clients, deciphering hieroglyphics is easier than parsing bankruptcy paperwork. I honestly believe I would receive more comments if I sent clients copies of my dental X-rays to review.

We set a date for the client to come in to review the documents with me page by page. The client signs the documents, which are then electronically filed with the bankruptcy court at the end of that same day. Although it is possible to file the required schedules of assets, exemptions, debts, income and expenses, as well statements regarding the client's Social Security number, their intention with respect to collateral for secured debts, names and addresses of co-debtors, among other information, within 14 days after a barebones Voluntary Petition is filed, my practice is to collect all relevant information in advance and to file all of the required documents at the same time the Voluntary Petition is filed. I take to heart the watchwords of George Armstrong Custer, "Avoid Unnecessary Surprises."

At the signing meeting, I review and rehearse with my client the questions the client will be asked at the Meeting of Creditors. The client receives a signed original copy of the bankruptcy documents at the conclusion of the signing meeting.

Filing bankruptcy triggers the application of the "automatic stay." As described in more detail elsewhere in this book, the automatic stay immediately stops creditors from taking any action to collect a debt from the debtor or from property belonging to the debtor. For example, creditors cannot bring or continue a collection lawsuit, garnish wages, foreclose real estate, assert a deficiency, repossess a car or other property, call, write or otherwise try to collect a debt from the debtor. If a collection lawsuit already had been started, it would come to a complete halt once the bankruptcy case was filed. Similarly, if a collection case had been lost and a judgment of wage garnishment entered, the wage garnishment would cease as soon as the bankruptcy case was filed. It might even be possible to have some of the garnished wages returned to the debtor. The automatic stay generally remains in effect until the debtor receives a discharge or the bankruptcy case ends. Creditors who violate the automatic stay by taking an action to collect a debt can be required to pay the debtor actual and punitive damages as well as the debtor's attorney's fees.

## NOTICE OF FILING (THE "341 NOTICE")

Shortly after a Chapter 7 bankruptcy case has been filed, a Chapter 7 Trustee is assigned to the case and a date and time is set for the Meeting of Creditors. In most bankruptcy jurisdictions, there is a panel of Chapter 7 Trustees who are randomly assigned to cases. The date of the Meeting of Creditors will depend upon the assigned Chapter 7 Trustee's schedule, but it usually is scheduled for a date approximately four weeks after the case is filed.

Meetings of Creditors are also required in other types of bankruptcy cases. Most jurisdictions have only one Trustee overseeing all Chapter 12 and Chapter 13 cases. In Chapter 11, no Trustee is assigned initially. The debtor begins Chapter 11 cases as the Debtor in Possession or "DIP."

A notice of the bankruptcy filing and the Meeting of Creditors (sometimes called the "341 Notice" because it is required by Section 341 of the Bankruptcy Code) is sent to all the creditors listed in the bankruptcy schedules. Regular bankruptcy creditors, such as banks and credit card issuers, and the debtor's attorney receive the notice electronically. Creditors who do not receive electronic notification and the client receive notice by mail, usually within a week of filing.

This notice provides the name and address of the debtor, the name, address, phone number and email address of the debtor's attorney, contact information for the Trustee assigned to the case, the date and time of the Meeting of Creditors, and the deadline for creditors to file an objection to discharge of their debts or to an exemption claimed by the debtor.

Usually, creditors in Chapter 7 cases are instructed not to file proofs of claims until they receive notice that the Chapter 7 Trustee has determined that the case is an asset case with proceeds that will be distributed to creditors. Very few Chapter 7 cases are asset cases. Most are "no-asset" cases. It makes no sense for creditors to file proof of claims in cases that are not expected to have nonexempt assets that could be sold to provide a recovery to creditors.

The notice also informs creditors that the filing of the bankruptcy case imposes an automatic stay against collection activities.

 ## COURT CONTROL OVER YOUR FINANCIAL AFFAIRS

The filing of a bankruptcy case creates a bankruptcy estate, theoretically including almost all of the debtor's property. Statutory exemptions under state and, where available, federal bankruptcy law, allow the debtor to exempt property from their bankruptcy estate and to keep the property from creditors.

In Chapter 7 cases, the bankruptcy estate is a snapshot on the date of filing. With a few exceptions, income and other property the debtor acquires after the day of filing belong to the debtor, not to the debtor's bankruptcy estate.

338 | FRESH START

With respect to the property that is in the debtor's estate at filing, the debtor should not sell or give away any of the property, even if an exemption for that property has been claimed, without the Chapter 7 Trustee's permission. In the vast majority of Chapter 7 cases, the Chapter 7 Trustee will close his administration of the estate and effectively turn over all the estate's exempt assets to the debtor at the conclusion of the Meeting of Creditors, usually about four weeks after filing.

## THE TRUSTEE

The Chapter 7 Trustee is appointed to administer the bankruptcy estate, including reviewing the bankruptcy schedules and statements, questioning the debtor at the Meeting of Creditors, collecting assets that are not exempt, and reversing preference payments and fraudulent transfers that would bring property improperly transferred by the debtor out of the bankruptcy estate back into the estate and provide a meaningful recovery to creditors.

The Chapter 7 Trustee receives a small, fixed fee for each case the Trustee administers. Most of the Chapter 7 Trustee's compensation comes in the form of commission. The more assets the Chapter 7 Trustee recovers and pays creditors, the more the Trustee earns. Although the fee structure gives the Chapter 7 Trustee a financial incentive to carefully examine the debtor, only a tiny percentage of Chapter 7 cases are asset cases requiring administration. Experienced Chapter 7 Trustees have an excellent sense of which cases are likely to produce a meaningful recovery for creditors. The asset cases requiring early investigation tend to be for debtors with sole proprietorships that could have nonexempt assets of value that might need to be preserved shortly after filing and prior to the Meeting of Creditors.

Trustees in Chapter 12 and Chapter 13 cases are involved in the confirmation of payment plans and in paying creditors. In Chapter 11 cases, except for Subchapter V small business cases, no Trustee is assigned, absent improper behavior by the debtor-in-possession.

# THE U.S. TRUSTEE

The U.S. Trustee is a division of the U.S. Department of Justice. It operates in 48 states. Alabama and North Carolina have a different, but functionally equivalent, overseer. The U.S. Trustee employs attorneys, auditors, and investigators, and works closely with their Department of Justice colleagues, to keep the bankruptcy system operating honestly.

In Chapter 7 cases, the U.S. Trustee reviews filings and audits cases generally for improper qualification for Chapter 7, including understating income or taking improper deductions on the Means Test, concealing or improperly transferring assets, or otherwise engaging in fraudulent behavior.

Running afoul of the U.S. Trustee most often results in case dismissal, either voluntary or by judicial decision, but could result in criminal prosecution.

# THE SECOND COURSE – PERSONAL FINANCIAL MANAGEMENT

Before you can receive a discharge in bankruptcy, you must complete a second course provided by a non-profit credit counseling agency. Congress requires the first course on credit counseling to dissuade people from filing bankruptcy. Since that mission -- to keep people out of bankruptcy -- was unsuccessful, Congress requires that filers take a second course, on personal financial management (also known as "budgeting"), to improve their ability to manage their finances in the future and to keep them from filing again.

Like the first course, the second course usually is taken on-line. Telephonic options also are available. In my practice, at the conclusion of the signing meeting, the client receives a signed original copy of the bankruptcy documents. Included in the documents is a schedule of income and a schedule of expenses. Together they comprise a budget. We recommend using that budget for the second course instead of creating a new budget.

While the first course is almost universally regarded as a waste of time, most of my clients, excluding the accountants, find the second course on budgeting worthwhile. An hour of time is required, but some clients spend even more time. As with the first course, the most important part is finishing and receiving a certificate of completion. Once you complete the personal financial management course, the agency will email you and your attorney a certificate of completion which must be filed with the bankruptcy court. Filing the certificate of completion with the bankruptcy court is a requirement for receiving a discharge.

 ## THE MEETING OF CREDITORS (THE "341 MEETING" OR "341 HEARING")

Approximately four weeks after filing, the Meeting of Creditors (also known as the "341 Meeting" or "341 Hearing" because it is required by

Section 341 of the Bankruptcy Code) is held. In some jurisdictions, the meeting is held in the bankruptcy courthouse but not in the courtroom. In other jurisdictions, the meeting is held in a federal office building at or near the offices of the U.S. Trustee. Due to Covid-19, where I practice, the meetings are held telephonically.

In Chapter 7 cases, the purpose of the Meeting of Creditors is to determine whether there are nonexempt assets that should be administered and, to a lesser extent, to verify that the debtor is eligible to file a Chapter 7 case. The Meeting of Creditors is run by the Chapter 7 Trustee. In addition to the Trustee, attending the meeting will be the debtor, the debtor's attorney, and any creditors of the debtor. Typically, the Trustee will swear the debtor in, ask a few questions about the reason for the filing and the preparation and signing of the bankruptcy documents. Then, depending upon the filing, the Trustee might ask how the debtor's property was valued, whether any property was sold or given away in the last few years, whether the debtor owned a business in the last few years and what assets the business might still have, whether there had been any "preference" payments, whether the debtor expects to receive a tax refund or a bonus, and whether the debtor is suing or planning on suing anyone. The Trustee will ask the debtor to confirm that the debtor understands that he or she must inform the debtor's attorney and the Trustee if anyone should die within six months from the filing date who leaves the debtor something in a will or life insurance policy. In most cases, the questioning lasts between six and ten minutes. If it appeared that there might be nonexempt assets or fraudulent transfers, the questioning would go longer.

Despite its name, creditors rarely attend the Meeting of Creditors. If they did, they would have the opportunity to ask the debtor questions under oath. Sophisticated creditors understand that they are highly unlikely to receive any payment in a Chapter 7 case, so attending the Meeting of Creditors is a waste of time. When creditors do show up, they tend to be unsophisticated creditors hoping to find out how much of their debts will be paid or family members bearing a grudge. I have witnessed a number of parents, ex-girlfriends and ex-spouses show up simply to bad mouth the debtor.

The exception to the creditors-do-not-attend rule is the sophisticated creditor who attends the meeting to lay the foundation for an objection to discharge, usually based on fraud. More than once, when my clients have failed to pay casino markers, lawyers for the casinos have attended the Meeting of Creditors. In addition, when my clients have ended business relationships with partners or lenders under unpleasant circumstances, lawyers for the aggrieved parties have attended the Meeting of Creditors. In each case, the lawyers asked the debtor questions about actions the debtor took or did not take, which the lawyers hoped would constitute the kind of fraudulent behavior that would enable them to challenge the dischargeability of their debts.

Prior to the Meeting of Creditors, the Chapter 7 Trustee will request a number of documents, which will vary among districts, but tend to include the following:

- Proof of Identification – usually driver's license and Social Security card
- Paystubs for the 60-days prior to filing
- Federal and state income tax returns, W2s and 1099s for the most recent year
- Bank statements showing the bank account balances on the date of filing

- Profit & Loss statements and Balance Sheets for sole proprietorships
- Appraisals or other valuations of house, car, other valuable assets, and business interests
- Recorded deed, mortgages, other liens, most recent mortgage statement for the house
- Retirement account and annuity statements
- Cash surrender value statement for whole life insurance policies
- Recent divorce documents
- Recent mortgage refinancing documents
- Documents regarding any current or planned lawsuits brought by the debtor
- Document declaring whether a Domestic Support Obligation is owed by the debtor

My practice is to take time during the signing meeting to review and rehearse all the questions a client might be asked at the Meeting of Creditors. As a result, being asked the questions by the Chapter 7 Trustee is like taking a test where all the questions are known in advance. Clients are nervous, but they easily breeze through the meeting, which rarely lasts longer than ten minutes. At the end of every meeting, I get the same reaction my children gave after being vaccinated by their pediatrician, "That wasn't so bad."

In Chapter 7, once the Meeting of Creditors has ended and the debtor has completed the second course, there usually is nothing more to do. Debtors are unlikely to see the bankruptcy judge, unless there is a reaffirmation hearing, or an adversary proceeding is brought by a creditor challenging the dischargeability of a debt. In my practice, in consumer cases, those matters do not arise.

In Chapter 13, there is a bit more activity after the Meeting of Creditors. A payment plan must be submitted and confirmed by the bankruptcy judge. The Chapter 13 Trustee may have strong opinions regarding what payments need to be included in the plan. Improper proofs of claims submitted by creditors may need to be challenged. Monthly plan payments will be made by the debtor to the Chapter 13 Trustee and then from the Trustee to creditors. Creditors are paid according to the priority of their claims established by the Bankruptcy Code. In some jurisdictions, secured debts may be paid by the Chapter 13 Trustee. In other jurisdictions, the debtor makes secured debt payments directly to the secured creditors.

In Chapter 11, there is a lot more activity after the Meeting of Creditors. A plan of reorganization must be submitted and confirmed by the bankruptcy court. Creditors must vote to approve the plan. Creditors can be expected to raise objections throughout the process to force liquidation or to gain an advantage over other creditors.

 DISCHARGE ORDER

In Chapter 7 cases, approximately two months after the Meeting of Creditors, roughly three to four months after filing, the debtor will receive an official discharge from the bankruptcy judge. The debtor's attorney will receive the discharge order electronically as soon as it enters. The debtor will receive it in the mail shortly thereafter. The discharge order prevents any creditor from attempting to collect any of the debts that were eligible for discharge. Debts that are not dischargeable include certain taxes, student loans, and any child or spousal support obligations. We advise clients to keep the discharge order in their permanent files.

The discharge order is a permanent injunction against creditors attempting to collect their debts. We advise clients that if they have any problems with creditors, they should send them a copy of the discharge order. If that does not work, we tell clients to let us know. By having the client first deal with the creditor, we lay the foundation for pursuing a violation of the discharge order. In over ten years of practice, only one client informed me that the discharge order was being violated – by letters sent to the client signed by "The Attorney General of the United States." That's how the letters were signed. Not with the Attorney General's name, with his title. Obviously, the letters were a fraudulent attempt to collect the debts. We dealt with the problem swiftly.

In Chapter 13 cases, the discharge order is entered after the completion of all payments under the plan, which may also include payments on secured debts, such as home mortgages, that are made directly by the debtor. An overwhelming percentage of Chapter 13 cases never result in a discharge.

Otherwise, the receipt of the discharge order concludes the bankruptcy case in the vast majority of cases. If the Chapter 7 Trustee is administering the debtor's estate, the case will continue until the creditors have been paid, but that activity generally requires little involvement by the debtor. That is all there is to it. The debtor gets a fresh start. Hurray!

Bankruptcy is faster, easier and better than you thought.

# About Andrew Balbus

Andrew Balbus is the founder of Balbus Law Firm, located in Danbury, Connecticut. His practice is limited to representing individuals and small businesses in bankruptcy cases in Connecticut and neighboring counties in New York.

Andrew Balbus received an LL.M. Master of Laws degree in bankruptcy law from St John's University School of Law where he also has been an Adjunct Professor. Mr. Balbus received his J.D. degree with honors from Harvard Law School. In addition to his outstanding legal education, he has a Masters of Business Administration (MBA) degree in finance from the Columbia University School of Business and a bachelor's degree, magna cum laude, in accounting/management science from Duke University. He is a member of the Phi Beta Kappa and Beta Gamma Sigma honor societies.

Mr. Balbus is the author of four articles regarding the application of the absolute priority rule to individuals in Chapter 11 published in the prestigious Norton Journal of Bankruptcy Law & Practice, which have been cited by bankruptcy and appellate court judges across the country. More recently, he authored an article on "Income Tax Refunds as Property of the Estate" for the 2018 Norton Annual Survey of Bankruptcy Law.

Prior to founding Balbus Law Firm, Mr. Balbus spent three decades as a lawyer, investment banker, business turnaround leader and entrepreneur. In 1999, Mr. Balbus founded Sellers' Market, the world's first "drop-off" store, a retail location to which people brought anything they wanted to sell. The business took advantage of on-line technology to sell virtually anything anywhere in the world, primarily using eBay auctions. The concept was widely imitated in the U.S. and abroad.

Prior to founding Sellers' Market, Mr. Balbus was President & COO of Sandberg & Sikorski, a 150-person manufacturer and distributor of fine gold and diamond jewelry. He led the company through a difficult transformation, including re-engineering its manufacturing and distribution operations, focusing on new marketing opportunities, and implementing programs to improve coordination, communication, and morale throughout the company. The end result was a complete turnaround and achievement of profitability levels that were among the highest in the U.S. jewelry manufacturing industry.

Prior to joining S&S, Mr. Balbus spent 10 years as an investment banker, specializing in corporate finance for emerging growth companies in the U.S. and abroad. His clients were involved in a diversity of businesses from high tech to low tech, from manufacturing to retailing, from mining gold to curing cancer. They included some well-known names, such as Benetton, Luxottica, Chaus and Office Depot. Many were located outside the U.S., in countries such as Mexico, Brazil, Spain, Italy and Ghana. On behalf of his clients, he bought and sold companies, took dozens of companies public and raised billions of dollars of debt and equity capital.

Balbus Law Firm utilizes Andrew Balbus' unique background in law, finance and turnaround management to take a multidisciplinary approach to the bankruptcy process. His knowledge and experience provide clients with an exceptional perspective in negotiating and restructuring debts and reorganizing businesses.

BALBUS
LAW FIRM

Made in the USA
Las Vegas, NV
24 September 2021